Fundamentals of Software Engineering

Fundamentals of Software Engineering

Helen Mason

MURPHY & MOORE
www.murphy-moorepublishing.com

Murphy & Moore Publishing,
1 Rockefeller Plaza,
New York City, NY 10020, USA

ISBN: 978-1-63987-250-3

Cataloging-in-Publication Data

Fundamentals of software engineering / Helen Mason.
 p. cm.
Includes bibliographical references and index.
ISBN 978-1-63987-250-3
1. Software engineering. 2. Engineering. I. Mason, Helen.
QA76.758 .F86 2022
005.1--dc23

For information on all Murphy & Moore Publications
visit our website at www.murphy-moorepublishing.com

 MURPHY & MOORE

Contents

Preface

The discipline of engineering which focuses on building robust software systems is termed as software engineering. The primary objective of software engineering is to create solutions which are able to meet their users' requirements. Software engineering is applied to small, medium and large-scale organizations. It utilizes engineering methods, processes, and techniques to create effective software solutions. According to the availability of resources, software development can be done by a team or an individual. Network control systems, operating systems, computer games and business applications are some common applications of software engineering. Software design, software development, software testing and software maintenance are few of its various sub-fields. Changing technology and new areas of specialization are evolving this field at a rapid pace. The topics included in this book on software engineering are of utmost significance and bound to provide incredible insights to readers. While understanding the long-term perspectives of the topics, it makes an effort in highlighting their impact as a modern tool for the growth of the discipline. For all those who are interested in software engineering, this book can prove to be an essential guide.

Given below is the chapter wise description of the book:

Chapter 1- Software engineering is an engineering branch associated with the design, development and maintenance of software products. A collection of executable programming code, associated libraries and documentations is called software. When such software is made for a specific requirement, it becomes a software product. This chapter serves as an introduction to software engineering.

Chapter 2- Software design is the process of defining software functions, objects, methods and structure of the programming codes, so that it matches the desired expectations. Software testing is the next step wherein the software is put through trials to ensure that it matches expected requirements and is error free. Software maintenance is the last step which is a continuous process by which a software product is modified and updated periodically. All these topics are covered in detail in this chapter.

Chapter 3- Software development is the collection of systematic operations involved in creating software products. It includes designing, preparing specifications, programming, testing, bug fixing and documentation. There are various methods used to develop software like aspect-oriented software development, rapid application model, spiral model, etc. This chapter deals with software development, its processes and the different types of software development in a detailed manner.

Chapter 4- User interface can be defined as the means through which the user communicates and controls the software application or hardware device. The process of building this method to facilitate user-system communication is known as user interface design. User interfaces are designed with ease of use and accessibility as a priority. The chapter sheds light on user interface and its design process.

Chapter 5- Software Engineering is used in a wide variety of fields. The development of artificial intelligence is one such area where the potential of software engineering is evident. Computational neuroscience and augmented reality are two other areas where software engineering has displayed promising possibilities. This chapter comprehensively summarizes all these applications of software engineering.

Indeed, my job was extremely crucial and challenging as I had to ensure that every chapter is informative and structured in a student-friendly manner. I am thankful for the support provided by my family and colleagues during the completion of this book.

Helen Mason

Software Engineering: An Introduction

Software engineering is an engineering branch associated with the design, development and maintenance of software products. A collection of executable programming code, associated libraries and documentations is called software. When such software is made for a specific requirement, it becomes a software product. This chapter serves as an introduction to software engineering.

Software

Software is a set of instructions, data or programs used to operate computers and execute specific tasks. Opposite of hardware, which describes the physical aspects of a computer, software is a generic term used to refer to applications, scripts and programs that run on a device. Software can be thought of as the variable part of a computer, and hardware the invariable part.

Software is often divided into categories. Application software refers to user-downloaded programs that fulfill a want or need. Examples of applications include office suites, database programs, web browsers, word processors, software development tools, image editors and communication platforms.

System software includes operating systems and any program that supports application software. The term middleware is sometimes used to describe programming that mediates between application and system software, or between two different kinds of application software. For example, middleware could be used to send a remote work request from an application in a computer that has one kind of operating system, to an application in a computer with a different operating system.

Additional categories of software are the utilities, which are small, useful programs with limited capabilities. Some utilities come with operating systems. Like applications, utilities tend to be separately installable and capable of being used independently from the rest of the operating system.

Similarly, applets are small applications that sometimes come with the operating system as accessories. They can also be created independently using Java or other programming languages.

Machine code is the lowest level of software. Other programming languages are translated into machine code so the computer can execute them. Software can be purchased or acquired in the following ways:

- Shareware: Usually distributed on a free or trial basis, with the intention of sale when the period is over.

- Liteware: A type of shareware with some capabilities disabled until the full version is purchased.

- Freeware: Can be downloaded for free but with copyright restrictions.

- Public domain software: Can be downloaded for free without restrictions.

- Open source software: A type of software where the source code is furnished and users agree not to limit the distribution of improvements.

- Proprietary software: Software that remains the property of its owner/creator and is used by end users or organizations under predefined conditions.

Today, much of the purchased software, shareware and freeware are directly downloaded over the internet. In these cases, software can be found on specific software industry vendor websites or application service providers. However, software can also be packaged onto CD-ROMs or diskettes and sold physically to a consumer.

A specialized type of software that allows hardware to run is firmware. This is a type of programming that is embedded onto a special area of the hardware's non-volatile memory, such as a microprocessor or read-only memory, on a one-time or infrequent basis so that thereafter it seems to be part of the hardware.

Although the terms computer science and software engineering are often used interchangeably, they are not the same. Computer science is the field of computing that centers on the study, implementation and analysis of algorithms. Software engineering, on the other hand, focuses on applying structured engineering principles to the development of software.

Design and Implementation

Design and implementation are the second and third steps in the overall Software Design Life Cycle, after the initial analysis of requirements. After user requirements are defined, software design aims to specify how to fulfill them.

A software design includes a description of the structure of the software that will be implemented, data models, interfaces between system components, and potentially the algorithms the software engineer used.

The design process transforms user requirements into a suitable form, which helps the computer programmer in software coding and implementation. The software engineers develop the software design iteratively, adding detail and correcting the design as they develop it.

The different types of software design include:

- Architectural design: The foundational design, which identifies the overall structure of the system, its main components, and their relationships with each other.

- High-level design: The second layer of design, which focuses on how the system, along with all of its components, can be implemented in forms of modules. It describes the relationships between the various modules and functions of the system, data flow, flow charts and data structures.

- Detailed design: The third layer of design, which focuses on all the implementation details necessary for the specified architecture.

The implementation phase is the process of converting a system specification into an executable system. If the software engineers used an incremental approach, the implementation phase may also involve refining the software specifications.

Software Quality

Software quality measures if the software meets its requirements, which are classified as either functional or non-functional:

- Functional requirements identify what the software should do. Functional requirements could be technical details, data manipulation and processing, calculations or any other specific function that specifies what an application aims to accomplish.

- Non-functional requirements, also known as "quality attributes," determine how the system should work. Non-functional requirements include such things as portability, disaster recovery, security, privacy and usability.

Software testing detects and solves technical issues in the software source code and assesses the overall usability, performance, security and compatibility of the product to ensure it meets its requirements.

The dimensions of software quality include:

- Accessibility: The degree to which the software can be comfortably used by diverse groups of people - including individuals who require adaptive technologies such as voice recognition and screen magnifiers.

- Compatibility: The suitability of the software for use in a variety of environments, such as different operating systems, devices and browsers.

- Efficiency: The ability of the software to perform well without wasting energy, resources, effort, time or money.

- Functionality: The ability of the software to carry out its specified or desired functions.

- Installability: The ability of the software to be installed in a specified environment.

- Localizability: The ability of the software to be used in various languages, time zones, etc.

- Maintainability: How easily the software can be modified to add features, improve features, fix bugs, etc.

- Performance: How fast the software performs under a particular load.

- Portability: The ability of the software to be easily transferred from one location to another.

- Reliability: The ability of the software to perform a required function under specific conditions for the specific period of time without any errors.

- Scalability: The measure of the software's ability to increase or decrease in performance in response to changes in the software's processing demands.

- Security: The ability of the software to protect against unauthorized access, invasion of privacy, theft, data loss, etc.

- Testability: The ability of the software to be easily tested.

- Usability: How easy it is to use the software.

Software Licensing and Patents

A software license is a document that provides legally-binding guidelines for the use and distribution of software. Typically, software licenses provide users with the right to one or more copies of the software without violating copyright. Additionally, the license outlines the responsibilities of the parties that enter into the license agreement and may place restrictions on how the end user can use the software.

Software licensing terms and conditions generally include fair use of the software, the limitations of liability, warranties as well as disclaimers and protections if the software or its use infringes on the intellectual property rights of others. Software licenses typically are proprietary, free or open source - depending on the terms under which users can redistribute or copy the software for future development or use.

Software patents are covered by the intellectual property suite of protections that grant the owner of the software exclusive rights to use the protected program. However, software patents are controversial in the United States and other countries for a variety of reasons, including the fact that software is already automatically covered by copyright protections and some think that additional protections may hamper innovation.

Currently, software may qualify for patent protection if it has an industrial or commercial use, and isn't just a business idea. The software must also be unique and not obvious to a person of average skill in the software industry. In addition, the owner has to describe the software in detail in an application submitted to the United States Patent and Trademark Office.

Software Engineering

Software engineering is defined as a process of analyzing user requirements and then designing, building, and testing software application which will satisfy those requirements.

- IEEE, in its standard 610.12-1990, defines software engineering as the application of a systematic, disciplined, which is a computable approach for the development, operation, and maintenance of software.

- Fritz Bauer defined it as 'the establishment and used standard engineering principles. It helps you to obtain, economically, software which is reliable and works efficiently on the real machines'.

- Boehm defines software engineering, which involves, 'the practical application of scientific

knowledge to the creative design and building of computer programs. It also includes associated documentation needed for developing, operating, and maintaining them.'

Software Crisis

- It was in the late 1960s when many software projects failed.

- Many software became over budget. Output was unreliable software which is expensive to maintain.

- Larger software was difficult and quite expensive to maintain.

- Lots of software not able to satisfy the growing requirements of the customer.

- Complexities of software projects increased whenever its hardware capability increased.

- Demand for new software increased faster compared with the ability to generate new software.

The Solution

Solution was to the problem was transforming unorganized coding effort into software engineering discipline. These engineering models helped companies to streamline operations and deliver software meeting customer requirements.

- The late 1970s saw the widespread uses of software engineering principles.

- In the 1980s saw the automation of software engineering process and growth of (CASE) Computer-Aided Software Engineering.

- The 1990s have seen an increased emphasis on the 'management' aspects of projects standard of quality and processes just like ISO 9001.

Popularity of Software Engineering

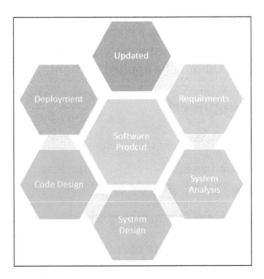

Here are the important reasons behind the popularity of software engineering:

- Large software: In our real life, it is quite more comfortable to build a wall than a house or building. In the same manner, as the size of the software becomes large, software engineering helps you to build software.

- Scalability: If the software development processes were based on scientific and engineering concepts, it is easier to re-create new software to scale an existing one.

- Adaptability: Whenever the software process was based on scientific and engineering, it is easy to re-create new software with the help of software engineering.

- Cost: Hardware industry has shown its skills and huge manufacturing has lower the cost of the computer and electronic hardware.

- Dynamic Nature: Always growing and adapting nature of the software. It depends on the environment in which the user works.

- Quality Management: Offers better method of software development to provide quality software products.

Relationship of Software Engineering with other Disciplines

Here, how software engineering related to other disciplines:

- Computer Science: Gives the scientific foundation for the software as electrical engineering mainly depends on physics.

- Management Science: Software engineering is labor-intensive work which demands both technical and managerial control. Therefore, it is widely used in management science.

- Economics: In this sector, software engineering helps you in resource estimation and cost control. Computing system must be developed, and data should be maintained regularly within a given budget.

- System Engineering: Most software is a component of a much larger system. For example, the software in an Industry monitoring system or the flight software on an airplane. Software engineering methods should be applied to the study of this type of systems.

Challenges of Software Engineering

Here are some critical challenges faced by software engineers:

- In safety-critical areas such as space, aviation, nuclear power plants, etc. the cost of software failure can be massive because lives are at risk.

- Increased market demands for fast turnaround time.

- Dealing with the increased complexity of software need for new applications.

- The diversity of software systems should be communicating with each other.

Attributes for Software Products

The characteristics of any software product include features which are displayed by the product when it is installed and put in use. They are not the services which are provided by the product. Instead, they have related to the products dynamic behavior and the use made of the product. Examples of these attributes are: Efficiency, reliability, robustness, maintainability, etc.

However, the relative importance of these characteristics varies from one software system to another.

Product Characteristics	Description
Maintainability	The software should evolve to meet the changing demands of the clients.
Dependability	Dependability includes various characteristics. Dependable software should never cause any physical or economic damage at the time of system failure.
Efficiency	The software application should overuse system resources like memory and processor cycle.
Usability	The software application should have specific UI and documentation.

Optimizing the above attribute is very challenging. For example, offering a better UI can reduce system efficiency.

Characteristics of Good Software

Any software should be judged by what it offers and what the methods which help you to use it are.

Every software must satisfy the following attributes:

- Operational,
- Transitional,
- Maintenance.

Here are some important characteristics of good software developed by software professionals:

Operational

This characteristic let us know about how well software works in the operations which can be measured on:

- Budget,
- Efficiency,
- Usability,
- Dependability,
- Correctness,
- Functionality,

- Safety,
- Security.

Transitional

This is an essential aspect when the software is moved from one platform to another:

- Interoperability,
- Reusability,
- Portability,
- Adaptability.

Maintenance

This aspect talks about how well software has the capabilities to adapt itself in the quickly changing environment:

- Flexibility,
- Maintainability,
- Modularity,
- Scalability.

Software Requirements

The software requirements are description of features and functionalities of the target system. Requirements convey the expectations of users from the software product. The requirements can be obvious or hidden, known or unknown, expected or unexpected from client's point of view.

Requirement Engineering

The process to gather the software requirements from client, analyze and document them is known as requirement engineering. The goal of requirement engineering is to develop and maintain sophisticated and descriptive 'System Requirements Specification' document.

Requirement Engineering Process

It is a four step process, which includes:

- Feasibility Study,
- Requirement Gathering,
- Software Requirement Specification,
- Software Requirement Validation.

Feasibility Study

When the client approaches the organization for getting the desired product developed, it comes up with rough idea about what all functions the software must perform and which all features are expected from the software. Referencing to this information, the analysts does a detailed study about whether the desired system and its functionality are feasible to develop.

This feasibility study is focused towards goal of the organization. This study analyzes whether the software product can be practically materialized in terms of implementation, contribution of project to organization, cost constraints and as per values and objectives of the organization. It explores technical aspects of the project and product such as usability, maintainability, and productivity and integration ability. The output of this phase should be a feasibility study report that should contain adequate comments and recommendations for management about whether or not the project should be undertaken.

Requirement Gathering

If the feasibility report is positive towards undertaking the project, next phase starts with gathering requirements from the user. Analysts and engineers communicate with the client and end-users to know their ideas on what the software should provide and which features they want the software to include.

Software Requirement Specification

SRS is a document created by system analyst after the requirements are collected from various stakeholders. SRS defines how the intended software will interact with hardware, external interfaces, speed of operation, response time of system, portability of software across various platforms, maintainability, speed of recovery after crashing, security, quality, limitations etc.

The requirements received from client are written in natural language. It is the responsibility of system analyst to document the requirements in technical language so that they can be comprehended and useful by the software development team.

SRS should come up with following features:

- User requirements are expressed in natural language.
- Technical requirements are expressed in structured language, which is used inside the organization.
- Design description should be written in Pseudo code.
- Format of forms and GUI screen prints.
- Conditional and mathematical notations for DFDs etc.

Software Requirement Validation

After requirement specifications are developed, the requirements mentioned are validated. User might ask for illegal, impractical solution or experts may interpret the requirements incorrectly.

This results in huge increase in cost if not nipped in the bud. Requirements can be checked against following conditions:

- If they can be practically implemented.

- If they are valid and as per functionality and domain of software.

- If there are any ambiguities.

- If they are complete.

- If they can be demonstrated.

Requirement Elicitation Process

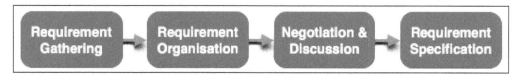

Requirement elicitation process can be depicted using the following diagram:

- Requirements gathering - The developers discuss with the client and end users and know their expectations from the software.

- Organizing Requirements - The developers prioritize and arrange the requirements in order of importance, urgency and convenience.

- Negotiation & discussion - If requirements are ambiguous or there are some conflicts in requirements of various stakeholders, if they are, it is then negotiated and discussed with stakeholders. Requirements may then be prioritized and reasonably compromised.

  The requirements come from various stakeholders. To remove the ambiguity and conflicts, they are discussed for clarity and correctness. Unrealistic requirements are compromised reasonably.

- Documentation - All formal & informal, functional and non-functional requirements are documented and made available for next phase processing.

Requirement Elicitation Techniques

Requirements Elicitation is the process to find out the requirements for an intended software system by communicating with client, end users, system users and others who have a stake in the software system development.

Interviews

Interviews are strong medium to collect requirements. Organization may conduct several types of interviews such as:

- Structured (closed) interviews, where every single information to gather is decided in advance, they follow pattern and matter of discussion firmly.

- Non-structured (open) interviews, where information to gather is not decided in advance, more flexible and less biased.

- Oral interviews.

- Written interviews.

- One-to-one interviews which are held between two persons across the table.

- Group interviews which are held between groups of participants. They help to uncover any missing requirement as numerous people are involved.

Surveys

Organization may conduct surveys among various stakeholders by querying about their expectation and requirements from the upcoming system.

Questionnaires

A document with pre-defined set of objective questions and respective options is handed over to all stakeholders to answer, which are collected and compiled. A shortcoming of this technique is, if an option for some issue is not mentioned in the questionnaire, the issue might be left unattended.

Task Analysis

Team of engineers and developers may analyze the operation for which the new system is required. If the client already has some software to perform certain operation, it is studied and requirements of proposed system are collected.

Domain Analysis

Every software falls into some domain category. The expert people in the domain can be a great help to analyze general and specific requirements.

Brainstorming

An informal debate is held among various stakeholders and all their inputs are recorded for further requirements analysis.

Prototyping

Prototyping is building user interface without adding detail functionality for user to interpret the features of intended software product. It helps giving better idea of requirements. If there is no software installed at client's end for developer's reference and the client is not aware of its own requirements, the developer creates a prototype based on initially mentioned requirements. The prototype is shown to the client and the feedback is noted. The client feedback serves as an input for requirement gathering.

Observation

Team of experts visit the client's organization or workplace. They observe the actual working of the existing installed systems. They observe the workflow at client's end and how execution problems are dealt. The team itself draws some conclusions which aid to form requirements expected from the software.

Software Requirements Characteristics

Gathering software requirements is the foundation of the entire software development project. Hence they must be clear, correct and well-defined. A complete Software Requirement Specifications must be:

- Clear,
- Correct,
- Consistent,
- Coherent,
- Comprehensible,
- Modifiable,
- Verifiable,
- Prioritized,
- Unambiguous,
- Traceable,
- Credible source.

Types of Software Requirements

We should try to understand what sort of requirements may arise in the requirement elicitation phase and what kinds of requirements are expected from the software system. Broadly software requirements should be categorized in two categories:

Functional Requirements

Requirements, which are related to functional aspect of software fall into this category. They define functions and functionality within and from the software system. Examples:

- Search option given to user to search from various invoices,
- User should be able to mail any report to management,
- Users can be divided into groups and groups can be given separate rights,

- Should comply business rules and administrative functions,
- Software is developed keeping downward compatibility intact.

Non-Functional Requirements

Requirements, which are not related to functional aspect of software, fall into this category. They are implicit or expected characteristics of software, which users make assumption of. Non-functional requirements include:

- Security,
- Logging,
- Storage,
- Configuration,
- Performance,
- Cost,
- Interoperability,
- Flexibility,
- Disaster recovery,
- Accessibility.

Requirements are categorized logically as:

- Must have: Software cannot be said operational without them,
- Should have: Enhancing the functionality of software,
- Could have: Software can still properly function with these requirements,
- Wish list: These requirements do not map to any objectives of software.

While developing software, 'Must have' must be implemented, 'Should have' is a matter of debate with stakeholders and negation, whereas 'could have' and 'wish list' can be kept for software updates.

User Interface Requirements

UI is an important part of any software or hardware or hybrid system. Software is widely accepted if it is:

- Easy to operate,
- Quick in response,
- Effectively handling operational errors,
- Providing simple yet consistent user interface.

User acceptance majorly depends upon how user can use the software. UI is the only way for users to perceive the system. A well performing software system must also be equipped with attractive, clear, consistent and responsive user interface. Otherwise the functionalities of software system cannot be used in convenient way. A system is said be good if it provides means to use it efficiently. User interface requirements are briefly mentioned below:

- Content presentation,
- Easy Navigation,
- Simple interface,
- Responsive,
- Consistent UI elements,
- Feedback mechanism,
- Default settings,
- Purposeful layout,
- Strategical use of color and texture,
- Provide help information,
- User centric approach,
- Group based view settings.

Software System Analyst

System analyst in an IT organization is a person, who analyzes the requirement of proposed system and ensures that requirements are conceived and documented properly & correctly. Role of an analyst starts during Software Analysis Phase of SDLC. It is the responsibility of analyst to make sure that the developed software meets the requirements of the client. System Analysts have the following responsibilities:

- Analyzing and understanding requirements of intended software,
- Understanding how the project will contribute in the organization objectives,
- Identify sources of requirement,
- Validation of requirement,
- Develop and implement requirement management plan,
- Documentation of business, technical, process and product requirements,
- Coordination with clients to prioritize requirements and remove and ambiguity,
- Finalizing acceptance criteria with client and other stakeholders.

Software Metrics and Measures

Software Measures can be understood as a process of quantifying and symbolizing various attributes and aspects of software. Software Metrics provide measures for various aspects of software process and software product.

Software measures are fundamental requirement of software engineering. They not only help to control the software development process but also aid to keep quality of ultimate product excellent. Let us see some software metrics:

- Size Metrics - LOC (Lines of Code), mostly calculated in thousands of delivered source code lines, denoted as KLOC.

  Function Point Count is measure of the functionality provided by the software. Function Point count defines the size of functional aspect of software.

- Complexity Metrics - McCabe's Cyclomatic complexity quantifies the upper bound of the number of independent paths in a program, which is perceived as complexity of the program or its modules. It is represented in terms of graph theory concepts by using control flow graph.

- Quality Metrics - Defects, their types and causes, consequence, intensity of severity and their implications define the quality of product.

  The number of defects found in development process and number of defects reported by the client after the product is installed or delivered at client-end, define quality of product.

- Process Metrics - In various phases of SDLC, the methods and tools used, the company standards and the performance of development are software process metrics.

- Resource Metrics - Effort, time and various resources used, represents metrics for resource measurement.

Software Reliability

Software reliability is defined as the probability of failure-free operation of a software system for a specified time in a specified environment. The key elements of the definition include probability of failure-free operation, length of time of failure-free operation and the given execution environment. Failure intensity is a measure of the reliability of a software system operating in a given environment. Example: An air traffic control system fails once in two years.

Factors Influencing Software Reliability

- Auser's perception of the reliability of software depends upon two categories of information:

  ○ The number of faults present in the software.

- ◦ The way users operate the system. This is known as the operational profile.
- The fault count in a system is influenced by the following:
  - ◦ Size and complexity of code.
  - ◦ Characteristics of the development process used.
  - ◦ Education, experience, and training of development personnel.
  - ◦ Operational environment.

Applications of Software Reliability

The applications of software reliability includes:

- Comparison of software engineering technologies:
  - ○ What is the cost of adopting a technology?
  - ○ What is the return from the technology - in terms of cost and quality?
- Measuring the progress of system testing: The failure intensity measure tells us about the present quality of the system: high intensity means more tests are to be performed.
- Controlling the system in operation: The amount of change to software for maintenance affects its reliability.
- Better insight into software development processes: Quantification of quality gives us a better insight into the development processes.

Functional and Non-functional Reliability Requirements

System functional requirements may specify error checking, recovery features, and system failure protection. System reliability and availability are specified as part of the non-functional requirements for the system.

System Reliability Specification

- Hardware reliability focuses on the probability a hardware component fails.
- Software reliability focuses on the probability a software component will produce an incorrect output. The software does not wear out and it can continue to operate after a bad result.
- Operator reliability focuses on the probability when a system user makes an error.

Failure Probabilities

If there are two independent components in a system and the operation of the system depends on them both then, $P(S) = P(A) + P(B)$.

If the components are replicated then the probability of failure is $P(S) = P(A)^n$ which means that all components fail at once.

Functional Reliability Requirements

- The system will check all operator inputs to see that they fall within their required ranges.

- The system will check all disks for bad blocks each time it is booted.

- The system must be implemented in using a standard implementation of Ada.

Non-functional Reliability Specification

The required level of reliability must be expressed quantitatively. Reliability is a dynamic system attribute. Source code reliability specifications are meaningless (e.g. N faults/1000 LOC). An appropriate metric should be chosen to specify the overall system reliability.

Hardware Reliability Metrics

Hardware metrics are not suitable for software since its metrics are based on notion of component failure. Software failures are often design failures. Often the system is available after the failure has occurred. Hardware components can wear out.

Software Reliability Metrics

Reliability metrics are units of measure for system reliability. System reliability is measured by counting the number of operational failures and relating these to demands made on the system at the time of failure. A long-term measurement program is required to assess the reliability of critical systems.

Probability of Failure on Demand

The probability system will fail when a service request is made. It is useful when requests are made on an intermittent or infrequent basis. It is appropriate for protection systems where service requests may be rare and consequences can be serious if service is not delivered. It is relevant for many safety-critical systems with exception handlers.

Rate of Fault Occurrence

Rate of fault occurrence reflects upon the rate of failure in the system. It is useful when system has to process a large number of similar requests that are relatively frequent. It is relevant for operating systems and transaction processing systems.

Reliability Metrics

Reliability metrics are used to quantitatively express the reliability of the software product. The option of which metric is to be used depends upon the type of system to which it applies & the requirements of the application domain.

Some reliability metrics which can be used to quantify the reliability of the software product are as follows:

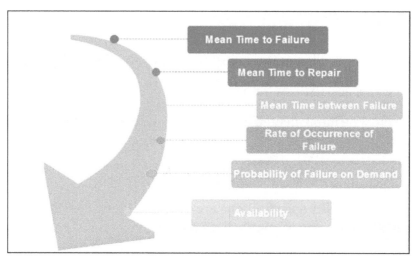

Reliability metrics.

Mean Time to Failure (MTTF)

MTTF is described as the time interval between the two successive failures. An MTTF of 200 mean that one failure can be expected each 200-time units. The time units are entirely dependent on the system & it can even be stated in the number of transactions. MTTF is consistent for systems with large transactions.

For example, it is suitable for computer-aided design systems where a designer will work on a design for several hours as well as for Word-processor systems. To measure MTTF, we can evidence the failure data for n failures. Let the failures appear at the time instants t_1, t_2.....t_n.

MTTF can be calculated as:

$$\sum_{i=1}^{n} \frac{t_{i+1} - t_i}{(n-1)}$$

Mean Time to Repair (MTTR)

Once failure occurs, some-time is required to fix the error. MTTR measures the average time it takes to track the errors causing the failure and to fix them.

Mean Time between Failure (MTBR)

We can merge MTTF & MTTR metrics to get the MTBF metric.

> MTBF = MTTF + MTTR

Thus, an MTBF of 300 denoted that once the failure appears, the next failure is expected to appear only after 300 hours. In this method, the time measurements are real-time & not the execution time as in MTTF.

Rate of Occurrence of Failure (ROCOF)

It is the number of failures appearing in a unit time interval. The number of unexpected events over a specific time of operation. ROCOF is the frequency of occurrence with which unexpected role is likely to appear. A ROCOF of 0.02 mean that two failures are likely to occur in each 100 operational time unit steps. It is also called the failure intensity metric.

Probability of Failure on Demand (POFOD)

POFOD is described as the probability that the system will fail when a service is requested. It is the number of system deficiency given several systems inputs. POFOD is the possibility that the system will fail when a service request is made.

A POFOD of 0.1 means that one out of ten service requests may fail. POFOD is an essential measure for safety-critical systems. POFOD is relevant for protection systems where services are demanded occasionally.

Availability (AVAIL)

Availability is the probability that the system is applicable for use at a given time. It takes into account the repair time & the restart time for the system. An availability of 0.995 means that in every 1000 time units, the system is feasible to be available for 995 of these. The percentage of time that a system is applicable for use, taking into account planned and unplanned downtime. If a system is down an average of four hours out of 100 hours of operation, its AVAIL is 96%.

Product Metrics

Product metrics are those which are used to build the artifacts i.e. requirement specification documents, system design documents etc. These metrics help in assessment if the product is good enough through reports on attributes like usability, reliability, maintainability & portability. In this measurements are taken from the actual body of the source code.

- Software size is thought to be reflective of complexity, development effort and reliability. Lines of Code (LOC), or LOC in thousands (KLOC), is an intuitive initial approach to measuring software size. The basis of LOC is that program length can be used as a predictor of program characteristics such as effort &ease of maintenance. It is a measure of the functional complexity of the program and is independent of the programming language.

- Function point metric is a method to measure the functionality of a proposed software development based on the count of inputs, outputs, master files, inquires, and interfaces.

- Test coverage metric estimate fault and reliability by performing tests on software products, assuming that software reliability is a function of the portion of software that is successfully verified or tested.

- Complexity is directly related to software reliability, so representing complexity is important. Complexity-oriented metrics is a method of determining the complexity of a program's control structure, by simplifying the code into a graphical representation. Representative metric is McCabe's Complexity Metric.

- Quality metrics measures the quality at various stages of software product development. An important quality metric is defect removal efficiency (DRE). DRE provides a measure of quality because of various quality assurance and control activities applied throughout the development process.

Project Management Metrics

Project metrics describe the project characteristics and execution. If there is good management of project by the programmer then this help us to achieve better products. Relationship exists between the development process and the ability to complete projects on time and within the desired quality objectives. Cost increase when developers use inadequate processes. Higher reliability can be achieved by using better development process, risk management process, configuration management process. These metrics tells about:

- Number of software developers.

- Staffing pattern over the life-cycle of the software.

- Cost and schedule.

- Productivity.

Process Metrics

Process metrics quantify useful attributes of the software development process & its environment. They tell if the process is functioning optimally as they report on attributes like cycle time & rework time. The goal of process metric is to do the right job on first time through the process. The quality of the product is a direct function of the process. So process metrics can be used to estimate, monitor and improve the reliability and quality of software. Process metrics describe the effectiveness and quality of the processes that produce the software product. Examples are:

- Effort required in the process.

- Time to produce the product.

- Effectiveness of defect removal during development.

- Number of defects found during testing.

- Maturity of the process.

Fault and Failure Metrics

A fault is a defect in a program which arises when programmer makes an error and causes failure when executed under particular conditions. These metrics are used to determine the failure-free execution software.

To achieve this goal, number of faults found during testing and the failures or other problems which are reported by the user after delivery are collected, summarized and analyzed. Failure metrics are based upon customer information regarding failures found after release of the software. The failure data collected is therefore used to calculate failure density, Mean Time Between Failures (MTBF) or other parameters to measure or predict software reliability.

Software Metrics for Reliability

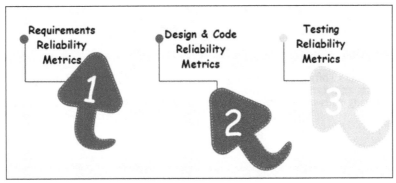

Types of Software Metrics.

The Metrics are used to improve the reliability of the system by identifying the areas of requirements. Different Types of Software Metrics are:

Requirements Reliability Metrics

Requirements denote what features the software must include. It specifies the functionality that must be contained in the software. The requirements must be written such that is no misconception between the developer & the client. The requirements must include valid structure to avoid the loss of valuable data.

The requirements should be thorough and in a detailed manner so that it is simple for the design stage. The requirements should not include inadequate data. Requirement Reliability metrics calculates the above-said quality factors of the required document.

Design and Code Reliability Metrics

The quality methods that exist in design and coding plan are complexity, size, and modularity. Complex modules are tough to understand & there is a high probability of occurring bugs. The reliability will reduce if modules have a combination of high complexity and large size or high complexity and small size. These metrics are also available to object-oriented code, but in this, additional metrics are required to evaluate the quality.

Testing Reliability Metrics

These metrics use two methods to calculate reliability:

- First, it provides that the system is equipped with the tasks that are specified in the requirements. Because of this, the bug due to the lack of functionality reduces.

- The second method is calculating the code, finding the bugs & fixing them. To ensure that the system includes the functionality specified, test plans are written that include multiple test cases. Each test method is based on one system state and tests some tasks that are based on an associated set of requirements. The goals of an effective verification program is to ensure that each elements is tested, the implication being that if the system passes the test, the requirements functionality is contained in the delivered system.

References

- Software, definition: searchapparchitecture.techtarget.com, Retrieved 22, june 2020

- What-is-software-engineering: guru99.com, Retrieved 16, May 2020

- Software-requirements, software-engineering: tutorialspoint.com, Retrieved 06, june 2020

- Software-engineering-software-reliability-metrics: javatpoint.com, Retrieved 21, . 2020

Software Design, Testing and Maintenance

Software design is the process of defining software functions, objects, methods and structure of the programming codes, so that it matches the desired expectations. Software testing is the next step wherein the software is put through trials to ensure that it matches expected requirements and is error free. Software maintenance is the last step which is a continuous process by which a software product is modified and updated periodically. All these topics are covered in detail in this chapter.

Software Design

The design phase of software development deals with transforming the customer requirements as described in the SRS documents into a form implementable using a programming language. The software design process can be divided into the following three levels of phases of design:

- Interface Design.

- Architectural Design.

- Detailed Design.

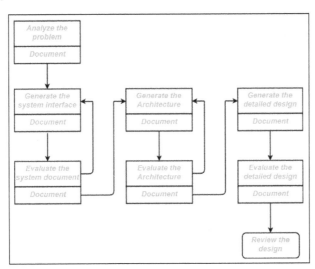

Interface Design

Interface design is the specification of the interaction between a system and its environment. this phase proceeds at a high level of abstraction with respect to the inner workings of the system i.e, during interface design, the internal of the systems are completely ignored and the system is treated as a black box. Attention is focussed on the dialogue between the target system and the users, devices, and other systems with which it interacts. The design problem statement produced during the problem analysis step should identify the people, other systems, and devices which are collectively called *agents*.

Interface design should include the following details:

- Precise description of events in the environment, or messages from agents to which the system must respond.

- Precise description of the events or messages that the system must produce.

- Specification on the data, and the formats of the data coming into and going out of the system.

- Specification of the ordering and timing relationships between incoming events or messages, and outgoing events or outputs.

Architectural Design

Architectural design is the specification of the major components of a system, their responsibilities, properties, interfaces, and the relationships and interactions between them. In architectural design, the overall structure of the system is chosen, but the internal details of major components are ignored.

Issues in architectural design include:

- Gross decomposition of the systems into major components.

- Allocation of functional responsibilities to components.

- Component interfaces.

- Component scaling and performance properties, resource consumption properties, reliability properties, and so forth.

- Communication and interaction between components.

The architectural design adds important details ignored during the interface design. Design of the internals of the major components is ignored until the last phase of the design.

Detailed Design

Design is the specification of the internal elements of all major system components, their properties, relationships, processing, and often their algorithms and the data structures. The detailed design may include:

- Decomposition of major system components into program units.

- Allocation of functional responsibilities to units.

- User interfaces.

- Unit states and state changes.

- Data and control interaction between units.

- Data packaging and implementation, including issues of scope and visibility of program elements.

- Algorithms and data structures.

Objectives of Software Design

- Correctness: A good design should be correct i.e. it should correctly implement all the functionalities of the system.

- Efficiency: A good software design should address the resources, time and cost optimization issues.

- Understandability: A good design should be easily understandable, for which it should be modular and all the modules are arranged in layers.

- Completeness: The design should have all the components like data structures, modules, and external interfaces, etc.

- Maintainability: A good software design should be easily amenable to change whenever a change request is made from the customer side.

Software Design Concepts

Concepts are defined as a principal idea or invention that comes in our mind or in thought to understand something. The software design concept simply means the idea or principle behind the design. It describes how you plan to solve the problem of designing software, the logic, or thinking behind how you will design software. It allows the software engineer to create the model of the system or software or product that is to be developed or built. The software design concept provides a supporting and essential structure or model for developing the right software. There are many concepts of software design and some of them are given below:

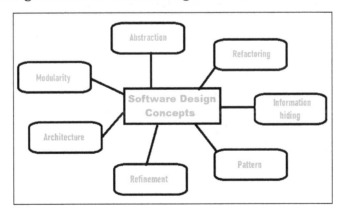

Following points should be considered while designing Software:

- Abstraction - Hide relevant data: Abstraction simply means to hide the details to reduce complexity and increases efficiency or quality. Different levels of Abstraction are necessary and must be applied at each stage of the design process so that any error that is present can be removed to increase the efficiency of the software solution and to refine the software solution. The solution should be described in broadways that cover a wide range of different things at a higher level of abstraction and a more detailed description of a solution of software should be given at the lower level of abstraction.

- Modularity - Subdivide the system: Modularity simply means to divide the system or project into smaller parts to reduce the complexity of the system or project. In the same way, modularity in design means to subdivide a system into smaller parts so that these parts can be created independently and then use these parts in different systems to perform different functions. It is necessary to divide the software into components known as modules because nowadays there is different software available like Monolithic software that is hard to grasp for software engineers. So, modularity is design has now become a trend and is also important.

- Architecture - Design a structure of something: Architecture simply means a technique to design a structure of something. Architecture in designing software is a concept that focuses on various elements and the data of the structure. These components interact with each other and use the data of the structure in architecture.

- Refinement - Removes impurities: Refinement simply means to refine something to remove any impurities if present and increase the quality. The refinement concept of software design is actually a process of developing or presenting the software or system in a detailed manner that means to elaborate a system or software. Refinement is very necessary to find out any error if present and then to reduce it.

- Pattern - A repeated form: The pattern simply means a repeated form or design in which the same shape is repeated   several times to form a pattern. The pattern in the design process means the repetition of a solution to a common recurring problem within a certain context.

- Information Hiding - Hide the information: Information hiding simply means to hide the information so that it cannot be accessed by an unwanted party. In software design, information hiding is achieved by designing the modules in a manner that the information gathered or contained in one module is hidden and it can't be accessed by any other modules.

- Refactoring - Reconstruct something: Refactoring simply means to reconstruct something in such a way that it does not affect the behavior or any other features. Refactoring in software design means to reconstruct the design to reduce and complexity and simplify it without affecting the behavior or its functions. Fowler has defined refactoring as "the process of changing a software system in a way that it won't affect the behavior of the design and improves the internal structure".

Object-Oriented Design

An object-oriented design determines which classes and objects are needed, and specify how they will interact. It encompasses object interaction to implement a solution for a system. Low level design details include how individual methods will accomplish their tasks.

Identifying Classes and Objects

The core activity of object-oriented design is determining the classes and objects that will make up the solution. The classes may be part of a class library, reused from a previous project, or newly written. One way to identify potential classes is to identify the objects discussed in the requirements. Objects are generally nouns, and the services that an object provides are generally verbs. A partial requirement document example is given below from which we can infer that not all nouns will correspond to a class or object in the final solution.

> The user must be allowed to specify each product by its primary characteristics, including its name and product number. If the bar code does not match the product, then an error should be generated to the message window and entered into the error log. The summary report of all transactions must be structured as specified in.

Guidelines for Discovering Objects

The guidelines for discovering objects encompass the following conventions:

- Limit responsibilities of each analysis class.

- Use clear and consistent names for classes and methods.

- Keep analysis classes simple.

Limit Responsibilities

Each class should have a clear and simple purpose for existence. Classes that contain many responsibilities are difficult to comprehend and maintain. A good test for limiting responsibilities lies in making attempts to explain the functionality of a class in a few sentences. As the design progresses and when more feedbacks are obtained from potential end-users, the project drifts and becomes more complicated. Therefore, it is probably good to have tiny objects. Smaller classes can be deployed in the project and later decisions can be made to merge it with other classes.

Use Clear and Consistent Names

Classes and methods should have suitable names. Class names should be nouns. The boundaries of the class tend to become too fuzzy when good names are not coined for the classes. Using too many simple classes is acceptable provided good and descriptive names are coined for the classes.

Keep Classes Simple

The classes should be kept simple without worrying about details like object relationships.

The class represents a group (classification) of objects with the same behaviors. Hence the class represents the concept of one such object. Generally, classes that represent objects should be given names that are singular nouns. Examples: Coin, Student, Message. The developer can instantiate as many objects as needed. Sometimes it is challenging to decide whether something should be represented as a class. For example, should an employee's address be represented as a set of instance variables or as an Address object. The more we examine the problem and its details, more clearly these issues become visible. When a class becomes too complex, it often should be decomposed into multiple smaller classes to distribute the responsibilities. The classes must be defined with the proper amount of detail. For example, it may be unnecessary to create separate classes for each type of appliance in a house and may be sufficient to define a more general Appliance class with appropriate instance data. It all depends on the details of the problem being solved. Identification of class also comprises the process of assigning responsibilities to each class.

Behavior Description

Every activity that a program must accomplish must be represented by one or more methods in one or more classes. We generally use verbs for the names of methods. In early stages it is not necessary to determine every method of every class – begin with primary responsibilities and evolve the design. The set of methods also dictate how your objects interact with each other to produce a solution. Sequence diagrams can help tracing object methods and interactions. The sequence diagram depicts the customer validation while logging on to the system.

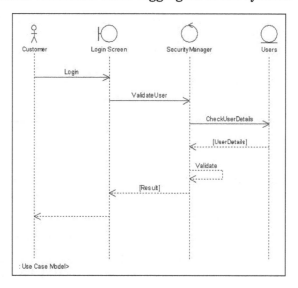

Cohesion between Methods

The methods of an object should be in harmony. If a method seems out of place, then your object might be better off by giving that responsibility to somewhere else. For example, getPosition(), getVelocity(), getAcceleration(), getColor(). Clear and unambiguous method names must be employed. Good names may prevent others to have a need for documentation and it gives a better understanding for other developers. If you cannot find a good name, it might mean that your object is not clearly defined, or you are trying to do too much inside your method.

Static Class Members

A static method is one that can be invoked through its class name. For example, the methods of the Math class are static:

    result = Math.sqrt(25)

Variables can be static as well. Determining whether a method or variable should be static is an important design decision.

Static Modifier

Static methods and variables are declared using the static modifier. It associates the method or variable with the class rather than with an object of that class. Static methods are sometimes called class methods and static variables are sometimes called class variables.

- Static Variables - Each object has its own data space, but if a variable is declared as static, only one copy of the variable exists. The memory space for a static variable is created when the class is first referenced. All objects instantiated from the class share its static variables. The change in value of a static variable in one object changes it for all others private static float price;

- Static Methods – Static methods are namespaced global functions. Static methods sometimes are called class methods.

```
class Helper

{

public static int cube (int num) {

return num * num * num;

}}
```

Because it is declared as static, the method can be invoked as value = Helper.cube(5);

- Static Class Members - Static methods and static variables often work together. The following example keeps track of how many objects have been created using a static variable, and makes that information available using a static method.

```
class MyClass {
    private static int count = 0;

    public MyClass () {
        count++;
    }

    public static int getCount () {
        return count;
    }
}
```

```
MyClass obj;

    for (int scan=1; scan <= 10;
scan+-)

        obj = new MyClass();

        System.out.println ("Objects
created: " +
            MyClass.getCount());
```

Class Relationships

Classes in a software system can have various types of relationships to each other. Three of the most common relationships:

- Dependency: A uses B.

- Aggregation: A has-a B.

- Inheritance: A is-a B.

Dependency

A dependency exists when one class relies on another in some way, usually by invoking the methods of the other. Numerous or complex dependencies among classes must be avoided as we do not want complex classes that depend on others. A good design strikes the right balance. Some dependencies occur between objects of the same class. A method of the class may accept an object of the same class as a parameter.

For example, the concat method of the String class takes as a parameter another String object,

> str3 = str1. concat (str2);

This drives home the idea that the service is being requested from a particular object.

Aggregation

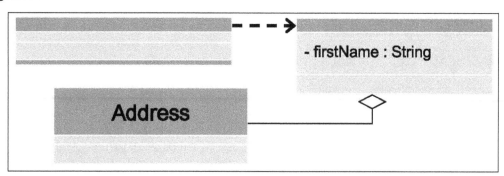

An aggregate is an object that is made up of other objects. Therefore aggregation is type of has-a relationship. E.g. A car has a chassis. In software, an aggregate object contains references to other objects as instance data. The aggregate object is defined in part by the objects that make it up. This is a special kind of dependency – the aggregate usually relies on the objects that compose it. The following example expresses aggregation in UML.

Inheritance

Classes with a set of similar attributes and operations may be organized into a hierarchical relationship. Common attributes and operations are factored out and assigned to a broad superclass (generalization):

- Generalization is the "is-a" relationship.

- Super classes are ancestors, subclasses are descendants.

A class can be iteratively refined into subclasses that inherit the attributes and operations of the superclass (specialization). The following figure provides an example for inheritance where "ball" is the superclass and the types of balls such as "football, baseball, basketball" are subclasses which inherit the properties of the superclass "ball".

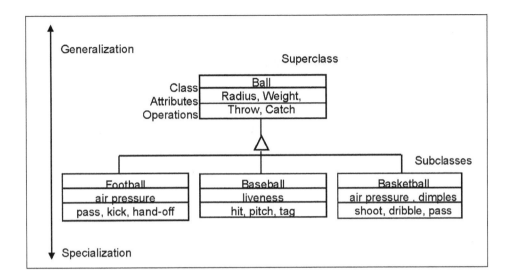

Class Design Principles (SOLID)

The object oriented design is comprised of five design principles called "SOLID" that facilitates agile software development. The SOLID principles are as follows:

- SRP: The Single Responsibility Principle.
- OCP: The Open/Closed Principle.
- LSP: The Liskov Substitution Principle.
- ISP: The Interface Segregation Principle.
- DIP: The Dependency Inversion Principle.

Single Responsibility Principle

A class should have one, and only one, reason to change. It should possess a single responsibility.

Open/Closed Principle

A principle that states we should add new functionalities by adding new code, not editing old code. Abstraction is the key for this principle. It aims at providing room for extension but not for modification.

Liskov Substitution Principle

All derived classes must be substitutable for their base classes. This principle guides us in the creation of abstractions. LSP Guides the Creation of Abstractions. Derived classes must be usable through the base class interface, without the need for the user to know the difference.

Interface Segregation Principle

Interface Segregation Principle splits interfaces to manage dependencies. Sometimes class methods have various groupings. These classes are used for different purposes and not all users rely upon all methods and they should not be forced to rely on method that they do not use. This lack of cohesion can cause serious dependency problems which are to be refactored.

Dependency Inversion Principle

Dependency Inversion Principle avoids the following actions such as, deriving from concrete classes, associating to concrete classes, aggregating concrete classes and dependencies on concrete components. The key factor of this principle states that "Details should depend on abstractions. Abstractions should not depend on details".

Benefits of Object Oriented Design

The Factory Pattern

Factories, Factory Methods and Abstract Factories are used to group together related objects and introduce a single point of entry to interact with them. For example, if an application needs to support multiple databases, the Factory pattern can be used to hide the database specific protocols to upper layers in the architecture and to determine which database configuration is currently being used. The beauty of this pattern is, if implemented correctly, additions to the factory (such as introducing a new database to support) do not require changes to the existing code, but only additions. This of course reduces testing complexity, hence saving time.

The Builder Pattern

The builder pattern assigns the building (construction) of complex objects (such as reports) to a Builder object. The cost benefit of this is that it allows for quick resolution of errors that may arise in handling these complex objects since there is a single construction point.

The Command Pattern

In this pattern, each "command" or request in an application is encapsulated in an object. This facilitates changing the request requirements, such as what information is submitted on a form, by changing only the single command object, without having a ripple effect on the rest of the application. Once again, testing complexity is reduced and time overhead is cut.

The Controller Pattern

There are several variants of the controller pattern, but the prominent one advocates using a single "controller" class for a distinct use case. The advantage here is ease of troubleshooting and a streamlined change process for requirement changes or updates.

The Mediator Pattern

A mediator defines how a set of complex objects works together. This is useful with complex business logic to make easy updates on change requests without having to redefine object relations throughout the application.

The Template Method Pattern

The template method pattern allows for a business process to be partially implemented, while delegating implementation-specific chunks to implementation objects. This facilitates the implementation of flexible requirements by allowing change and easy prototyping in cases where the product behavior is experimental or not completely specified or agreed upon.

The Adapter Pattern

The adapter pattern accommodates the creation of an adapter to emulate a similar process in another branch of the product. This obviously saves time, both during development and testing, for applications that have similar behaviors in multiple parts of the application (such as creating records in the database). It also makes the application more extensible to new features that continue the trend of the similar behaviors.

The Decorator Pattern

The decorator pattern allows the behavior of the application to change dynamically. If implemented correctly, it can change or add behaviors to the current application without modifying existing code. This naturally lends itself to flexible requirements, as well as reduces development time on upgrades.

Component-Based Design

The concept of component-based design envisions building websites out of ready-made elements (components), which are designed and programmed segments to be used as building blocks for your website.

In other words, components are like LEGO bricks, which you can assemble in various ways to build your subpages by composing and arranging them in various ways in order to achieve the desired goal. A component is like a ready-made element, which you can fill with any content or add graphic elements to it. What is more, components are not tied to specific a subpage, which means that you can use them throughout your website. Examples of such components include text blocks, a photo banner, a contact form, or a call-to-action block. If you find yourself in a need to come up with a new landing page in a pinch, you can easily and quickly build one using a library of ready-made components. That means you don't have to pay the developers to code it from scratch since all the elements were coded ahead of time.

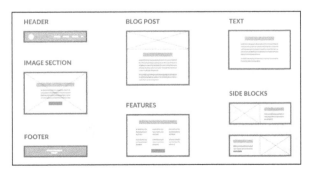

Benefits of Component-based Websites

One of the most important ones is definitely versatility in reusing these building blocks since they enable you to freely shape and rearrange your website without the help of developers. The components are intuitive and easy to use, and more importantly, they don't require you to have any web development knowledge. They are designed in such a way as to make any website administrator able to easily modify and add required sections and build new subpages. In other words, you can simply click your way to a new subpage if you need one.

All changes in design or code modifications of a given element are easier. You can modify the design of the component template, and all subpages containing the component will immediately adapt and reflect the changes. This is a great time-saver, since all changes have to be made just once, and the effect is visible immediately on all subpages that use the given component.

By building a component-based website, in reality, you're building a website management system. The resulting tool is both effective and easy to use, and as an additional perk, it offers outstanding potential in terms of modification to website administrator. Building such a website requires creating a basic structure, which enables the administrator to freely shape the subpages, as well as designing and coding elements, which can be added to the structure.

Component-level Design

Steps 1 and 2: Identify Classes

- Most classes from the problem domain are analysis classes created as part of the analysis model.

- The infrastructure design classes are introduced as components during architectural design.

Step 3: Class Elaboration

- Specify message details when classes or components collaborate.

- Identify appropriate interfaces for each component.

- Elaborate attributes and define data structures required to implement them.

- Describe processing flow within each operation in detail.

Collaboration Details

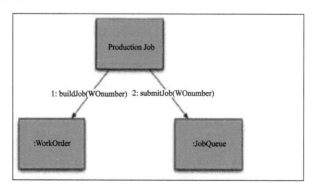

Messages can be elaborated by expanding their syntax in the following manner: [guard condition] sequence expression (return value) := message name (argument list) The following example of "ProductionJob" depicts the collaboration details for job production module.

Appropriate Interfaces

PrintJob interface "initiateJob", which does not exhibit sufficient cohesion because it performs three different sub functions – refactoring can be performed.

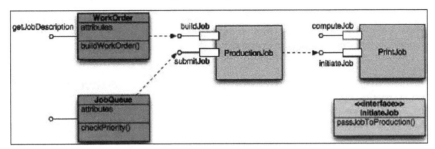

Elaborate Attributes

Analysis classes will typically only list names of general attributes (ex. paperType). All the attributes during component design are listed. UML syntax:

```
name: type-expression = initial-value { property string }
```

For example, paperType can be broken into weight, size, and color. The weight attribute would be:

```
paperType-weight: string = "A" { contains 1 of 4 values – A, B, C, or D }
```

Describe Processing Flow

The process follow is described in detail using activity diagram. The activity diagram for compute-PaperCost( ) is shown below which provides a detail description of the modules.

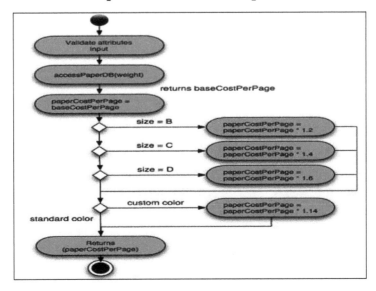

Step 4: Persistent Data

The persistent data sources are described (databases and files) and the classes required to manage them are identified.

Step 5: Elaborate Behavior

It is sometimes necessary to model the behavior of a design class. Transitions from state to state have the form:

Event-name (parameter-list) [guard-condition] / action expression

The behavior of the system is elaborated using a state diagram to depict the transition of states during work flow. The following state diagram provides the transition of states for BuildingJob-Data.

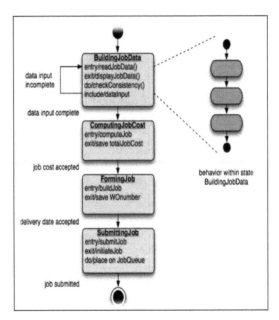

Step 6: Elaborate Deployment Diagrams

Deployment diagrams are elaborated to represent the location of key packages or components.

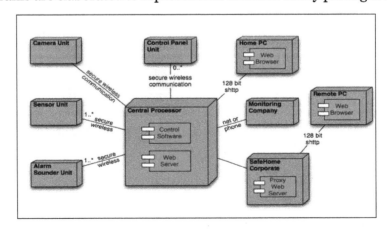

Step 7: Redesign/Reconsider

The first component-level model you create will not be as complete, consistent, or accurate as the nth iteration you apply to the model. The best designers will consider many alternative design solutions before settling on the final design model.

Design Reuse

Design reuse is the process of building new software applications and tools by reusing previously developed designs. New features and functionalities may be added by incorporating minor changes.

Design reuse involves the use of designed modules, such as logic and data, to build a new and improved product. The reusable components, including code segments, structures, plans and reports, minimize implementation time and are less expensive. This avoids reinventing existing software by using techniques already developed and to create and test the software. Design reuse is used in a variety of fields, from software and hardware to manufacturing and aeronautics.

Design reuse involves many activities utilizing existing technologies to cater to new design needs. The ultimate goal of design reuse is to help the developers create better products maximizing it's value with minimal resources, cost and effort.

Today, it is almost impossible to develop an entire product from scratch. Reuse of design becomes necessary to maintain continuity and connectivity. In the software field, the reuse of the modules and data helps save implementation time and increases the possibility of eliminating errors due to prior testing and use.

Design reuse requires that a set of designed products already exist and the design information pertaining to the product is accessible. Large software companies usually have a range of designed products. Hence the reuse of design facilitates making new and better software products. Many software companies have incorporated design reuse and have seen considerable success. The effectiveness of design reuse is measured in terms of production, time, cost and quality of the product. These key factors determine whether a company has been successful in making design reuse a solution to its new software needs and demands. With proper use of existing technology and resources, a company can benefit in terms of cost, time, performance and product quality.

A proper process requires an intensive design reuse process model. There are two interrelated process methodologies involved in the systematic design reuse process model.

The data reuse process is as follows:

- Gathering Information: This involves the collection of information, processing and modeling to fetch related data.

- Information Reuse: This involves the effective use of data.

The design reuse process has four major issues:

- Retrieve,

- Reuse,

- Repair,

- Recover.

These are generally referred to as the four Rs. In spite of these challenges, companies have used the design reuse concept as a successfully implemented concept in the software field at different levels, ranging from low level code reuse to high level project reuse.

Reuse Based Software Engineering

Reused based software engineering can be categorized as the following:

- Application system reuse,

- Component reuse,

- Function reuse.

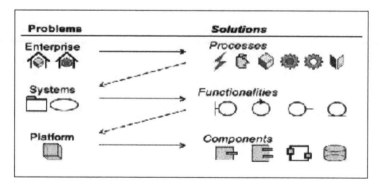

Application System Reuse

The whole of an application system may be reused either by incorporating it without change into other systems (COTS reuse) or by developing application families. Widely practised as software systems are implemented as application families and COTS reuse is becoming increasingly common.

Component Reuse

Components of an application from sub-systems to single objects may be reused. Component reuse is seen as the key to effective and widespread reuse through component based software engineering. Component reuse must allow easy access and retrieval to the components, the component size must be suitable and the functionalities must be easy to comprehend.

Function Reuse

Software components that implement a single well-defined function may be reused. Function reuse is common in some application domains (e.g. engineering) where domain-specific libraries of reusable functions have been established.

Benefits of Reuse

- Increased reliability - Components exercised in working systems are tried and tested under real conditions.

- Reduced process risk - Less uncertainty in development costs.

- Effective use of specialists - The components are reused instead of application experts develop components instead of repeating the same on multiple projects.

- Standards compliance - Embed standards in reusable components (e.g. menu format).

- Accelerated development - Avoid original development and hence speed-up production which may reduce testing time as well.

Requirements for Design with Reuse

The requirements for design with reuse comprises of the following:

- It must be possible to find appropriate reusable components.

- The re-user of the component must be confident that the components will be reliable and will behave as specified.

- The components must be documented so that they can be understood and, where appropriate, modified.

Reuse Problems

The challenges encountered during reusing of components are as follows:

- Increased maintenance costs - If source code of components is not available, then other parts for modification must be engineered around the components which are inflexible.

- Not-invented-here syndrome - Some developers resist reuse due to matter of trust, and question of creativity.

- Lack of tool support.

- Maintaining a component library as an effective library for reuse can be difficult and expensive.

- Finding and adapting reusable components.

Generator-based Reuse

Program generators involve the reuse of standard patterns and algorithms. These are embedded in the generator and parameterised by user commands from which a program is then automatically generated. Generator-based reuse is possible when domain abstractions and their mapping to executable code can be identified. A domain specific language is used to compose and control these abstractions.

Types of Program Generator

- Application generators for business data processing.

- Parser and lexical analyser generators for language processing.

- Code generators in CASE tools.

Reuse through Program Generation

Reuse through program generation involves obtaining a well-defined application description which contains the details of the application. The application domain knowledge is gathered, the description and knowledge are fed into the program generator which automatically generates the program which has access to the database.

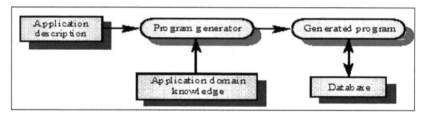

Component-based Development

Component-based software engineering (CBSE) is an approach to software development that re-lies on reuse. Components are more abstract than object classes and can be considered to be stand-alone service providers. Components provide a service without regard to where the component is executing or its programming language. Components can range in size from simple functions to entire application systems and are independent – very loosely coupled. Components are encapsu-lated to wrap functionalities. The components are obtained from the repositories which are com-posed to develop a component based system.

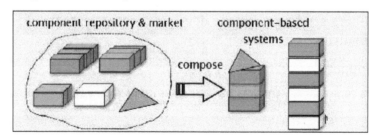

Component Interfaces

Component interface provides the interaction between components of a system. A component en-compasses two functionalities in terms of interface:

- Provides interface – It defines the services that are provided by the component to other components.

- Requires interface – It defines the services that specifies what services must be made available for the component to execute as specified.

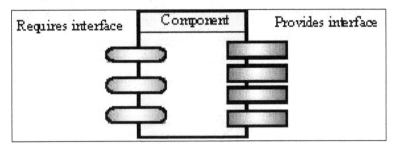

Example: Printing Services Component.

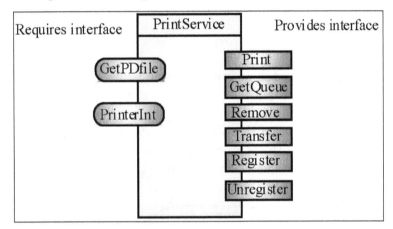

- Requires – GetPDFile – to get printer description file for a printer type, and PrinterInt – to transfer commands to a specific printer.

- Provides – Print, GetOueue, Remove, Transfer, Register and Unregister.

Components – Different Levels of Abstractions

Components possess different levels of abstraction as follows:

- Functional abstraction - The component implements a single function such as a mathematical function.

- Casual groupings - The component is a collection of loosely related entities that might be data declarations, functions, etc.

- Data abstractions - The component represents a data abstraction or class in an objectoriented language.

- Cluster abstractions - The component is a group of related classes that work together (sometimes called a framework).

- System abstraction - The component is an entire self-contained system. Provides interface is the so-called API (application programming interface).

CBSE Processes

The system requirements are modified to reflect the components that are available. CBSE usually involves a prototyping or an incremental development process with components being 'glued together' using a scripting language. The process involves designing the system architecture. Based on the architecture the components are specified, the suitable components that can be reused are determined and are incorporated in the architecture for the development of component based software development.

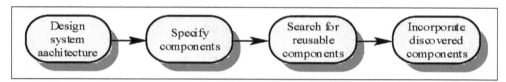

Development with Reuse

The development with reuse methodology involves establishing a well-defined outline of the system requirements. The requirements are analysed and the components that can be reused are determined and selected. Based on the selected components the requirements are modified and the architectural system is well established. The reusable components are determined and the components are specified based on the reusable components that are suitable for development of the system. The specified components are later incorporated in the development of the system.

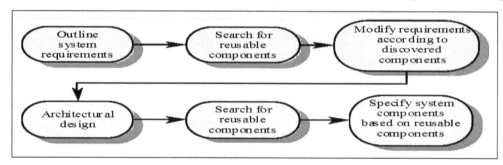

CBSE Problems

The challenges that are encountered during component based software development are as follows:

- Component incompatibilities may mean that cost and schedule savings are less than expected.

- Finding and understanding components.

- Managing evolution as requirements change in situations where it may be impossible to change the system components.

Application Frameworks

Frameworks are a sub-system design made up of a collection of abstract and concrete classes and the interfaces between them. The sub-system is implemented by adding components to fill in parts of the design and by instantiating the abstract classes in the framework. Frameworks are moderately large entities that can be reused. The framework classes include:

System Infrastructure Frameworks

System infrastructure framework supports the development of system infrastructures such as communications, user interfaces and compilers. Best developed of these three is particularly for GUI.

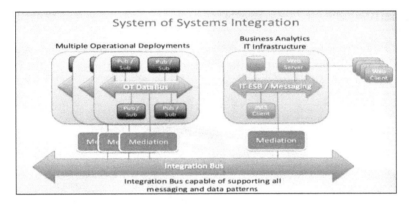

Middleware Integration Frameworks

Standards and classes that support component communication and information exchange encompass middleware integration framework. Examples – CORBA, COM, DCOM, JavaBeans.

Enterprise Application Frameworks

Enterprise Application Frameworks supports the development of specific types of application such as telecommunications or financial systems.

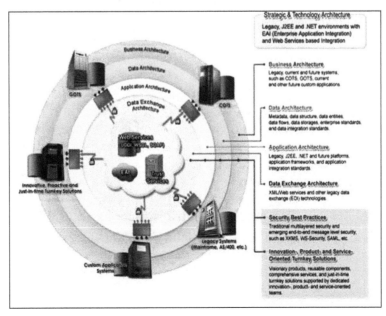

Extending Frameworks

Frameworks are generic and are extended to create a more specific application or sub-system. Extending the framework involves:

- Adding concrete classes that inherit operations from abstract classes in the framework.

- Adding methods that are called in response to events that are recognised by the framework (call backs).

Model-View Controller

Model-View Controller provides a system infrastructure framework for GUI design. It allows multiple presentations of an object and separate interactions with these presentations. MVC framework involves the instantiation of a number of patterns.

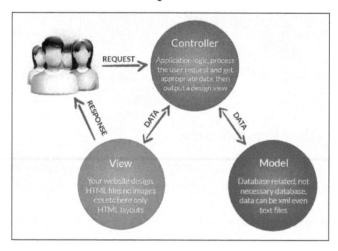

The controller possesses the application logic which processes the users request and gets appropriate response. View provides the visual design and model comprises of the database, sometimes these can be xml or even text files.

COTS Product Reuse

COT is the acronym for Commercial Off-The-Shelf systems. COTS systems are usually complete application systems that offer an API (Application Programming Interface). Building large systems by integrating COTS systems is now a viable development strategy for some types of system such as E-commerce systems.

Component Reusability

Component reusability should reflect stable domain abstractions such as fundamental concepts in the application domain that change slowly – e.g. bank accounts, university students. It should hide state representation and be as independent as possible. Component reusability should publish exceptions through the component interface; different applications will have different requirements for exception handling and the applications handle them rather than trying to handle them in the component.

Reusability Enhancement

- Name generalisation - Names in a component may be modified so that they are not a direct reflection of a specific application entity.

- Operation generalisation- Operations may be added to provide extra functionality and application specific operations may be removed.

- Exception generalisation- Application specific exceptions are removed and exception management added to increase the robustness of the component.

- Component certification - Component is certified as reusable.

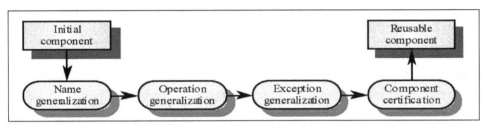

Software Testing

Software Testing is a method to check whether the actual software product matches expected requirements and to ensure that software product is Defect free. It involves execution of software/system components using manual or automated tools to evaluate one or more properties of interest. The purpose of software testing is to identify errors, gaps or missing requirements in contrast to actual requirements.

Some prefer saying Software testing as a White Box and Black Box Testing. In simple terms, Software Testing means the Verification of Application Under Test (AUT).

Importance of Software Engineering

Software Testing is Important because if there are any bugs or errors in the software, it can be identified early and can be solved before delivery of the software product. Properly tested software product ensures reliability, security and high performance which further results in time saving, cost effectiveness and customer satisfaction.

Testing is important because software bugs could be expensive or even dangerous. Software bugs can potentially cause monetary and human loss, and history is full of such examples.

- In April 2015, Bloomberg terminal in London crashed due to software glitch affected more than 300,000 traders on financial markets. It forced the government to postpone a 3bn pound debt sale.

- Nissan cars recalled over 1 million cars from the market due to software failure in the airbag sensory detectors. There have been reported two accidents due to this software failure.

- Starbucks was forced to close about 60 percent of stores in the U.S and Canada due to software failure in its POS system. At one point, the store served coffee for free as they were unable to process the transaction.

- Some of Amazon's third-party retailers saw their product price is reduced to 1p due to a software glitch. They were left with heavy losses.

- Vulnerability in Windows 10. This bug enables users to escape from security sandboxes through a flaw in the win32k system.

- In 2015 fighter plane F-35 fell victim to a software bug, making it unable to detect targets correctly.

- China Airlines Airbus A300 crashed due to a software bug on April 26, 1994, killing 264 innocents live.

- In 1985, Canada's Therac-25 radiation therapy machine malfunctioned due to software bug and delivered lethal radiation doses to patients, leaving 3 people dead and critically injuring 3 others.

- In April of 1999, a software bug caused the failure of a $1.2 billion military satellite launch, the costliest accident in history.

- In May of 1996, a software bug caused the bank accounts of 823 customers of a major U.S. bank to be credited with 920 million US dollars.

Benefits of Software Testing

Here are the benefits of using software testing:

- Cost-Effective: It is one of the important advantages of software testing. Testing any IT project on time helps you to save your money for the long term. In case if the bugs caught in the earlier stage of software testing, it costs less to fix.

- Security: It is the most vulnerable and sensitive benefit of software testing. People are looking for trusted products. It helps in removing risks and problems earlier.

- Product quality: It is an essential requirement of any software product. Testing ensures a quality product is delivered to customers.

- Customer Satisfaction: The main aim of any product is to give satisfaction to their customers. UI/UX Testing ensures the best user experience.

Testing in Software Engineering

As per ANSI/IEEE 1059, Testing in Software Engineering is a process of evaluating a software product to find whether the current software product meets the required conditions or not. The testing process involves evaluating the features of the software product for requirements in terms of any missing requirements, bugs or errors, security, reliability and performance.

Types of Software Testing

Typically Testing is classified into three categories:

- Functional Testing.

- Non-Functional Testing or Performance Testing.

- Maintenance (Regression and Maintenance).

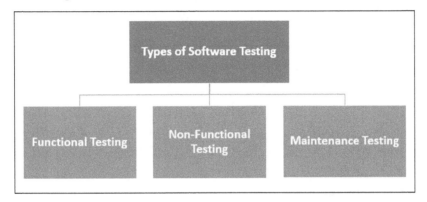

Testing Category	Types of Testing
Functional Testing	Unit Testing
	Integration Testing
	Smoke
	UAT (User Acceptance Testing)
	Localization
	Globalization
	Interoperability
	So on
Non-Functional Testing	Performance
	Endurance
	Load
	Volume
	Scalability
	Usability
	So on
Maintenance	Regression
	Maintenance

Testing Strategies in Software Engineering

Here are important strategies in software engineering:

- Unit Testing: This software testing approach is followed by the programmer to test the unit of the program. It helps developers to know whether the individual unit of the code is working properly or not.

- Integration testing: It focuses on the construction and design of the software. You need to see that the integrated units are working without errors or not.

- System testing: In this method, your software is compiled as a whole and then tested as a whole. This testing strategy checks the functionality, security, portability, amongst others.

Program Testing

Program Testing in software testing is a method of executing an actual software program with the aim of testing program behavior and finding errors. The software program is executed with test case data to analyse the program behavior or response to the test data. A good program testing is one which has high chances of finding bugs.

Computer Bug

In 1947, Harvard University was operating a room-sized computer called the Mark II. It encompassed mechanical relays and glowing vacuum tubes. The technicians program the computer by reconfiguring it and they had to change the occasional vacuum tube. A moth flew into the computer and was zapped by the high voltage when it landed on a relay. Bugs can also be known as:

- Defect,

- Fault,

- Problem,

- Error,

- Incident,

- Anomaly,

- Variance,

- Failure,

- Inconsistency,

- Product Anomaly,

- Product Incidence,

- Feature.

Defective Software

The programs that are developed contain defects which are hard to predict in the future, however it is highly likely, that the software we will develop in the future will not be significantly better.

Sources of Problems

The problems can arise from various sources such as:

- Requirements Definition: Erroneous, incomplete, inconsistent requirements.
- Design: Fundamental design flaws in the software.
- Implementation: Mistakes in chip fabrication, wiring, programming faults, malicious code.
- Support Systems: Poor programming languages, faulty compilers and debuggers, misleading development tools.
- Inadequate Testing of Software: Incomplete testing, poor verification, mistakes in debugging.
- Evolution: Sloppy redevelopment or maintenance, introduction of new flaws in attempts to fix old flaws, incremental escalation to inordinate complexity.

Adverse Effects of Faulty Software

Faulty software causes many adverse effects such as:

- Money Management: Fraud, violation of privacy, shutdown of stock exchanges and banks, negative interest rates.
- Control of Elections: Wrong results (intentional or non-intentional).
- Control of Jails: Technology-aided escape attempts and successes, accidental release of inmates, failures in software controlled locks.
- Law Enforcement: False arrests and imprisonments.

Bug in Space Code

Project Mercury's FORTRAN code had the following fault: DO I = 1.10 instead of... DO I = 1...10. The fault was discovered in an analysis of why the software did not seem to generate results that were sufficiently accurate. The erroneous 1.10 would cause the loop to be executed exactly once.

Military Aviation Problems

An F-18 crashed because of a missing exception condition: if... then... without the else clause that was thought could not possibly arise. In simulation, an F-16 program bug caused the virtual plane to flip over whenever it crossed the equator, as a result of a missing minus sign to indicate south latitude.

Year Ambiguities

In 1992, Mary Bandar received an invitation to attend a kindergarten in Winona, Minnesota, along with others born in '88. Mary was 104 years old at the time. Mr. Blodgett's auto insurance rate tripled when he turned 101. He was the computer program's first driver over 100, and his age was interpreted as 1. This is a double blunder because the program's definition of a teenager is someone under 20.

AT&T Bug

In mid-December 1989, AT&T installed new software in 114 electronic switching systems. On January 15, 1990, 5 million calls were blocked during a 9 hour period nationwide. The bug was traced to a C program that contained a break statement within a switch clause nested within a loop. The switch clause was part of a loop. Initially, the loop contained only if clauses with break statements to exit the loop. When the control logic became complicated, a switch clause was added to improve the readability of the code.

Bank Generosity

A Norwegian bank ATM consistently dispersed 10 times the amount required. Many people joyously joined the queues as the word spread. A software flaw caused a UK bank to duplicate every transfer payment request for half an hour. The bank lost 2 billion British pounds. The bank eventually recovered the funds but lost half a million pounds in potential interest.

Making Rupee

An Australian man purchased $104,500 worth of Sri Lankan Rupees. The next day he sold the Rupees to another bank for $440,258. The first bank's software had displayed a bogus exchange rate in the Rupee position. A judge ruled that the man had acted without intended fraud and could keep the extra $335,758.

Bug in BoNY Software

The Bank of New York (BoNY) had a $32 billion overdraft as the result of a 16-bit integer counter that went unchecked. BoNY was unable to process the incoming credits from security transfers, while the NY Federal Reserve automatically debited BoNY's cash account.

Specification

You have to know what your product is before you can say if it has a bug -"if you can't say it, you can't do it". A specification defines the product being created and includes the functional requirements that describe the features the product will support (E.g. on a word processor save, print, check spelling, change font etc.) and non-functional requirements that focuses on the constraints of the product (E.g. Security, reliability, user friendliness, platform etc.).

Software Bugs

A software bug occurs when at least one of these rules is true:

- The software does not do something that the specification says it should do.

- The software does something that the specification says it should not do.

- The software does something that the specification does not mention.

- The software does not do something that the product specification does not mention but should.

- The software is difficult to understand, hard to use or slow.

Most bugs are not because of mistakes in the code, the estimation of the bugs uncovered at various phases is as follows:

- Specification (~= 55%).

- Design (~= 25%).

- Code (~= 15%).

- Other (~= 5%).

Relative Cost of Bugs

The bugs that are found at later phases cost more to fix. Cost to fix a bug increases exponentially (10^x) i.e. it increases tenfold as time increases. E.g. a bug found during specification costs $1 to fix. If the bug is found in design cost is $10, if found in code cost is $100 and if found in released software cost is $1000. The cost keeps increasing tenfold as the time increases.

Bug Free Software

Software is in the news for the wrong reason such as security breach, Mars Lander lost, hackers getting credit card information, etc. The development of bug free software is difficult when software gets more features and supports more platforms, it becomes increasingly difficult to make it create bug-free. The common questions that arise with the development of bug free software are:

- Why can't software engineers develop software that just works?

- Do you think bug free software is unattainable?

- Are their technical barriers that make this impossible?

- Is it just a question of time before we can do this?

- Are we missing technology or processes?

Process

Software testing can be divided into two steps:

- Verification: it refers to the set of tasks that ensure that software correctly implements a specific function. Example: Verification: "Are we building the product right?"

- Validation: it refers to a different set of tasks that ensure that the software that has been built is traceable to customer requirements. Example: Validation: "Are we building the right product?"

Other Types of Software Testing

Software Testing can be broadly classified into two types:

- Manual Testing: Manual testing includes testing software manually, i.e., without using any automated tool or any script. In this type, the tester takes over the role of an end-user and tests the software to identify any unexpected behavior or bug. There are different stages for manual testing such as unit testing, integration testing, system testing, and user acceptance testing.

- Testers use test plans, test cases, or test scenarios to test software to ensure the completeness of testing. Manual testing also includes exploratory testing, as testers explore the software to identify errors in it.

- Automation Testing: Automation testing, which is also known as Test Automation, is when the tester writes scripts and uses software to test the product. This process involves automation of a manual process. Automation Testing is used to re-run the test scenarios that were performed manually, quickly, and repeatedly.

- Apart from regression testing, automation testing is also used to test the application from load, performance, and stress point of view. It increases the test coverage, improves accuracy, and saves time and money in comparison to manual testing.

Different Levels of Software Testing

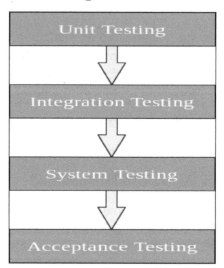

Software level testing can be majorly classified into 4 levels:

- Unit Testing: A level of the software testing process where individual units/components of a software/system are tested. The purpose is to validate that each unit of the software performs as designed.

- Integration Testing: A level of the software testing process where individual units are combined and tested as a group. The purpose of this level of testing is to expose faults in the interaction between integrated units.

- System Testing: A level of the software testing process where a complete, integrated system/software is tested. The purpose of this test is to evaluate the system's compliance with the specified requirements.

- Acceptance Testing: A level of the software testing process where a system is tested for acceptability. The purpose of this test is to evaluate the system's compliance with the business requirements and assess whether it is acceptable for delivery.

Black Box Testing

Black box testing is a software testing technique where the functionalities of the system is tested without comprehending or looking into the internal structure. The characteristics of black-box testing comprises of the following:

- Program is treated as a black box.

- Implementation details do not matter.

- Requires an end-user perspective.

- Criteria are not precise.

- Test planning can begin early.

Black box testing is also known as specification-based testing. Black box testing refers to test activities using specification-based testing methods and criteria to discover program errors based on program requirements and product specifications. The major testing focuses on the following:

- Specification-based function errors.

- Specification-based component/system behavior errors.

- Specification-based performance errors.

- User-oriented usage errors.

- Black box interface errors.

Black box testing comprises of testing software against a specification of its external behavior without knowledge of internal implementation details. It can be applied to software "units" (e.g., classes) or to entire programs. The external behavior is defined in API docs, functional specs, requirements specs, etc. Black box testing purposely disregards the program's control structure and the attention is focused primarily on the information domain (i.e., data that goes in, data that comes out). The goal is to derive sets of input conditions (test cases) that fully exercise the external functionality.

Information Domain: Inputs and Outputs

Inputs encompass of individual input values and hence many different values are tried for each individual input. The combinations of inputs include:

- Individual inputs that are not independent from each other.

- Programs process multiple input values together, not just one at a time.

- Try many different combinations of inputs in order to achieve good coverage of the input domain.

In addition to the particular combination of input values chosen, the ordering and timing of the inputs can also make a difference.

Defining the Input Domain

- Boolean value:

    ○ T or F.

- Numeric value in a particular range:

    ○ 99 <= N <= 99.

    ○ Integer, Floating point.

Equivalence Partitioning

Typically the universe of all possible test cases is so large that you cannot try them all. You have to select a relatively small number of test cases to actually run, but which test cases to choose. Equivalence partitioning helps answer this question.

Partition the test cases into "equivalence classes". Each equivalence class contains a set of "equivalent" test cases. Two test cases are considered to be equivalent if we expect the program to process them both in the same way (i.e., follow the same path through the code). If you expect the program to process two test cases in the same way, only test one of them, thus reducing the number of test cases you have to run.

- First-level partitioning: Valid vs. Invalid test cases.

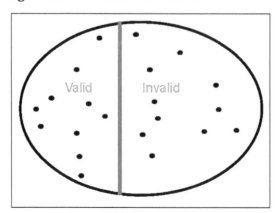

- Partition the valid and invalid test cases into equivalence classes.

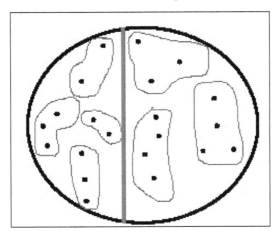

- Create a test case for at least one value from each equivalence class.

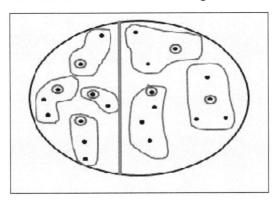

When designing test cases, you may use different definitions of "equivalence", each of which will partition the test case space differently. Test multiple values in each equivalence class as many times you're not sure if you have defined the equivalence classes correctly or completely, and testing multiple values in each class is more thorough than relying on a single value.

Examples

1. int Add (n1, n2, n3...):

- Equivalence Definition 1: partition test cases by the number of inputs (1, 2, 3, etc.).

- Equivalence Definition 2: partition test cases by the number signs they contain (positive, negative, both).

- Equivalence Definition 3: partition test cases by the magnitude of operands (large numbers, small numbers, both).

2. string Fetch (URL):

- Equivalence Definition 1: partition test cases by URL protocol ("http", "https", "ftp", "file", etc.).

- Equivalence Definition 2: partition test cases by type of file being retrieved (HTML, GIF, JPEG, Plain Text, etc.).

- Equivalence Definition 3: partition test cases by length of URL (very short, short, medium, long, very long, etc.).

Techniques

Following are some techniques that can be used for designing black box tests:

- Equivalence Partitioning: It is a software test design technique that involves dividing input values into valid and invalid partitions and selecting representative values from each partition as test data.

- Boundary Value Analysis: It is a software test design technique that involves the determination of boundaries for input values and selecting values that are at the boundaries and just inside/outside of the boundaries as test data.

- Cause-Effect Graphing: It is a software test design technique that involves identifying the cases (input conditions) and effects (output conditions), producing a Cause-Effect Graph, and generating test cases accordingly.

Advantages

- Tests are done from a user's point of view and will help in exposing discrepancies in the specifications.

- Tester need not know programming languages or how the software has been implemented.

- Tests can be conducted by a body independent from the developers, allowing for an objective perspective and the avoidance of developer-bias.

- Test cases can be designed as soon as the specifications are complete.

Disadvantages

- Only a small number of possible inputs can be tested and many program paths will be left untested.

- Without clear a specification, which is the situation in many projects, test cases will be difficult to design.

- Tests can be redundant if the software designer/developer has already run a test case.

White Box Testing

White box testing is testing based on analysis of internal logic (design, code, etc.). (But expected results still come from requirements). It is also known as structural testing. White-box testing concerns techniques for designing tests; it is not a level of testing. White-box testing techniques apply primarily to lower levels of testing (e.g., unit and component). The major testing focuses on:

- Program structures:
    - Program statements and branches.
    - Various kinds of program paths.
- Program internal logic and data structures.
- Program internal behaviors and states.
- Logic coverage:
    - Statement: Each statement executed at least once.
    - Branch: Each branch traversed (and every entry point taken) at least once.
    - Condition: Each condition True at least once and False at least once.
    - Branch/Condition: Both branch and condition coverage achieved.
    - Compound Condition: All combinations of condition values at every branch statement covered (and every entry point taken).
    - Path: All program paths traversed at least once.
- Dataflow coverage.
- Path conditions and symbolic evaluation.
- Other white-box testing strategies (e.g., "fault-based testing").

White box is a testing methodology to test the internal structures and working of software. White box testing also known as structural testing is testing based on analysis of internal logic (design, code, etc.).

- Test model: Control program chart (graph).
- Test case design: Various white-box testing methods generate test cases based on a given control program graph for a program.

The goal of white box testing is to:

- Guarantee that all independent paths within a module have been exercised at least once.
- Exercise all logical decisions on their true and false sides.
- Execute all loops at their boundaries and within their operational bounds.
- Exercise internal data structures to assure their validity.
- Exercise all data define and use paths.

Techniques

One of the most popular testing techniques for white box testing is called code coverage analysis, this technique tries to eliminate any gaps in the test case suite, and it identifies sections of an app that are not used by test cases. Once these gaps are found, we can create cases to see and verify parts of the code that is untested; this results in a more polished product at the end.

Following are some coverage analysis techniques:

- Statement Coverage: In this method, we try to traverse all statements in the code at least one time. This assures that all of the code is tested.

- Branch Coverage: This method is planned to traverse each branch of the decision points in the code. This makes sure that all decisions are at least tested once.

There are some other testing techniques too, here are just a few:

- Condition Coverage: In this testing technique, we make sure that all conditions are covered in the code, for an example:

```
READ A, B
IF (A == 0 || B == 0)
PRINT '0'
```

As you can see, here we have 2 conditions: A == 0 and B == 0. Now, these conditions receive TRUE and FALSE as values. One possible example can be:

```
#TC1 - A = 0, B = 110
#TC2 - A = 10, B = 0
```

- Multiple Condition Coverage: This is a bit more advanced than the last one. As you can guess, we test all possible combinations and all possible outcomes at least once. Here is a decent example:

```
READ A, B
IF (A == 0 || B == 0)
PRINT '0'

#TC1: A = 0, B = 0
#TC2: A = 0, B = 10
#TC3: A = 110, B = 0
#TC4: A = 110, B = 5
```

Hence, we require 4 test cases for 2 conditions. Hence if there are n conditions then we will require 2^n test cases.

- Basis Path Testing: In this technique, we make control flow graph and then we calculate its cyclomatic complexity which is the number of independent paths. Using the cyclomatic complexity, we can find the minimal number of test cases we can design for each independent path of the flow graph.

- Loop Testing: Loops are one of the most used tools in a programmer's weaponry. As these are at the core of so many algorithms, it only makes sense to have a testing technique based on loops. There can be 3 types of loops: Simple, nested and concatenated. Let's take a look at how a tester will deal with the tech of these types:

  - Simple Loops: For a loop that is simple in design and has the size n, we can design some test cases that do the following:

    - Skip said loop.

    - Only traverse the loop once.

    - Have 2 passes.

    - Have any number of passes that is less than its size.

    - n-1 and n+1 pass through the loop.

  - Nested Loops: For code with nested loops, we start with the innermost loop and then go outwards till we can reach to the outermost loop.

  - Concatenated loops: In the case of these loops. We use simple loop test once after another and in case the concatenated loop is not independent, we can deal with them as we did with nested loops.

Advantages

Now that we have seen what this testing method is and how it works. Let's take a look at some of the pros of this:

- It has simple and clear rules to let a tester know when the testing is done.

- The techniques are easy to automate, this results in a developer having to hire fewer testers and smaller expenses.

- It shows bottlenecks which makes the optimization quite easy for the programmers.

- A testing team can get started with their work without having to wait for the development team to complete the UI development.

- As all code paths are at covered in the code in most of the cases, the testing of code is more through.

- It helps in removing parts of the code that are not essential to the functionality of the program.

Disadvantages

- It is quite taxing on resources. To get the testing done, you will need someone who knows your code very well to be on the testing team and who is a good programmer himself. This type of skill level increases the expenses of the testing.

- In many cases, being able to test every possible condition in the code is not possible due to time constraints or budget limitations.

- As it is based on checking the functionality of the existing code, you can't find the missing functionality in the program.

- If any part of the code is redesigned and re-written, testers need to write the test cases again.

Gray Box Testing

Gray Box Testing is a software testing technique which is a combination of Black Box Testing technique and White Box Testing technique. In Black Box Testing technique, tester is unknown to the internal structure of the item being tested and in White Box Testing the internal structure is known to tester. The internal structure is partially known in Gray Box Testing. This includes access to internal data structures and algorithms for purpose of designing the test cases.

Gray Box Testing is named so because the software program is like a semi-transparent or grey box inside which tester can partially see. It commonly focuses on context-specific errors related to web systems.

Objective of Gray Box Testing

The objective of Gray Box Testing is:

- To provide combined advantages of both black box testing and white box testing.

- To combine the input of developers as well as testers.

- To improve overall product quality.

- To reduce the overhead of long process of functional and non-functional testings.

- To provide enough free time to developers to fix defects.

- To test from the user point of view rather than a designer point of view.

Gray Box Testing Techniques

- Matrix Testing: In matrix testing technique, business and technical risks which are defined by the developers in software programs are examined. Developers define all the variables that exist in the program. Each of the variables has an inherent technical and business risk and can be used with varied frequencies during its life cycle.

- Pattern Testing: To perform the testing, previous defects are analyzed. It determines the cause of the failure by looking into the code. Analysis template includes reasons for the defect. This helps test cases designed as they are proactive in finding other failures before hitting production.

- Orthogonal Array Testing: It is mainly a black box testing technique. In orthogonal array testing, test data have numbers of permutations and combinations. Orthogonal array testing is preferred when maximum coverage is required when there are very few test cases and test data is large. This is very helpful in testing complex applications.

- Regression Testing: Regression testing is testing the software after every change in the software to make sure that the changes or the new functionalities are not affecting the existing functioning of the system. Regression testing is also carried out to ensure that fixing any defect has not affected other functionality of the software.

Advantages of Gray Box Testing

- Users and developers have clear goals while doing testing.

- Gray box testing is mostly done by the user perspective.

- Testers are not required to have high programming skills for this testing.

- Gray box testing is non-intrusive.

- Overall quality of the product is improved.

- In gray box testing, developers have more time for defect fixing.

- By doing gray box testing, benefits of both black box and white box testing is obtained.

- Gray box testing is unbiased. It avoids conflicts between a tester and a developer.

- Gray box testing is much more effective in integration testing.

Disadvantages of Gray Box Testing

- Defect association is difficult when gray testing is performed for distributed systems.

- Limited access to internal structure leads to limited access for code path traversal.

- Because source code cannot be accessed, doing complete white box testing is not possible.

- Gray box testing is not suitable for algorithm testing.

- Most of the test cases are difficult to design.

Software Maintenance

Software maintenance is the process of modification or making changes in the system after delivery to overcome errors and faults in the system that were not uncovered during the early stages of the development cycle.

The IEEE Standard for Software Maintenance (IEEE 1219) gave the definition for software maintenance as: "The process of modifying a software system or component after delivery to correct faults, improves performance or other attributes, or adapt to a changed environment".

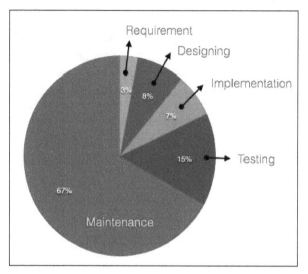

Maintenance Principles

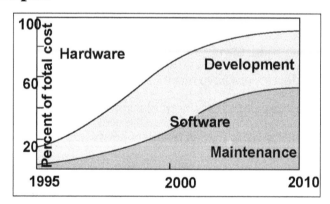

The IEEE/EIA 12207 Standard defines maintenance as modification to code and associated documentation due to a problem or the need for improvement.

Nature of Maintenance

Modification requests are logged and tracked, the impact of proposed changes are determined, code and other software artifacts are modified, testing is conducted, and a new version of the software product is released. Maintainers can learn from the developer´s knowledge of the software.

Need for Maintenance

Maintenance must be performed in order to:

- Correct faults.

- Improve the design.

- Implement enhancements.

- Interface with other systems.

- Adapt programs so that different hardware, software, system features, and telecommunications facilities can be used.

- Migrate legacy software.

- Retire software.

Tasks of a Maintainer

The maintainer does the following functions:

- Maintain control over the software's day-to-day functions.

- Maintain control over software modification.

- Perfecting existing functions.

- Preventing software performance from degrading to unacceptable levels.

Majority of Maintenance Costs

Maintenance consumes a major share of software life cycle financial resources. But studies and
surveys have shown that "over 80% of the maintenance effort is used for non-corrective actions.
Quality of software design, construction, documentation, and testing affects software maintenance
costs.

Evolution of Software

Lehman has studied software maintenance and evolution for over 20 years, leading to 'Lehman's
Laws'. E.g. increasing complexity — as a program is evolved, its complexity increases unless work
is done to maintain or reduce it.

Categories of Maintenance

Maintenance can be categorized into the following:

- Corrective maintenance: Reactive modification of a software product performed after delivery to correct discovered problems.

- Adaptive maintenance: Modification of a software product performed after delivery to keep
  a software product usable in a changed or changing environment.

- Perfective maintenance: Modification of a software product after delivery to improve performance or maintainability.

- Preventive maintenance: Modification of a software product after delivery to detect and
  correct latent faults in the software product before they become effective faults.

Key to Maintenance

The key to effective maintenance lies in development. Depending upon the development of the product the maintenance of the product is determined.

- Higher quality ⇒ less (corrective) maintenance.

- Anticipating changes ⇒ less (adaptive and perfective) maintenance.

- Better tuning to user needs ⇒ less (perfective) maintenance.

- Less code ⇒ less maintenance.

The distribution of maintenance activities are shown in the figure below:

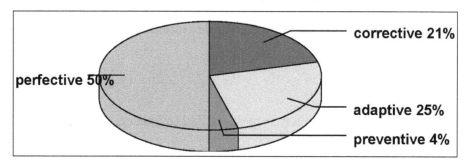

Major Causes of Maintenance Problems

Some of the major factors which causes problem in maintenance is as follows:

- Unstructured code.

- Insufficient domain knowledge.

- Insufficient documentation.

The key issues in software maintenance include:

- Limited Understanding.

- Shift in type of maintenance.

- Impact Analysis.

- Maintainability.

- Alignment with organizational objectives.

- Staffing.

- Process.

- Organizational aspects of maintenance.

- Outsourcing.

- Cost Estimation.
- Specific Measures.

Limited Understanding

The maintainers make changes or corrections to software that they did not write, so they should quickly understand the software. 40%-60% of the maintenance effort is devoted to understanding the software. Comprehension is difficult in the absence of documentation and when the original developers are unavailable. The maintainers must quickly understand the software and should make modifications to overcome the issues in the system.

Shift in Type of Maintenance

Shift in type of maintenance over time can be projected as follows:

- Introductory stage: Emphasis on user support.
- Growth stage: Emphasis on correcting faults.
- Maturity: Emphasis on enhancements.
- Decline: Emphasis on technology changes.

Impact Analysis

The objectives of impact analysis are:

- Determination of the scope of the change in order to plan and implement the work.
- Development of accurate estimates of resources needed to perform the work.
- Analysis of the cost/benefits of the requested change.
- Communication to others of the complexity of a given change.

Maintainability

IEEE [IEEE610.12-90] defines maintainability as the ease with which software can be maintained, enhanced, adapted, or corrected to satisfy specified requirements and the presence of systematic and mature processes, techniques, and tools helps to enhance the maintainability of a system.

Alignment with Organizational Objectives

The return on investment for software maintenance is less clear than the initial development. The view at senior management level is often a major activity consuming significant resources with no clear quantifiable benefit for the organization.

Staffing

Maintenance is often not viewed as glamorous work. Software maintenance personnel are frequently viewed as second-class citizens and morale therefore suffers.

Process

A software process is a set of activities, methods, practices, and transformations which people use to develop and maintain software and the associated products. At the process level, software maintenance activities share much in common with software development (for example, software configuration management is a crucial activity in both).

Organizational Aspects of Maintenance

The team that develops the software is not necessarily assigned to maintain the software once it is operational. The important factor is the delegation or assignment of the maintenance responsibility to a single group or person, regardless of the organization´s structure.

Outsourcing

Software maintenance which is not missioning critical can be outsourced. Outsourcing companies typically spend a number of months assessing the software before they will enter into a contractual relationship. One report states that 50% of outsourcers provide services without any clear service level agreement.

Cost Estimation

Impact analysis identifies systems and products affected by a software change request and yields an estimate of the resources required. ISO/IEC14764 states "the two most popular approaches to estimating resources for software maintenance are the use of parametric models and the use of experience".

Specific Measures

- Analysability: Measures of the maintainer´s effort or resources expended in trying to diagnose deficiencies or causes of failure, or in identifying parts to be modified.

- Changeability: Measures of the maintainer´s effort associated with implementing a specified modification.

- Stability: Measures of the unexpected behavior of software, including that encountered during testing.

- Testability: Measures of the maintainers and users effort in trying to test the modified software.

Maintenance Processes

The maintenance process commences with the modification request to improvise the system. When the request is received the classification and identification the modules is done for analysis. After analysis, design for the improvisation of the system is done and it is implemented. The modified system is then tested and delivered to the customers.

Maintenance process varies considerably depending on the types of software being maintained, the development processes used in an organization and people involved in the process. The maintenance process is shown in the figure below, where a change request is received to modify the system. The impact analysis is done and the release of the new modified version is planned. The modifications that were specified are implemented and the modified system is released. Maintenance process also takes care of fault repair, system enhancement and platform adaptation.

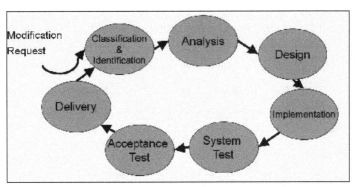

The IEEE 1219-98 Maintenance Process Activities.

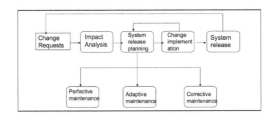

Unique Maintenance Activities

- Transition – A sequence of activities during which software is transferred progressively from the developer to the maintainer.

- Modification request acceptance/rejection - Work over a certain size/effort/complexity may be rejected by maintainers and rerouted to a developer.

- Modification Request and Problem Report Help Desk - End-user support function that triggers the assessment, prioritization, and costing of modification requests.

- Impact Analysis.

- Software Support - Help and advice to users concerning a request for information (for example, business rules, validation, data meaning and ad-hoc requests/reports).

Supporting Activities

Supporting activities include software maintenance planning, software configuration management, verification and validation, software quality assurance, reviews, audits, and user training.

Maintenance Planning Activity

- Release/version planning activity involves.

- Collecting the dates of availability of individual requests.

- Agree with users on the content of subsequent releases/versions.

- Identify potential conflicts and develop alternatives.

- Assess the risk of a given release and develop a back-out plan in case problems arise.

- Inform all the stakeholders.

A software maintenance plan should specify how users will request software modifications or report problems. At the highest level, the maintenance organization will have to conduct business planning activities (budgetary, financial, and human resources) just like all other divisions of the organization.

Software Configuration Management

Software configuration management procedures should provide for the verification, validation, and audit of each step required identifying, authorizing, implementing, and releasing the software product. It is not sufficient to simply track Modification Requests or Problem Reports. The software product and any changes made to it must be controlled.

Software Quality

The activities and techniques for Software Quality Assurance (SQA), V&V, reviews, and audits must be selected in concert with all the other processes to achieve the desired level of quality.

Software Rejuvenation

Software rejuvenation includes the following actions:

- Re-documentation: It is the creation or revision of alternative representations of software at the same level of abstraction. It generates data interface tables, call graphs, component/ variable cross references etc.

- Restructuring: It is the transformation of the system's code without changing its behavior.

- Reverse Engineering: Reverse engineering involves analyzing a system to extract information about the behavior and/or structure.

- Design Recovery: It is the recreation of design abstractions from code, documentation, and domain knowledge. It generates structure charts, entity relationship diagrams, DFDs, requirements models.

- Re-engineering: Examination and alteration of a system to reconstitute it in another form. It is also known as renovation, reclamation. It is often not undertaken to improve maintainability, but to replace aging legacy software.

Re-Engineering process involves the following activities:

- Decide what to re-engineer and comprehend whether it is whole software or a part of it.

- Perform Reverse Engineering, in order to obtain specifications of existing software.

- Restructure Program if required. For example, changing function-oriented programs into object-oriented programs.

- Re-structure data as required.

- Apply Forward engineering concepts in order to get re-engineered software.

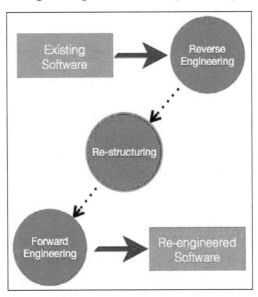

Reengineering is done in the following occurrences:

- When system changes are mostly confined to part of the system then re-engineer that part.

- When hardware or software support becomes obsolete.

- When tools to support re-structuring are available.

Re-engineered System

The development of a new system involves establishing a well-defined system specification and the proceeding with the design a and implementation to come up with a new system. In a reengineered system, a existing software is taken and the system is understood thoroughly to make the transformation to develop a reengineered system.

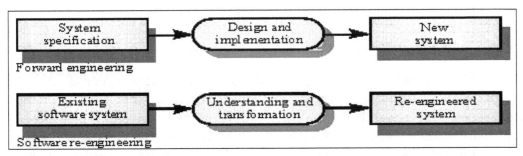

Advantages of Re-engineering

- Reduced risk: There is a high risk in new software development. There may be development problems, staffing problems and specification problems.

- Reduced cost: The cost of re-engineering is often significantly less than the costs of developing new software.

Benefits of Software Maintenance

Bug Fixes

Software maintenance packages provided by vendors offer peace-of-mind protection by keeping you covered for bugs and software problems. Like any other product, most software packages are under warranty for a specific period of time. Once these warranties expire, however, you may be required to pay out of pocket for fixes, much like you would for your vehicle. Maintenance programs allow your software to stay in warranty so you do not have to come up with cash should an error occur. Implementing the right software system is a long term investment and maintaining an active warranty will help to ensure this.

Improved Performance with Regular Upgrades

Most maintenance programs will include an upgrade component. Under a maintenance program, you will be entitled to free upgrades – usually once per year. These upgrades often address issues reported by other software users and can greatly improve functionality and performance. Considering the overall cost of upgrades over time, this component of software maintenance is often all that is necessary to make the program worthwhile. Depending on the vendor, upgrades may also reflect changes requested by customers and will also mean you receive a system based on the most up-to-date technology, features and software. If you had any custom work done as part of your original implementation and purchase, make sure to check that this custom work will also be upgraded, and not at an additional cost.

Adapt to a Changing Environment

Technology and the business environment are the two of the fastest changing aspects of our world. It is increasingly important to make sure that your business is always taking advantage of the best that your software has to offer and that your software matches the business requirements of the time. Regular updates and maintenance will allow you to keep up with market trends and ensure your business is as efficient and effective as it can be.

Predictive Cash Flow

The last benefit, but one of the most significant from a financial perspective, is the ability to gain control over your software expenditure. If you are covered for software bugs and receive regular upgrades, your overall IT expenditures will be reduced to a single monthly (or yearly) fee – your maintenance fee. This eliminates the guessing game of IT expenditure and eliminates large unexpected upfront costs down the road. For on-premises solutions, most maintenance packages range in cost from 15%-22% of total license costs. For cloud-based systems (and often one of the benefits) is that these maintenance fees are typically built right into monthly license fees.

Software Risk Management

Risk is an uncertainty. We don't know whether a particular event will occur or not, but if it does has a negative impact on a project. An example would be that team is working on a project and the developer walks out of project and other person is recruited in his place and he doesn't work on the same platform and converts it into the platform he is comfortable with. Now the project has to yield the same result in the same time span. That is the risk of schedule relies on whether they will be able to complete the project on time.

Risk is the probability of suffering loss. Risk provides an opportunity to develop the project better.

Risk exposure= Size (loss)* probability of (loss)

There is a difference between a problem and risk. Problem is some event which has already occurred but risk is something that is unpredictable.

Need for Risk Management

The need for risk management can be expressed using Murphy's Laws. The law expresses that if anything can go wrong, it will go wrong. Of things that could go wrong, the one that causes the most damage will occur.

Project risks are defined as the undesirable event, the chance this event might occur and the consequences of all possible outcomes, Risk management attempts to identify such events, minimize their impact & provide a response if the event is detected. The essence of project management is risk management.

Risk Characteristics

The two characteristics of risk:

- Uncertainty: The risk may or may not happen, that is, there are no 100% risks (those, instead, are called constraints).

- Loss: The risk becomes a reality and unwanted consequences or losses occur.

Risk Categorization

Risks can be categorized broadly into project risks, technical risks, business risks, known risks, undreamt risks, predictable and unpredictable risks.

- Project risks: They threaten the project plan. If they become real, it is likely that the project schedule will slip and that costs will increase.

- Technical risks: They threaten the quality and timeliness of the software to be produced. If they become real, implementation may become difficult or impossible.

- Business risks: They threaten the viability of the software to be built. If they become real, they jeopardize the project or the product. Business risk can be further categorized into the following:

  ○ Market risk: Building an excellent product or system that no one really wants.

  ○ Strategic risk: Building a product that no longer fits into the overall business strategy for the company.

  ○ Sales risk: Building a product that the sales force doesn't understand how to sell.

  ○ Management risk: Losing the support of senior management due to a change in focus or a change in people.

  ○ Budget risk: Losing budgetary or personnel commitment.

- Known risks: Those risks that can be uncovered after careful evaluation of the project plan, the business and technical environment in which the project is being developed, and other reliable information sources (e.g., unrealistic delivery date).

- Predictable risks: Those risks that are extrapolated from past project experience (e.g., past turnover).

- Unpredictable risks: Those risks that can and do occur, but are extremely difficult to identify in advance.

- Undreamt risk: Those risks that are extremely challenging to handle, which are of undreamt scale to confront.

Reactive vs. Proactive Risk Strategies

- Reactive risk strategies: Reactive risk strategies are based on the tag "Don't worry, I'll think of something". The majority of software teams and managers rely on this approach. Nothing is done about risks until something goes wrong. When something goes wrong the team then flies into action in an attempt to correct the problem rapidly (firefighting). Crisis management is the choice of management techniques.

- Proactive risk strategies: The primary objective is to avoid risk and to have a contingency plan in place to handle unavoidable risks in a controlled and effective manner.

Software risk management begins with the notion that software risk is an issue that needs to be managed. Software risk at its core stems from problems within the software itself, i.e., the source code that is introduced during development. Software risk management must then address two Software types of issues:

- Software failure and non-performance.

- Project and program management and delivery.

Software risk management takes a proactive approach Software risk by providing an approach and methodology to look for areas where a software defect impacts the usability of the software for end users and the business. For example, a catastrophic failure as the result of a software bug that does not allow the software to run correctly or at all is a type of software risk that must be managed.

Software risk as an impact on project management, program management, or delivery is one in which software defects and complexity impact the ability to release software on-time or within budget. The impact here is in delays and costs to the business that must be absorbed. For example, a defect found late in the development process could result in re-work that takes days or weeks to correct thereby delaying a project.

Principles and Best Practices

What are the ways that you can address software risk management? A set of software risk management principles and best practices can serve as a guide to help ensure that the risk of critical issues is mitigated. Currently, most software risk management relies on testing. But testing is not necessarily enough to truly manage risk. And it's important to note that the old adage, "You can't manage what you don't measure" very much applies to managing software risk.

- Identify the riskiest areas and components within your applications and systems.

- Identify the root-cause for the majority of defects that result in system failures (i.e., the "killer defects").

- Understand the importance of quantifying transaction and object risk in addition to risk-based testing.

- Learn how to optimize your test efficiency while expanding your coverage:

  ○ Leverage structural quality analysis to supplement your risk-based testing.

  ○ Understand the complexity of the underlying system components.

  ○ Quantify the degree to which complex system components have changed.

- Make sure you have a scorecard or dashboard for measuring and tracking the levels of software risk in each release of your most mission critical applications.

Software Risk Management Plan

Creating a software risk management plan helps to both jump start managing software risk as well as making it on ongoing part of your software development process. A software risk management plan should typically include:

- Jump Start Your Risk Management.

- Look at Integration Level Risk.

- Look at System Level Risk.

- Measure your level of software risk in your critical applications.

These steps comprise the basis of comprehensive risk management. Of course, as you develop your software risk management plan, incorporate procedures and processes that make the most sense to your business. But recall that system-level risks are the greatest threats and it is these threats that require the most mitigation.

Risk Mitigation

An effective strategy for dealing with risk must consider the following three issues (these are not mutually exclusive):

- Risk mitigation (i.e., avoidance).

- Risk monitoring.

- Risk management and contingency planning.

Risk mitigation (avoidance) is the primary strategy and is achieved through a plan. Example: Risk of high staff turnover. The strategy for reducing staff turnover involves meeting with the current staff to determine causes for turnover (e.g., poor working conditions, low pay and competitive job market). Mitigate those causes that are under our control before the project starts. Once the project commences, assume turnover will occur and develop techniques to ensure continuity when people leave. Project teams are organized so that information about each development activity is widely dispersed. The documentation standards are defined and mechanisms are established to ensure that documents are developed in a timely manner. Peer reviews of all work are conducted so that more than one person is "up to speed". The backup staff member for every critical technologist is assigned to avoid risks that arise due to the absence of the critical technologist.

During risk monitoring, the project manager monitors factors that may provide an indication of whether a risk is becoming more or less likely. Risk management and contingency planning assume that mitigation efforts have failed and that the risk has become a reality. RMMM steps incur additional project cost as large projects may have identified 30 – 40 risks. Risk is not limited to the software project itself but can occur after the software has been delivered to the user.

Software Safety and Hazard Analysis

These are software quality assurance activities that focus on the identification and assessment of potential hazards that may affect software negatively and cause an entire system to fail. If hazards can be identified early in the software process, software design features can be specified that will either eliminate or control potential hazards.

RMMM Plan

The RMMM plan may be a part of the software development plan or may be a separate document. Once RMMM has been documented and the project has begun, the risk mitigation, and monitoring steps begin. Risk mitigation is a problem avoidance activity and risk monitoring is a project tracking activity.

Risk monitoring has three objectives that include the assessment whether the predicted risks do, in fact, occur. It ensures that risk aversion steps defined for the risk are being properly applied and collects information that can be used for future risk analysis. The findings from risk monitoring may allow the project manager to ascertain what risks caused which problems throughout the project.

Risk Response Process Control

The Risk Management Plan should specify the risks, risk responses, and mechanisms used to control the process. Risks must be continuously monitored for risk triggers. Potential risk events should be identified early in a project and monitoring for such events immediately commence. Each risk is assigned to a specific person who has the expertise and authority to identify and provide a response to an event. Risk response process control needs an environment where problems are readily reported, embraced and solved. Changes in any aspect of the project need to be documented and communicated. The authority to approve a change must be assigned and the changes must be communicated to the team. Written forms are employed to track hardware, software and document changes. The members who are notified of changes, when the change is made and the change that is made must be documented.

Software Change Management

Software change management is a process of identifying changes that are to be done in the software. It facilitates and controls making changes to the software for the effective development of the project.

Change management is a planned approach to integrating change which includes formal processes for assessing the impact of the change on both the people it affects and the way they do their jobs. The application of techniques gains acceptance and understanding of the change and change in behavior takes advantage of the new functionality. Change is the interplay among various forces that are involved in growing something new. Deep change comes only through real growth i.e. through learning and unlearning. 70% of all change initiatives fail due to failure to address human component of change.

Implementation of large scale business transformation initiatives, like SAP, by nature result in significant and fundamental change such as:

- Changes in the job of the people.
- Change in job and work content.
- Change in the people you work with.
- The tools (systems, reports, etc.) of the job and how people interface with them change.
- Implementing the initiative requires additional, unfamiliar work, maybe in unfamiliar locations.
- New skills, behaviors will be required.
- Employee assignment.

- Controls (over process and information) will change.

- Change in information that is provided, accessed, and shared.

Change management helps determine how people will react to these changes, and therefore, the ultimate success of the transformation of the vision, knowledge, & responsibility.

Software Change Management is also called software configuration management (SCM). It is an umbrella activity that is applied throughout the software process. The goal is to maximize productivity by minimizing mistakes caused by confusion when coordinating software development. SCM identifies, organizes, and controls modifications to the software being built by a software development team. SCM activities are formulated to identify change, control change, ensure that change is being properly implemented, and report changes to others who may have an interest.

SCM is initiated when the project begins and terminates when the software is taken out of operation. View of SCM from various roles:

- Project manager - An auditing mechanism.

- SCM manager - A controlling, tracking, and policy making mechanism.

- Software engineer - A changing, building and access control mechanism.

- Customer - A quality assurance and product identification mechanism.

Software Configuration

The output from the software process makes up the software configuration:

- Computer programs (both source code files and executable files).

- Work products that describe the computer programs (Documents targeted at both technical practitioners and users).

- Data (contained within the programs themselves or in external files).

The major danger to a software configuration is change. First Law of System Engineering states "No matter where you are in the system life cycle, the system will change, and the desire to change it will persist throughout the life cycle".

Software change originated when errors detected in the software need to be corrected. New business or market conditions dictate changes in product requirements or business rules. Software changes occur when new customer needs demands modification of data produced by information systems, functionality delivered by products, or services delivered by a computer-based system. Reorganization or business growth/downsizing causes changes in project priorities or software engineering team structure. Budgetary or scheduling constraints cause a redefinition of the system or product.

Configuration Management System – Elements

- Configuration elements include a set of tools coupled with a file management (e.g., database) system that enables access to and management of each software configuration item.

- Process elements comprises of a collection of procedures and tasks that define an effective approach to change management for all participants.

- Construction elements consist of a set of tools that automate the construction of software by ensuring that the proper set of valid components (i.e., the correct version) is assembled.

- Human elements are a set of tools and process features used by a software team to implement effective SCM.

Baseline for SCM

The baseline for SCM concept focuses on helping practitioners to control change without seriously impeding justifiable change.

A specification or product that has been formally reviewed and agreed upon, and that thereafter serves as the basis for further development, and that can be changed only through formal change control procedures.

It is a milestone in the development of software and is marked by the delivery of one or more Computer Software Configuration Items (CSCIs) that have been approved as a consequence of a formal technical review.

Baseline Process

The baseline process involves the following:

- A series of software engineering tasks produces a CSCI.

- The CSCI is reviewed and possibly approved.

- The approved CSCI is given a new version number and placed in a project database (i.e., software repository).

- A copy of the CSCI is taken from the project database and examined/modified by a software engineer.

- The baseline of the modified CSCI goes back.

Automated SCM Repository

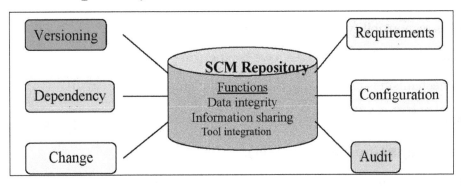

Functions of an SCM Repository

- Data integrity: It validates entries, ensures consistency, cascades modifications.

- Information sharing: It shares information among developers and tools, manages and controls multi-user access.

- Tool integration: It establishes a data model that can be accessed by many software engineering tools, controls access to the data.

- Data integration: It allows various SCM tasks to be performed on one or more CSCIs.

- Methodology enforcement: It defines an entity-relationship model for the repository that implies a specific process model for software engineering.

- Document standardization: It defines objects in the repository to guarantee a standard approach for creation of software engineering documents.

Primary Objectives of the SCM Process

The Primary Objectives of the SCM Process includes:

- Identification of all items that collectively define the software configuration.

- Manage changes to one or more of these items.

- Facilitate construction of different versions of an application.

- Ensure the software quality is maintained as the configuration evolves over time.

- Provide information on changes that have occurred.

SCM

Software change management focuses on addressing the following issues:

- How does a software team identify the discrete elements of a software configuration?

- How does an organization manage the many existing versions of a program (and its documentation) in a manner that will enable change to be accommodated efficiently?

- How an organization control changes does before and after software is released to a customer?

- Who has responsibility for approving and ranking changes?

- How can we ensure that changes have been made properly?

- What mechanism is used to apprise others of changes that are made?

SCM TASKS

- Concentric layers (from inner to outer):

  ○ Identification,

- ○ Change control,

- ○ Version control,

- ○ Configuration auditing,

- ○ Status reporting.

- CSCIs flow outward through these layers during their life cycle.

- CSCIs ultimately become part of the configuration of one or more versions of a software application or system.

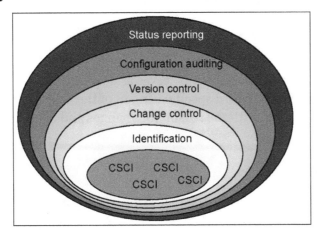

Identification Task

Identification separately names each CSCI and then organizes it in the SCM repository using an object-oriented approach. Objects start out as basic objects and are then grouped into aggregate objects. Each object has a set of distinct features that identifies it such as a name that is unambiguous to all other objects, a description that contains the CSCI type, a project identifier, and change and/or version information, a list of resources needed by the object and object realization (i.e., the document, the file, the model, etc.).

Change Task

Change control is a procedural activity that ensures quality and consistency as changes are made to a configuration object. A change request is submitted to a configuration control authority, which is usually a change control board (CCB). The request is evaluated for technical merit, potential side effects, overall impact on other configuration objects and system functions, and projected cost in terms of money, time, and resources.

An engineering change order (ECO) is issued for each approved change request. It describes the change to be made, the constraints to follow, and the criteria for review and audit. The baseline CSCI is obtained from the SCM repository where access control governs which software engineers have the authority to access and modify a particular configuration object. The Synchronization control helps to ensure that parallel changes performed by two different people don't overwrite one another.

Version Control Task

Version control is a set of procedures and tools for managing the creation and use of multiple occurrences of objects in the SCM repository. Required version control capabilities include:

- A SCM repository that stores all relevant configuration objects.

- A version management capability that stores all versions of a configuration object (or enables any version to be constructed using differences from past versions).

- A make facility that enables the software engineer to collect all relevant configuration objects and construct a specific version of the software.

- Issues tracking (bug tracking) capability that enables the team to record and track the status of all outstanding issues associated with each configuration object.

The SCM repository maintains a change set. It serves as a collection of all changes made to a baseline configuration and is used to create a specific version of the software. It captures all changes to all files in the configuration along with the reason for changes and details of who made the changes and when the changes were made.

Configuration Auditing Task

Configuration auditing is an SQA activity that helps to ensure that quality is maintained as changes are made. It complements the formal technical review and is conducted by the SQA group. It addresses the following questions:

- Has the change specified in the ECO been made? Have any additional modifications been incorporated?

- Has a formal technical review been conducted to assess technical correctness?

- Has the software process been followed, and have software engineering standards been properly applied?

- Has the change been "highlighted" and "documented" in the CSCI? Have the change data and change author been specified? Do the attributes of the configuration object reflect the change?

- Have SCM procedures for noting the change, recording it, and reporting it been followed?

- Have all related CSCIs been properly updated?

A configuration audit ensures that the correct CSCIs (by version) have been incorporated into a specific build and all the documentation is up-to-date and consistent with the version that has been built.

Status Reporting Task

Configuration status reporting (CSR) is also called status accounting. It provides information about each change to those personnel in an organization with a need to know. It addresses the questions and answers what happened, who did it, when did it happen, and what else will be affected. The sources of entries for configuration status reporting occurs when each time a CSCI is assigned new or updated information, each time a change is approved by the CCB and an ECO is issued and each time a configuration audit is conducted. The configuration status report is placed in an on-line database or on a website for software developers and maintainers to read. It is given to management and practitioners to keep them apprised of important changes to the project CSCIs.

References

- Software-engineering-software-design-process: geeksforgeeks.org, Retrieved 25, june 2020

- Benefits-of-object-oriented-design, technologies: ayokasystems.com, Retrieved 25, june 2020

- Software-testing-introduction-importance: guru99.com, Retrieved 10, 2020

- Gray-box-testing-software-testing: geeksforgeeks.org, Retrieved 25, june 2020

- The-importance-of-software-maintenance: bluelinkerp.com, Retrieved 25, june 2020

- Software-risk-management, castsoftware.com, Retrieved 05, July 2020

3

Processes and Methods of Software Development

Software development is the collection of systematic operations involved in creating software products. It includes designing, preparing specifications, programming, testing, bug fixing and documentation. There are various methods used to develop software like aspect-oriented software development, rapid application model, spiral model, etc. This chapter deals with software development, its processes and the different types of software development in a detailed manner.

Software development is the collective processes involved in creating software programs, embodying all the stages throughout the systems development life cycle (SDLC).

SDLC methodologies support the design of software to meet a business need, the development of software to meet the specified design and the deployment of software to production. A methodology should also support maintenance, although that option may or may not be chosen, depending on the project in question.

The waterfall model, the original SDLC method, is linear and sequential, generally following these stages in order:

1) Identification of required software.

2) Analysis of the software requirements.

3) Detailed specification of the software requirements.

4) Software design.

5) Programming.

6) Testing.

7) Maintenance.

The waterfall and similar models are considered predictive methodologies, in contrast to adaptive models such as agile software development (ASD), rapid application development (RAD), joint application development (JAD), the fountain model, the spiral model, build and fix and synchronize-and-stabilize. Frequently, several models are combined into some sort of hybrid methodology as is the case with open source software development (OSSD).

Software Development Process

A software development process or life cycle is a structure imposed on the development of a software product. There are several models for such processes, each describing approaches to a variety of tasks or activities that take place during the process.

Processes

More and more software development organizations implement process methodologies.

The Capability Maturity Model (CMM) is one of the leading models. Independent assessments can be used to grade organizations on how well they create software according to how they define and execute their processes.

There are dozens of others, with other popular ones being ISO 9000, ISO 15504, and Six Sigma.

The process of software development services goes through a series of stages in stepwise fashion that almost every developing company follows. Known as the 'software development life cycle,' these six steps include planning, analysis, design, development & implementation, testing & deployment and maintenance.

- Planning: Without the perfect plan, calculating the strengths and weaknesses of the project, development of software is meaningless. Planning kicks off a project flawlessly and affects its progress positively.

- Analysis: This step is about analyzing the performance of the software at various stages and making notes on additional requirements. Analysis is very important to proceed further to the next step.

- Design: Once the analysis is complete, the step of designing takes over, which is basically building the architecture of the project. This step helps remove possible flaws by setting a standard and attempting to stick to it.

- Development and Implementation: The actual task of developing the software starts here with data recording going on in the background. Once the software is developed, the stage of implementation comes in where the product goes through a pilot study to see if it's functioning properly.

- Testing: The testing stage assesses the software for errors and documents bugs if there are any.

- Maintenance: Once the software passes through all the stages without any issues, it is to undergo a maintenance process wherein it will be maintained and upgraded from time to time to adapt to changes.

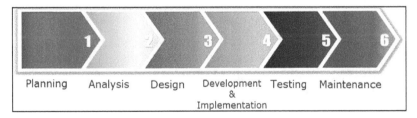

Process Activities/Steps

Software Engineering processes are composed of many activities, notably the following:

- Requirements Analysis

    Extracting the requirements of a desired software product is the first task in creating it.

While customers probably believe they know what the software is to do, it may require skill and experience in software engineering to recognize incomplete, ambiguous or contradictory requirements.

- Specification

Specification is the task of precisely describing the software to be written, in a mathematically rigorous way. In practice, most successful specifications are written to understand and fine-tune applications that were already well-developed, although safety-critical software systems are often carefully specified prior to application development. Specifications are most important for external interfaces that must remain stable.

- Software architecture

The architecture of a software system refers to an abstract representation of that system. Architecture is concerned with making sure the software system will meet the requirements of the product, as well as ensuring that future requirements can be addressed.

- Implementation

Reducing a design to code may be the most obvious part of the software engineering job, but it is not necessarily the largest portion.

- Testing

Testing of parts of software, especially where code by two different engineers must work together, falls to the software engineer.

- Documentation

An important task is documenting the internal design of software for the purpose of future maintenance and enhancement.

- Training and Support

A large percentage of software projects fail because the developers fail to realize that it doesn't matter how much time and planning a development team puts into creating software if nobody in an organization ends up using it. People are occasionally resistant to change and avoid venturing into an unfamiliar area, so as a part of the deployment phase, its very important to have training classes for the most enthusiastic software users (build excitement and confidence), shifting the training towards the neutral users intermixed with the avid supporters, and finally incorporate the rest of the organization into adopting the new software. Users will have lots of questions and software problems, which lead to the next phase of software.

- Maintenance

Maintaining and enhancing software to cope with newly discovered problems or new requirements could take far more time than the initial development of the software. Not only may it be necessary to add code that does not fit the original design but also just determining how software works at some point after it is completed may require significant effort by a software engineer. About 60% of all software engineering work is maintenance, but this statistic can be misleading. A small part of that is fixing bugs. Most maintenance is extending systems to do new things, which in many ways can be considered new work.

Process Models

A decades-long goal has been to find repeatable, predictable processes or methodologies that improve productivity and quality. Some try to systematize or formalize the seemingly unruly task of writing software. Others apply project management techniques to writing software. Without project management, software projects can easily be delivered late or over budget. With large numbers of software projects not meeting their expectations in terms of functionality, cost, or delivery schedule, effective project management is proving difficult.

Waterfall Processes

The best-known and oldest process is the waterfall model, where developers follow these steps in order. They state requirements, analyze them, design a solution approach, architect a software framework for that solution, develop code, test, deploy, and maintain. After each step is finished, the process proceeds to the next step.

Iterative Processes

Iterative development prescribes the construction of initially small but ever-larger portions of a software project to help all those involved to uncover important issues early before problems or faulty assumptions can lead to disaster. Commercial developers prefer iterative processes because it allows a potential of reaching the design goals of a customer who does not know how to define what he wants.

Agile software development processes are built on the foundation of iterative development. To that foundation they add a lighter, more people-centric viewpoint than traditional approaches. Agile processes use feedback, rather than planning, as their primary control mechanism. The feedback is driven by regular tests and releases of the evolving software.

Agile processes seem to be more efficient than older methodologies, using less programmer time to produce more functional, higher quality software, but have the drawback from a business perspective that they do not provide long-term planning capability. In essence, they say that they will provide the most bang for the buck, but won't say exactly when that bang will be.

Extreme Programming, XP, is the best-known agile process. In XP, the phases are carried out in extremely small (or "continuous") steps compared to the older, "batch" processes. The (intentionally incomplete) first pass through the steps might take a day or a week, rather than the months or years of each complete step in the Waterfall model. First, one writes automated tests, to provide concrete goals for development. Next is coding (by a pair of programmers), which is complete when all the tests pass, and the programmers can't think of any more tests that are needed. Design and architecture emerge out of refactoring, and come after coding. Design is done by the same people who do the coding. The incomplete but functional system is deployed or demonstrated for the users (at least one of which is on the development team). At this point, the practitioners start again on writing tests for the next most important part of the system.

While Iterative development approaches have their advantages, software architects are still faced with the challenge of creating a reliable foundation upon which to develop. Such a foundation often requires a fair amount of upfront analysis and prototyping to build a development model. The development model often relies upon specific design patterns and entity relationship diagrams (ERD). Without this upfront foundation, Iterative development can create long term challenges that are significant in terms of cost and quality.

Critics of iterative development approaches point out that these processes place what may be an unreasonable expectation upon the recipient of the software: that they must possess the skills and experience of a seasoned software developer. The approach can also be very kind of house you want, let me build you one and see if you like it. If you don't, we'll tear it all down and start over." A large pile of building-materials, which are now scrap, can be the final result of such a lack of upfront discipline. The problem with this criticism is that the whole point of iterative programming is that you don't have to build the whole house before you get feedback from the recipient. Indeed, in a sense conventional programming places more of this burden on the recipient, as the requirements and planning phases take place entirely before the development begins, and testing only occurs after development is officially over.

Software Release Life Cycle

Software release cycle is a process in software engineering which ensures the timely release of a software application from its coding to final release, in a well defined manner. The basic purpose of defining a software cycle is to assess the stability of a software product under development, at each level or stage of a lifecycle and accordingly developing the product for the next subsequent level, until it finally releases.

Generally, a software release lifecycle consists of five stages viz. pre-alpha, alpha, Beta, Release candidate, general availability. However, a project management or business team may visualize and define the software release lifecycle in their own way, depending upon their approach.

Let's go through each of these stages, to understand the concept of the software release life cycle.

Pre-alpha

All the activities done prior to the alpha release of a software product, falls in the phase of pre-alpha stage. These activities are nothing, but the development process of a software product, consisting of several milestones, where each milestone reflects the achievement of successful implementation and execution of the certain specific tasks.

Generally, the activities covered under pre-alpha phase comprises of requirement gathering & analysis, designing, development and unit testing.

Requirement Gathering and Analysis

This phase of pre-alpha stage consist of gathering of requirement and thereafter their analysis, feasibility study, etc. to consider and validate the implementation of these requirements in a software product. The Project Manager, Business Manager, developers and the client or the owner are accountable for the gathering & analysis of the requirements, so that they can make out a well define plan, to carry out the software development process.

Designing

Requirement gathering and analysis phase is followed by the designing phase, where the output of the former phase works as the resource for the latter. A design team is deployed, to work out and comes out with the structural view or may be called blueprint of a product, incorporating the specified requirements. This design helps the development team in visualizing and understanding an overview of a product, along with the need of certain hardware or software requirements, required in its development.

Development

Designing phase is followed by the implementation or the development phase. In development phase, a development team, equipped with all sort of resources such as SRS, software design, etc. and backed up by the design and other teams, carries out the task of development process and implementing specified requirements and specifications in the software product.

Unit Testing

Each unit developed by the developers, is evaluated by the developer itself, to assess the compliance of specified requirements and specifications by each individual unit, along with their stability, for going through the integration process and facing further testing techniques.

In pre-alpha stage, pre-alpha versions of a software product are being released such as milestone versions, where each milestone reflects the achievement in incorporating certain or specific functionalities or requirements in a product.

Alpha

It is one of first type of testing performed on a software product, after its initial development. Generally, alpha testing is an in-house testing process, performed within the organization by the testers or the developers.

During alpha testing, firstly white box testing techniques are performed by the developers, followed by the black box testing and gray box testing by the testing team.

The alpha released product, is generally of unstable nature, and may not be able to sustain further testing. Further, an alpha version of software does not ensure the compliance of all specified requirements but covers the majority of requirements.

Beta

The software product is deployed on the customer site, for getting tested by the intended users or the client in the real environment. It may be seen as the last testing phase, before the product is released in the market.

Basically, a software product is handed over to the targeted users, just before its release, so as to assess the usability and performance features of a software product.

Further, a beta phase may consist of two levels.

Open Beta: In open beta, a product is released and open to public, for testing the software application, in a real environment.

Closed Beta: In closed beta, product is being handed over to limited and specific users, to perform beta testing over a software product.

Release Candidate

It is considered as the beta version of a software product, and may be seen as the final product to be released, unless no serious issues or defects arise. At this moment of time, it is ensured that the product, which has gone through multiple beta cycles, does not needs any further improvement and no more changes, is required in the product. Thus, the version is potentially seen as the final product, to be ready for the market release.

General Availability

The final stable software product is released and is made available in the market for its selling and purchase, after completing all marketing formalities and commercialization activities, which may include security and compliance testing, along with the nationwide or the worldwide availability of the product.

Aspect-Oriented Software Development

Aspect-oriented software development (AOSD) is a software design solution that helps address the modularity issues that are not properly resolved by other software approaches, like procedural, structured and object-oriented programming (OOP). AOSD complements, rather than replaces, these other types of software approaches.

AOSD is also known as aspect-oriented programming (AOP).

AOSD features are as follows:

- Considered a subset of post-object programming technologies.

- Better software design support through isolating application business logic from supporting and secondary functions.

- Provides complementary benefits and may be used with other agile processes and coding standards.

- Key focus - Identification, representation and specification of concerns, which also may be cross-cutting.

- Provides better modularization support of software designs, reducing software design, development and maintenance costs.

- Modularization principle based on involved functionalities and processes.

- Because concerns are encapsulated into different modules, localization of crosscutting concerns is better promoted and handled.

- Provides tools and software coding techniques to ensure modular content support at the source code level.

- Promotes reusability of code used for the modularization of cross-cutting concerns.

- Smaller code size, due to tackling cross cutting concerns.

- Reduced efficiency from increased overhead.

Iterative and Incremental Development

Iterative development was created as a response to inefficiencies and problems found in the waterfall model. Modified Waterfall, Rational Unified Process (RUP) and most, if not all, agile models are based on iterations.

General idea is to develop a system through iterations (repeated cycles) and incrementally (in small portions of time). Through them team members or stakeholders can learn from their mistakes and apply that knowledge on the next iteration.

Working through iterations means that the development of the application is split into smaller chunks. In each iteration features are defined, designed, developed and tested. Iteration cycles are repeated until fully functional software is ready to be delivered to production. The process does not try to start with the full set of requirements and design. Instead, team tries to prepare just what is needed for the successful delivery of the next iteration.

Some models have different names for iteration like sprint or time-boxed. Iterations can be limited in time; they end after the agreed period independently of the size of the scope that was done. Alternative way of doing iterations is to limit them in scope. They last until the agreed scope is fully finished (developed and tested).

It is a common practice that each iteration is finished with a demo to stakeholders. That demo is used as the learning process with the objective to correct the way next iteration is done or modify the scope. Since working model is available much earlier, it is much easier to spot problems before it is too late or too expensive to take corrective actions.

This way of developing is in stark contrast with the waterfall model where each phase of the software development life-cycle (SDLC) needs to be fully completed until the next one starts.

One of the main advantages of iterative development is that it allows more flexibility to adapt to changes. Unlike the waterfall model where unforeseen problems often surface late in the project and are very costly to fix, iterative approach, on the other hand, goes through short cycles that allow the team to learn, adapt and change the direction in the next iteration.

Not everyone can use iterative development effectively. Iterative development is much harder than the waterfall model. It requires higher level of technical excellence, more discipline and buyout from the whole team. It often requires that team members are capable of performing more than one type of tasks (for example develop and test or work on both front-end and back-end).

Changes need to be done across all roles when they come from the waterfall process. Two of those roles that are often most affected are integration engineers and testers.

Integration Engineers

Integration phase in iterative development is very short or, when done right, continuous. While in the waterfall model this phase can take even several weeks for bigger projects, iterations require it to be very short and done often. If, for example, testers need to test some functionality as soon as the code is done, integration and deployment needs to be almost instantaneous. There are many tools currently in use that facilitate the integration and deployment. Some of them are Puppet and Chef for configuration management and Jenkins, Hudson, Bamboo and Travis for Continuous Integration, Delivery and Deployment. Everything, or almost everything, should be scripted and run on certain events.

Testers

Testers (especially when used to only manual testing) are among those who have most difficulties adapting to the iterative process when they're coming from the waterfall, especially if they are used to test the application after it is done. Switch to iterations forces them to act in a different way and think in forms of specific functionalities that should be verified instead of a fully developed system.

They need to work in parallel with developers in order to meet iteration deadlines.

Often there is no time to perform manual testing after the code of some specific functionality is finished. High level of automation is required. While developers are writing the code, testers need to write scripts that will verify functionalities that code will create. Automation requires certain coding skills that testers might not posses. As a result, test automation might be left to developers while testers continue being focused on manual testing (both are required to certain extent). However, in those cases testers might feel that part of their work and security it brings is taken away from them.

Advantages

End products are often more aligned to client needs due to abilities to demo functionalities done in each iteration and adjust depending on the feedback. Higher level of automation required for successful iterations allows faster detection of problems and creation of reliable and repeatable processes. That same automation, after initial investment, leads to reduction in costs and time to market. Interdependency among team members increases the shared knowledge within the team leading to a better understanding.

Some of those changes can be applied to the waterfall model but in many cases they are not. The incentives for doing them are not big since they might not be perceived as necessities. For example, Continuous Integration has big potential savings in non-waterfall projects due to the need to perform installations, deployments, testing and other tasks often and fast. In the waterfall model intention is to do the integration once (after the development phase is finished) so the investment for scripts and jobs that will perform repeatable and scheduled processes does not look like it provides enough return.

In most situations, iterative and incremental process contains the complexity and mitigates risks within a defined time box. This allows the team to continually review and adapt the solution according to the realities of the ever-changing situation.

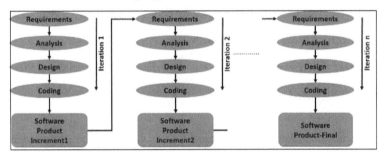

Iterative Incremental Model – Strengths

The advantages or strengths of Iterative Incremental model are –

- You can develop prioritized requirements first.

- Initial product delivery is faster.

- Customers gets important functionality early.

- Lowers initial delivery cost.

- Each release is a product increment, so that the customer will have a working product at hand all the time.

- Customer can provide feedback to each product increment, thus avoiding surprises at the end of development.

- Requirements changes can be easily accommodated.

Iterative Incremental Model – Weaknesses

The disadvantages of the Iterative Incremental model are –

- Requires effective planning of iterations.

- Requires efficient design to ensure inclusion of the required functionality and provision for changes later.

- Requires early definition of a complete and fully functional system to allow the definition of increments.

- Well-defined module interfaces are required, as some are developed long before others are developed.

- Total cost of the complete system is not lower.

Situations when Iterative Incremental Model can be used

Iterative Incremental model can be used when –

- Most of the requirements are known up-front but are expected to evolve over time.

- The requirements are prioritized.

- There is a need to get the basic functionality delivered fast.

- A project has lengthy development schedules.

- A project has new technology.

- The domain is new to the team.

Incremental Funding Methodology

In today's financially constrained IT industry, software development projects are unlikely to be funded unless they return clearly defined, low-risk value to the business. Demands for shorter investment periods, faster time-to-market, and increased operational agility require new and radical approaches to software development that draw upon the expertise of both software and financial stakeholders. Only by opening the traditional black box of software development to rigorous financial analysis, and by embracing software development as a value-creation activity, can organizations position themselves to maximize the returns on their software investments.

IFM is a financially informed approach to software development, designed to maximize returns through delivering functionality in 'chunks' of customer valued features, carefully sequenced so as to optimize Net Present Value (NPV). IFM applies a financially rigorous analysis to the delivery sequence in order to compare alternate options and when necessary to change the dynamics of a project in order to secure executive buy-in and funding.

The initial IFM concepts were drawn from several years of experience in winning competitive contracts for systems integration and application development projects. To succeed in this highly competitive environment, the bid has to meet the budget, the development costs have to be low enough to ensure a reasonable margin for the bidder, and the margin must be justified against the risks. Clearly these ideas are not new and are true for any competitive procurement. However, as the IT industry continues to tighten its belt, and margins become progressively tighter, competitive differentiation cannot always be achieved through technical or price innovation. A different approach is necessary.

The initial IFM concepts were drawn from several years of experience in winning competitive contracts for systems integration and application development projects. To succeed in this highly competitive environment, the bid has to meet the budget, the development costs have to be low enough to ensure a reasonable margin for the bidder, and the margin must be justified against the risks. Clearly these ideas are not new and are true for any competitive procurement. However, as the IT industry continues to tighten its belt, and margins become progressively tighter, competitive differentiation cannot always be achieved through technical or price innovation. A different approach is necessary.

By optimizing the time at which value is returned to the customer, instead of concentrating only on controlling risk and cost, it is possible to present a uniquely differentiated value proposition even in circumstances that preclude traditional differentiation. By categorizing customer requirements in terms of units of value, it is often possible to sequence their development and delivery in such a way as to reduce initial investment costs, generate early revenue, and in the right circumstances to even transition a project to early self-funding status. Furthermore, the overall project cost is amortized into more manageable portions, each part of which has accountability for its returns. This is the essence of IFM.

IFM can be applied in conjunction with any iterative software development process such as the Rational Unified Process (RUP) or eXtreme Programming (XP).

Rapid Application Development

The RAD (Rapid Application Development) model is based on prototyping and iterative development with no specific planning involved. The process of writing the software itself involves the planning required for developing the product.

Rapid Application Development focuses on gathering customer requirements through workshops or focus groups, early testing of the prototypes by the customer using iterative concept, reuse of the existing prototypes (components), continuous integration and rapid delivery.

Rapid application development is a software development methodology that uses minimal planning in favor of rapid prototyping. A prototype is a working model that is functionally equivalent to a component of the product.

In the RAD model, the functional modules are developed in parallel as prototypes and are integrated to make the complete product for faster product delivery. Since there is no detailed preplanning, it makes it easier to incorporate the changes within the development process.

RAD projects follow iterative and incremental model and have small teams comprising of developers, domain experts, customer representatives and other IT resources working progressively on their component or prototype.

The most important aspect for this model to be successful is to make sure that the prototypes developed are reusable.

RAD Model Design

RAD model distributes the analysis, design, build and test phases into a series of short, iterative development cycles.

Following are the various phases of the RAD Model –

Business Modeling

The business model for the product under development is designed in terms of flow of information and the distribution of information between various business channels. A complete business analysis is performed to find the vital information for business, how it can be obtained, how and when is the information processed and what are the factors driving successful flow of information.

Data Modeling

The information gathered in the Business Modeling phase is reviewed and analyzed to form sets of data objects vital for the business. The attributes of all data sets is identified and defined. The relation between these data objects are established and defined in detail in relevance to the business model.

Process Modeling

The data object sets defined in the Data Modeling phase are converted to establish the business information flow needed to achieve specific business objectives as per the business model. The process model for any changes or enhancements to the data object sets is defined in this phase. Process descriptions for adding, deleting, retrieving or modifying a data object are given.

Application Generation

The actual system is built and coding is done by using automation tools to convert process and data models into actual prototypes.

Testing and Turnover

The overall testing time is reduced in the RAD model as the prototypes are independently tested during every iteration. However, the data flow and the interfaces between all the components need to be thoroughly tested with complete test coverage. Since most of the programming components have already been tested, it reduces the risk of any major issues.

The following illustration describes the RAD Model in detail:

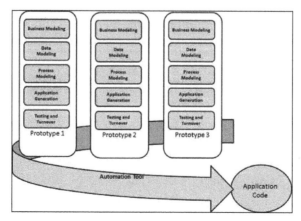

RAD Model Vs Traditional SDLC

The traditional SDLC follows a rigid process models with high emphasis on requirement analysis and gathering before the coding starts. It puts pressure on the customer to sign off the requirements before the project starts and the customer doesn't get the feel of the product as there is no working build available for a long time.

The customer may need some changes after he gets to see the software. However, the change process is quite rigid and it may not be feasible to incorporate major changes in the product in the traditional SDLC.

The RAD model focuses on iterative and incremental delivery of working models to the customer. This results in rapid delivery to the customer and customer involvement during the complete development cycle of product reducing the risk of non-conformance with the actual user requirements.

RAD Model - Application

RAD model can be applied successfully to the projects in which clear modularization is possible. If the project cannot be broken into modules, RAD may fail.

The following pointers describe the typical scenarios where RAD can be used –

- RAD should be used only when a system can be modularized to be delivered in an incremental manner.

- It should be used if there is a high availability of designers for modeling.

- It should be used only if the budget permits use of automated code generating tools.

- RAD SDLC model should be chosen only if domain experts are available with relevant business knowledge.

- Should be used where the requirements change during the project and working prototypes are to be presented to customer in small iterations of 2-3 months.

RAD Model - Pros and Cons

RAD model enables rapid delivery as it reduces the overall development time due to the reusability of the components and parallel development. RAD works well only if high skilled engineers are available and the customer is also committed to achieve the targeted prototype in the given time frame. If there is commitment lacking on either side the model may fail.

The advantages of the RAD Model are as follows –

- Changing requirements can be accommodated.

- Progress can be measured.

- Iteration time can be short with use of powerful RAD tools.

- Productivity with fewer people in a short time.

- Reduced development time.

- Increases reusability of components.

- Quick initial reviews occur.

- Encourages customer feedback.

- Integration from very beginning solves a lot of integration issues.

The disadvantages of the RAD Model are as follows –

- Dependency on technically strong team members for identifying business requirements.

- Only system that can be modularized can be built using RAD.

- Requires highly skilled developers/designers.

- High dependency on modeling skills.

- Inapplicable to cheaper projects as cost of modeling and automated code generation is very high.

- Management complexity is more.

- Suitable for systems that are component based and scalable.

- Requires user involvement throughout the life cycle.

- Suitable for project requiring shorter development times.

Spiral Model

Spiral model is one of the most important Software Development Life Cycle models, which provides support for Risk Handling. In its diagrammatic representation, it looks like a spiral with many loops. The exact number of loops of the spiral is unknown and can vary from project to project. Each loop of the spiral is called a Phase of the software development process. The exact number of phases needed to develop the product can be varied by the project manager depending upon the project risks. As the project manager dynamically determines the number of phases, so the project manager has an important role to develop a product using spiral model.

The Radius of the spiral at any point represents the expenses (cost) of the project so far, and the angular dimension represents the progress made so far in the current phase.

Each phase of Spiral Model is divided into four quadrants as shown in the above figure. The functions of these four quadrants are discussed below-

1. Objectives determination and identify alternative solutions: Requirements are gathered from the customers and the objectives are identified, elaborated and analyzed at the start of every phase. Then alternative solutions possible for the phase are proposed in this quadrant.

2. Identify and resolve Risks: During the second quadrant all the possible solutions are evaluated to select the best possible solution. Then the risks associated with that solution is identified and the risks are resolved using the best possible strategy. At the end of this quadrant, Prototype is built for the best possible solution.

3. Develop next version of the Product: During the third quadrant, the identified features are developed and verified through testing. At the end of the third quadrant, the next version of the software is available.

4. Review and plan for the next Phase: In the fourth quadrant, the Customers evaluate the so far developed version of the software. In the end, planning for the next phase is started.

A risk is any adverse situation that might affect the successful completion of a software project. The most important feature of the spiral model is handling these unknown risks after the project has started. Such risk resolutions are easier done by developing a prototype. The spiral model supports coping up with risks by providing the scope to build a prototype at every phase of the software development.

Below diagram shows the different phases of the Spiral Model:

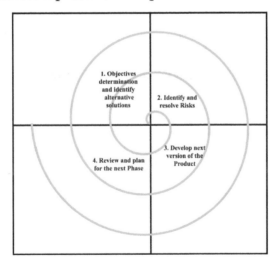

Prototyping Model also support risk handling, but the risks must be identified completely before the start of the development work of the project. But in real life project risk may occur after the development work starts, in that case, we cannot use Prototyping Model. In each phase of the Spiral Model, the features of the product dated and analyzed and the risks at that point of time are identified and are resolved through prototyping. Thus, this model is much more flexible compared to other SDLC models.

Reason why Spiral Model is called a Meta Model

The Spiral model is called as a Meta Model because it subsumes all the other SDLC models. For example, a single loop spiral actually represents the Iterative Waterfall Model. The spiral model incorporates the stepwise approach of the Classical Waterfall Model. The spiral model uses the approach of Prototyping Model by building a prototype at the start of each phase as a risk handling technique. Also, the spiral model can be considered as supporting the evolutionary model – the iterations along the spiral can be considered as evolutionary levels through which the complete system is built.

Advantages of Spiral Model

Below are some of the advantages of the Spiral Model:

- Risk Handling: The projects with many unknown risks that occur as the development proceeds, in that case, Spiral Model is the best development model to follow due to the risk analysis and risk handling at every phase.

- Good for large projects: It is recommended to use the Spiral Model in large and complex projects.

- Flexibility in Requirements: Change requests in the Requirements at later phase can be incorporated accurately by using this model.

- Customer Satisfaction: Customer can see the development of the product at the early phase of the software development and thus, they habituated with the system by using it before completion of the total product.

Disadvantages of Spiral Model

Below are some of the main disadvantages of the spiral model:

- Complex: The Spiral Model is much more complex than other SDLC models.

- Expensive: Spiral Model is not suitable for small projects as it is expensive.

- Too much dependable on Risk Analysis: The successful completion of the project is very much dependent on Risk Analysis. Without very highly experienced expertise, it is going to be a failure to develop a project using this model.

- Difficulty in time management: As the number of phases is unknown at the start of the project, so time estimation is very difficult.

Waterfall Model

Classical waterfall model is the basic software development life cycle model. It is very simple but idealistic. Earlier this model was very popular but nowadays it is not used. But it is very important because all the other software development life cycle models are based on the classical waterfall model.

Classical waterfall model divides the life cycle into a set of phases. This model considers that one phase can be started after completion of the previous phase. That is the output of one phase will be the input to the next phase. Thus the development process can be considered as a sequential flow in the waterfall. Here the phases do not overlap with each other. The different sequential phases of the classical waterfall model are shown in the below figure:

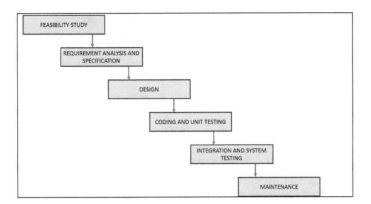

Let us now learn about each of these phases in brief details:

1. Feasibility Study: The main goal of this phase is to determine whether it would be financially and technically feasible to develop the software. The feasibility study involves understanding the problem and then determine the various possible strategies to solve the problem. These different identified solutions are analyzed based on their benefits and drawbacks, the best solution is chosen and all the other phases are carried out as per this solution strategy.

2. Requirements analysis and specification: The aim of the requirement analysis and specification phase is to understand the exact requirements of the customer and document them properly. This phase consists of two different activities.

    •   Requirement gathering and analysis: Firstly all the requirements regarding the software are gathered from the customer and then the gathered requirements are analyzed. The goal of the analysis part is to remove incompleteness (an incomplete requirement is one in which some parts of the actual requirements have been omitted) and inconsistencies (inconsistent requirement is one in which some part of the requirement contradicts with some other part).

    •   Requirement specification: These analyzed requirements are documented in a software requirement specification (SRS) document. SRS document serves as a contract between development team and customers. Any future dispute between the customers and the developers can be settled by examining the SRS document.

3. Design: The aim of the design phase is to transform the requirements specified in the SRS document into a structure that is suitable for implementation in some programming language.

4. Coding and Unit testing: In coding phase software design is translated into source code using any suitable programming language. Thus each designed module is coded. The aim of the unit-testing phase is to check whether each module is working properly or not.

5. Integration and System testing: Integration of different modules are undertaken soon after they have been coded and unit tested. Integration of various modules is carried out incrementally over a number of steps. During each integration step, previously planned modules are added to the partially integrated system and the resultant system is tested.

Finally, after all the modules have been successfully integrated and tested, the full working system is obtained and system testing is carried out on this.

System testing consists three different kinds of testing activities as described below :

- α-testing: α-testing is the system testing performed by the development team.

- β-testing: β-testing is the system testing performed by a friendly set of customers.

- Acceptance testing: After the software has been delivered, the customer performed the acceptance testing to determine whether to accept the delivered software or to reject it.

6. Maintenance: Maintenance is the most important phase of a software life cycle. The effort spent on maintenance is the 60% of the total effort spent to develop a full software. There are basically three types of maintenance:

Corrective Maintenance: This type of maintenance is carried out to correct errors that were not discovered during the product development phase.

Perfective Maintenance: This type of maintenance is carried out to enhance the functionalities of the system based on the customer's request.

Adaptive Maintenance: Adaptive maintenance is usually required for porting the software to work in a new environment such as work on a new computer platform or with a new operating system.

Advantages of Classical Waterfall Model

Classical waterfall model is an idealistic model for software development. It is very simple, so it can be considered as the basis for other software development life cycle models. Below are some of the major advantages of this SDLC model:

- This model is very simple and is easy to understand.

- Phases in this model are processed one at a time.

- Each stage in the model is clearly defined.

- This model has very clear and well understood milestones.

- Process, actions and results are very well documented.

- This model works well for smaller projects.

Drawbacks of Classical Waterfall Model

Classical waterfall model suffers from various shortcomings, basically we can't use it in real projects, but we use other software development lifecycle models which are based on the classical waterfall model. Below are some major drawbacks of this model:

No feedback path: In classical waterfall model evolution of a software from one phase to another phase is like a waterfall. It assumes that no error is ever committed by developers during any phases. Therefore, it does not incorporate any mechanism for error correction.

Difficult to accommodate change requests: This model assumes that all the customer requirements can be completely and correctly defined at the beginning of the project, but actually customers' requirements keep on changing with time. It is difficult to accommodate any change requests after the requirements specification phase is complete.

No overlapping of phases: This model recommends that new phase can start only after the completion of the previous phase. But in real projects, this can't be maintained. To increase the efficiency and reduce the cost, phases may overlap.

V-Model

The V-Model is a unique, linear development methodology used during a software development life cycle (SDLC). The V-Model focuses on a fairly typical waterfall-esque method that follows strict, step-by-step stages. While initial stages are broad design stages, progress proceeds down through more and more granular stages, leading into implementation and coding, and finally back through all testing stages prior to completion of the project.

The Process of the V-Model

Much like the traditional waterfall model, the V-Model specifies a series of linear stages that should occur across the life cycle, one at a time, until the project is complete. For this reason V-Model is not considered an agile development method, and due to the sheer volume of stages and their integration, understanding the model in detail can be challenging for everyone on the team, let alone clients or users.

The V-shape of the V-Model method represents the various stages that will be passed through during the software development life cycle. Beginning at the top-left stage and working, over time, toward the top-right tip, the stages represent a linear progression of development similar to the waterfall model.

The nine stages involved in the typical V-Model and how they all come together to generate a finished product are discussed below:

Requirements

During this initial phase, system requirements and analysis are performed to determine the feature set and needs of users. Just as with the same phase from the waterfall model or other similar methods, spending enough time and creating thorough user requirement documentation is critical during this phase, as it only occurs once.

Another component unique to the V-Model is that during each design stage, the corresponding tests are also designed to be implemented later during the testing stages. Thus, during the requirements phase, acceptance tests are designed.

System Design

Utilizing feedback and user requirement documents created during the requirements phase, this next stage is used to generate a specification document that will outline all technical components such as the data layers, business logic, and so on.

System Tests are also designed during this stage for later use.

Architecture Design

During this stage, specifications are drawn up that detail how the application will link up all its various components, either internally or via outside integrations. Often this is referred to as high-level design.

Integration tests are also developed during this time.

Module Design

This phase consists of all the low-level design for the system, including detailed specifications for how all functional, coded business logic will be implemented, such as models, components, interfaces, and so forth.

Unit tests should also be created during the module design phase.

Implementation/Coding

At this point, halfway through the stages along the process, the actual coding and implementation occur. This period should allot for as much time as is necessary to convert all previously generated design and specification docs into a coded, functional system. This stage should be fully complete once the testing phases begin.

Unit Testing

Now the process moves back up the far side of the V-Model with inverse testing, starting with the unit tests developed during the module design phase. Ideally, this phase should eliminate the vast majority of potential bugs and issues, and thus will be the lengthiest testing phase of the project.

That said, just as when performing unit testing with other development models, unit tests cannot (or should not) cover every possible issue that can occur in the system, so the less granular testing phases to follow should fill in these gaps.

Integration Testing

Testing devised during the architecture design phase are executed here, ensuring that the system functions across all components and third-party integrations.

System Testing

The tests created during system design are next executed, largely focusing on performance and regression testing.

Acceptance Testing

Lastly, acceptance testing is the process of implementing all tests created during the initial requirements phase and should ensure that the system is functional in a live environment with actual data, ready for deployment.

Advantages of the V-Model

- Suited for Restricted Projects: Due to the stringent nature of the V-Model and its linear design, implementation, and testing phases, it's perhaps no wonder that the V-Model has been heavily adopted by the medical device industry in recent years. In situations where the project length and scope are well-defined, the technology is stable, and the documentation & design specifications are clear, the V-Model can be a great method.

- Ideal for Time Management: Along the same vein, V-Model is also well-suited for projects that must maintain a strict deadline and meet key milestone dates throughout the process. With fairly clear and well understood stages that the whole team can easily comprehend and prepare for, it is relatively simple to create a time line for the entire development life cycle, while generating milestones for each stage along the way. Of course, the use of BM in no way ensures milestones will always be met, but the strict nature of the model itself enforces the need to keep to a fairly tight schedule.

Disadvantages of the V-Model

- Lacks Adaptability: Similar to the issues facing the traditional waterfall model on which the V-Model is based, the most problematic aspect to the V-Model is its inability to adapt to any necessary changes during the development life cycle. For example, an overlooked issue within some fundamental system design, that is then only discovered during the implementation phase, can present a severe setback in terms of lost man-hours as well as increased costs.

- Timeline Restrictions: While not an inherent problem with the V-Model itself, the focus on testing at the end of the life cycle means that it's all too easy to be pigeonholed at the end of the project into performing tests in a rushed manner to meet a particular deadline or milestone.

- Ill-Suited for Lengthy Life Cycles: Like the waterfall model, the V-Model is completely linear and thus projects cannot be easily altered once the development train has left the station. V-Model is therefore poorly suited to handle long-term projects that may require many versions or constant updates/patches.

- Encourages 'Design-by-Committee' Development: While V-Model is certainly not the only development model to fall under this criticism, it cannot be denied that the strict and methodical nature of the V-Model and its various linear stages tend to emphasize a development cycle befitting managers and users, rather than developers and designers. With a method like V-Model, it can be all too easy for project managers or others to overlook the vast complexities of software development in favor of trying to meet deadlines, or to simply feel overly confident in the process or current progress, based solely on what stage in the life cycle is actively being developed.

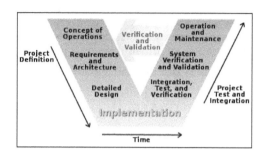

Extreme Programming

Agile Manifesto

A team of software developers published the Agile Manifesto in 2001, highlighting the importance of the development team, accommodating changing requirements and customer involvement.

The Agile Manifesto states that –

We are uncovering better ways of developing software by doing it and helping others do it. Through this work, we have come to value –

- Individuals and interactions over processes and tools.

- Working software over comprehensive documentation.

- Customer collaboration over contract negotiation.

- Responding to change over following a plan.

That is, while there is value in the items on the right, we value the items on the left more.

Characteristics of Agility

Following are the characteristics of Agility –

- Agility in Agile Software Development focuses on the culture of the whole team with multi-discipline, cross-functional teams that are empowered and self-organizing.

- It fosters shared responsibility and accountability.

- Facilitates effective communication and continuous collaboration.

- The whole-team approach avoids delays and wait times.

- Frequent and continuous deliveries ensure quick feedback that in in turn enable the team align to the requirements.

- Collaboration facilitates combining different perspectives timely in implementation, defect fixes and accommodating changes.

- Progress is constant, sustainable, and predictable emphasizing transparency.

Software Engineering Trends

The following trends are observed in software engineering –

- Gather requirements before development starts. However, if the requirements are to be changed later, then following is usually noticed –

  o Resistance to the changes at a later stage of development.

  o There is a requirement of a rigorous change process that involves a change control board that may even push the changes to later releases.

  o The delivery of a product with obsolete requirements, not meeting the customer's expectations.

  o Inability to accommodate the inevitable domain changes and technology changes within the budget.

- Find and eliminate defects early in the development life cycle in order to cut the defect-fix costs.

  o Testing starts only after coding is complete and testing is considered as a tester's responsibility though the tester is not involved in development.

  o Measure and track the process itself. This becomes expensive because of.

  o Monitoring and tracking at the task level and at the resource level.

  o Defining measurements to guide the development and measuring every activity in the development.

  o Management intervention.

- Elaborate, analyze, and verify the models before development.

  o A model is supposed to be used as a framework. However, focus on the model and not on the development that is crucial will not yield the expected results.

- Coding, which is the heart of development is not given enough emphasis. The reasons being –

  o Developers, who are responsible for the production, are usually not in constant communication with the customers.

  o Coding is viewed as a translation of design and the effective implementation in code is hardly ever looped back into the design.

- Testing is considered to be the gateway to check for defects before delivery.

  o Schedule overruns of the earlier stages of development are compensated by overlooking the test requirements to ensure timely deliveries.

  o This results in cost overruns fixing defects after delivery.

- o   Testers are made responsible and accountable for the product quality though they were not involved during the entire course of development.

- Limiting resources (mainly team) to accommodate budget leads to –

  - o   Resource over allocation.

  - o   Team burnout.

  - o   Loss in effective utilization of team competencies.

  - o   Attrition.

Extreme programming: A way to handle the specific needs of software development

Software Engineering involves –

- Creativity.

- Learning and improving through trials and errors.

- Iterations.

Extreme Programming builds on these activities and coding. It is the detailed (not the only) design activity with multiple tight feedback loops through effective implementation, testing and refactoring continuously.

Extreme Programming is based on the following values –

- Communication.

- Simplicity.

- Feedback.

- Courage.

- Respect.

XP is a lightweight, efficient, low-risk, flexible, predictable, scientific, and fun way to develop a software.

eXtreme Programming (XP) was conceived and developed to address the specific needs of software development by small teams in the face of vague and changing requirements.

Extreme Programming is one of the Agile software development methodologies. It provides values and principles to guide the team behavior. The team is expected to self-organize. Extreme Programming provides specific core practices where –

- Each practice is simple and self-complete.

- Combination of practices produces more complex and emergent behavior.

Embrace Change

A key assumption of Extreme Programming is that the cost of changing a program can be held mostly constant over time.

This can be achieved with −

- Emphasis on continuous feedback from the customer.
- Short iterations.
- Design and redesign.
- Coding and testing frequently.
- Eliminating defects early, thus reducing costs.
- Keeping the customer involved throughout the development.
- Delivering working product to the customer.

Extreme Programming in a Nutshell

Extreme Programming involves −

- Writing unit tests before programming and keeping all of the tests running at all times. The unit tests are automated and eliminates defects early, thus reducing the costs.
- Starting with a simple design just enough to code the features at hand and redesigning when required.
- Programming in pairs (called pair programming), with two programmers at one screen, taking turns to use the keyboard. While one of them is at the keyboard, the other constantly reviews and provides inputs.
- Integrating and testing the whole system several times a day.
- Putting a minimal working system into the production quickly and upgrading it whenever required.
- Keeping the customer involved all the time and obtaining constant feedback.

Iterating facilitates the accommodating changes as the software evolves with the changing requirements.

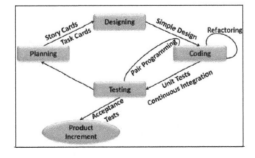

Why is it Called "Extreme?"

Extreme Programming takes the effective principles and practices to extreme levels:

- Code reviews are effective as the code is reviewed all the time.

- Testing is effective as there is continuous regression and testing.

- Design is effective as everybody needs to do refactoring daily.

- Integration testing is important as integrate and test several times a day.

- Short iterations are effective as the planning game for release planning and iteration planning.

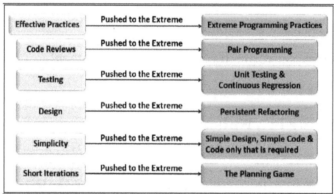

Kent Beck, Ward Cunningham and Ron Jeffries formulated extreme Programming in 1999. The other contributors are Robert Martin and Martin Fowler.

In Mid-80s, Kent Beck and Ward Cunningham initiated Pair Programming at Tektronix. In the 80s and 90s, Smalltalk Culture produced Refactoring, Continuous Integration, constant testing, and close customer involvement. This culture was later generalized to the other environments.

In the Early 90s, Core Values were developed within the Patterns Community, Hillside Group. In 1995, Kent summarized these in Smalltalk Best Practices, and in 1996, Ward summarized it in episodes.

In 1996, Kent added unit testing and metaphor at Hewitt. In 1996, Kent had taken the Chrysler C3 project, to which Ron Jeffries was added as a coach. The practices were refined on C3.

Scrum practices were incorporated and adapted as the planning game. In 1999, Kent published his book, 'Extreme Programming Explained'. In the same year, Fowler published his book, Refactoring.

Extreme Programming has been evolving since then, and the evolution continues through today.

Success in Industry

The success of projects, which follow Extreme Programming practices, is due to –

- Rapid development.

- Immediate responsiveness to the customer's changing requirements.

- Focus on low defect rates.

- System returning constant and consistent value to the customer.

- High customer satisfaction.

- Reduced costs.

- Team cohesion and employee satisfaction.

Extreme Programming Advantages

Extreme Programming solves the following problems often faced in the software development projects:

- Slipped schedules: and achievable development cycles ensure timely deliveries.

- Cancelled projects: Focus on continuous customer involvement ensures transparency with the customer and immediate resolution of any issues.

- Costs incurred in changes: Extensive and ongoing testing makes sure the changes do not break the existing functionality. A running working system always ensures sufficient time for accommodating changes such that the current operations are not affected.

- Production and post-delivery defects: Emphasis is on: the unit tests to detect and fix the defects early.

- Misunderstanding the business and domain: Making the customer a part of the team ensures constant communication and clarifications.

- Business changes: Changes are considered to be inevitable and are accommodated at any point of time.

- Staff turnover: Intensive team collaboration ensures enthusiasm and good will. Cohesion of multi-disciplines fosters the team spirit.

Lean Software Development

Lean development is the application of Lean principles to software development. Lean got its start in manufacturing, as a way to optimize the production line to minimize waste and maximize value to the customer. These two goals are also relevant to software development, which also follows a repeatable process, requires particular quality standards, and relies on the collaboration of a group of specialized workers in order to get done.

Of course, there are some major differences between manufacturing and software development, as well - namely, that manufacturing deals with the production of physical goods, while the value being created in software development is created within the mind of the developer.

Applying Lean principles to knowledge work requires a shift in mindset however, in terms of how value, waste, and other key Lean concepts are defined.

Lean Development Principles

The seven principles of Lean development are: Eliminate Waste, Build Quality In, Create Knowledge, Defer Commitment, Deliver Fast, Respect People, and Optimize the Whole. In their book, Lean Software Development: An Agile Toolkit, Mary and Tom Poppendieck outlined how these Lean principles can be applied to software development. Here is a brief summary of each of these principles, as well as practical tips on how to apply them in software development.

Eliminate Waste

One of the key elements of practicing Lean is to eliminate anything that does not add value to the customer. There are seven wastes (or *muda)* defined in the Toyota school of Lean manufacturing. They are:

- Over-production: Manufacturing an item before it is required.

- Unnecessary transportation: Moving inventory from place to place, which puts it at risk for damage without adding any value.

- Inventory: Holding inventory adds cost without adding any value to the customer; excess inventory takes up valuable space, increases lead times, and delays innovation.

- Motion: Literally refers to unnecessary movement of workers on the shop floor.

- Defects: Quality issues result in rework or scrap and can add tremendous additional costs to organizations who don't habitually find ways to eliminate sources of defects.

- Over-processing: Using advanced, expensive tools to do what could be done with simpler tools

- Waiting: When inventory waits between value-adding steps.

Tom and Mary Poppendieck translated those wastes to software development. Each of these wastes should be systematically eliminated in order to maximize customer value:

- Unnecessary code or functionality: Delays time to customer, slows down feedback loops.

- Starting more than can be completed: Adds unnecessary complexity to the system, results in context-switching, handoff delays, and other impediments to flow.

- Delay in the software development process: Delays time to customer, slows down feedback loops.

- Unclear or constantly changing requirements: Results in rework, frustration, quality issues, lack of focus.

- Bureaucracy: Delays speed.

- Slow or ineffective communication: Results in delays, frustrations, and poor communication to stakeholders which can impact IT's reputation in the organization.

- Partially done work: Does not add value to the customer or allow team to learn from work.

- Defects and quality issues: Results in rework, abandoned work, and poor customer satisfaction.

- Task switching: Results in poor work quality, delays, communication breakdowns, and low team morale.

Build Quality In

It might seem self-evident - every team wants to build quality into their work. But unless this is part of a disciplined practice, it's far easier said than done. In trying to ensure quality, many teams actually create waste - through excessive testing, for example, or an excessive logging of defects.

In recent decades, many Lean development teams have found success by applying the following Lean development tools to build quality into their work. In Lean development, quality is everyone's job - not just QA's.

These are some of the most popular Lean development tools for building quality in:

- Pair programming: Avoid quality issues by combining the skills and experience of two developers instead of one.

- Test-driven development: Writing criteria for code before writing the code to ensure it meets business requirements.

- Incremental development and constant feedback.

- Minimize wait states: Reduce context switching, knowledge gaps, and lack of focus.

- Automation: Automate any tedious, manual process or any process prone to human error.

Create Knowledge

The Lean development principle of Create Knowledge is another one that seems simple, but requires discipline and focus to implement. This principle encourages Lean teams to provide the infrastructure to properly document and retain valuable learning. This can be done by using any combination of the following tools:

- Pair Programming.

- Code reviews.

- Documentation.

- Wiki – to let the knowledge base build up incrementally.

- Thoroughly commented code.

- Knowledge sharing sessions.

- Training.

- Use tools to manage requirements or user stories.

Defer Commitment

This Lean development principle is easily misused. Defer Commitment does not mean that teams should be flaky or irresponsible about their decision-making. Rather, the opposite: This Lean principle encourages team to demonstrate responsibility by keeping their options open and continuously collecting information, rather than making decisions without the necessary data.

To defer commitment means to not plan (in excessive detail) for months in advance, to not commit to ideas or projects without a full understanding of the business requirements, and to constantly be collecting and analyzing information regarding any important decisions.

Deliver Fast

Every team wants to deliver fast, to put value into the hands of the customer as quickly as possible. The question isn't why teams want to deliver fast, but rather, what slows them down. Here are a few common culprits:

- Thinking too far in advance about future requirements.

- Blockers that aren't responded to with urgency.

- Over-engineering solutions and business requirements.

The Lean way of delivering quickly isn't working longer hours and weekends, or working recklessly for the sake of speed. Lean development is based on this concept: Build a simple solution, put it in front of customers, enhance incrementally based on customer feedback. This is important, especially in software, because speed to market is an incredible competitive advantage.

Respect People

The Lean principle of Respect for People is often one of the most neglected, especially in the fast-paced, burnout-ridden world of software development. It applies to every aspect of the way Lean teams operate, from how they communicate, handle conflict, hire and onboard new team members, deal with process improvement, and more. Lean development teams can encourage respect for people by communicating proactively and effectively, encouraging healthy conflict, surfacing any work-related issues as a team, and empowering each other to do their best work.

Optimize the Whole

Sub optimization is a serious issue in software development, and is often a self-fulfilling prophecy. In their book, Mary and Tom Poppendieck describe two vicious cycles that Lean development teams often fall into.

The first is releasing sloppy code for the sake of speed. When developers feel pressured to deliver at all costs, they release code that may or may not meet quality requirements. This increases the complexity of the code base, resulting in more defects. With more defects, there is more work to do, putting more pressure on developers to deliver quickly so the cycle continues.

The second is an issue with testing. When testers are overloaded, it creates a long cycle time between when developers write code and when testers are able to give feedback on it. This means that developers continue writing code that may or may not be defective, resulting in more defects and therefore requiring more testing.

As the antidote to sub optimization, optimizing the whole is a Lean development principle that encourages Lean organizations to eliminate these sorts of vicious cycles by operating with a better understanding of capacity and the downstream impact of work.

It's based on the idea that every business represents a value stream — the sequence of activities required to design, produce, and deliver a product or service to customers. If our goal is to deliver as much value to our customers as quickly as possible, then we have to optimize our value streams to be able to do just that. To understand how to optimize our value streams, first we have to properly identify them.

After identifying how value flows through their teams, many organizations decide to organize their software development teams to be complete, multi-disciplined, co-located product teams, which enables them to have everything they need to deliver a request from start to finish, without reference to other teams. This is an approach popularized by Spotify, that has been adopted by many Lean organizations as a way to optimize the whole and increase the speed of value delivery.

Test-Driven Development

TDD can be defined as a programming practice that instructs developers to write new code only if an automated test has failed. This avoids duplication of code. TDD means "Test Driven Development". The primary goal of TDD is to make the code clearer, simple and bug-free.

Test-Driven Development starts with designing and developing tests for every small functionality of an application. In TDD approach, first, the test is developed which specifies and validates what the code will do.

In the normal Testing process, we first generate the code and then test. Tests might fail since tests are developed even before the development. In order to pass the test, the development team has to develop and refactors the code. Refactoring a code means changing some code without affecting its behavior.

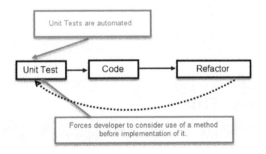

The simple concept of TDD is to write and correct the failed tests before writing new code (before development). This helps to avoid duplication of code as we write a small amount of code at a time in order to pass tests. (Tests are nothing but requirement conditions that we need to test to fulfill them).

Test-Driven development is a process of developing and running automated test before actual development of the application. Hence, TDD sometimes also called as Test First Development.

Ways to Perform TDD Test

Following steps define how to perform TDD test,

- Add a test.
- Run all tests and see if any new test fails.
- Write some code.
- Run tests and Refactor code.
- Repeat.

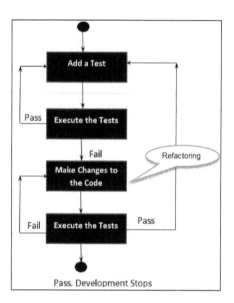

TDD Cycle Defines

- Write a test.
- Make it run.
- Change the code to make it right i.e. Refactor.
- Repeat process.

Some Clarifications About TDD

- TDD is neither about "Testing" nor about "Design".

- TDD does not mean "write some of the tests, then build a system that passes the tests.

- TDD does not mean "do lots of Testing."

TDD Vs. Traditional Testing

TDD approach is primarily a specification technique. It ensures that your source code is thoroughly tested at confirmatory level:

- With traditional testing, a successful test finds one or more defects. It is same as TDD. When a test fails, you have made progress because you know that you need to resolve the problem.

- TDD ensures that your system actually meets requirements defined for it. It helps to build your confidence about your system.

- In TDD more focus is on production code that verifies whether testing will work properly. In traditional testing, more focus is on test case design. Whether the test will show the proper/improper execution of the application in order to fulfill requirements.

- In TDD, you achieve 100% coverage test. Every single line of code is tested, unlike traditional testing.

- The combination of both traditional testing and TDD leads to the importance of testing the system rather than perfection of the system.

- In Agile Modeling (AM), you should "test with a purpose". You should know why you are testing something and what level its need to be tested.

Acceptance TDD and Developer TDD

There are two levels of TDD

Acceptance TDD (ATDD): With ATDD you write a single acceptance test. This test fulfills the requirement of the specification or satisfies the behavior of the system. After that write just enough production/functionality code to fulfill that acceptance test. Acceptance test focuses on the overall behavior of the system. ATDD also was known as Behavioral Driven Development (BDD).

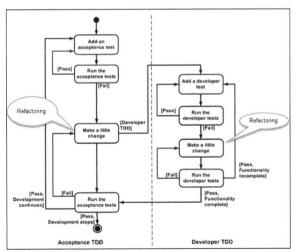

Developer TDD: With Developer TDD you write single developer test i.e. unit test and then just enough production code to fulfill that test. The unit test focuses on every small functionality of the system. Developer TDD is simply called as TDD.

The main goal of ATDD and TDD is to specify detailed, executable requirements for your solution on a just in time (JIT) basis. JIT means taking only those requirements in consideration that are needed in the system. So increase efficiency.

Scaling TDD via Agile Model Driven Development (AMDD)

TDD is very good at detailed specification and validation. It fails at thinking through bigger issues such as overall design, use of the system, or UI. AMDD addresses the Agile scaling issues that TDD does not.

Thus AMDD used for bigger issues.

The lifecycle of AMDD

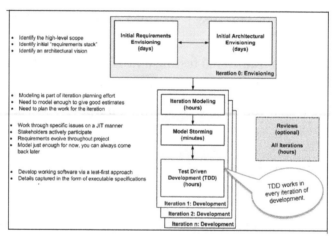

In Model-driven Development (MDD), extensive models are created before the source code is written. Which in turn have.

In above figure, each box represents a development activity.

Envisioning is one of the TDD process of predicting/imagining tests which will be performed during the first week of the project. The main goal of envisioning is to identify the scope of the system and architecture of the system. High-level requirements and architecture modeling is done for successful envisioning.

It is the process where not a detailed specification of software/system is done but exploring the requirements of software/system which defines the overall strategy of the project.

Iteration 0: Envisioning

There are two main sub-activates:

- Initial requirements envisioning.

It may take several days to identify high-level requirements and scope of the system. The main focus is to explore usage model, Initial domain model, and user interface model (UI).

- Initial Architectural envisioning.

It also takes several days to identify architecture of the system. It allows setting technical directions for the project. The main focus is to explore technology diagrams, User Interface (UI) flow, domain models, and Change cases.

Iteration Modeling

Here team must plan the work that will be done for each iteration:

- Agile process is used for each iteration, i.e. during each iteration, new work item will be added with priority.

- First higher prioritized work will be taken into consideration. Work items added may be reprioritized or removed from items stack any time.

- The team discusses how they are going to implement each requirement. Modeling is used for this purpose.

- Modeling analysis and design is done for each requirement which is going to implement for that iteration.

Model Storming

This is also known as Just in time Modeling:

- Here modeling session involves a team of 2/3 members who discuss issues on paper or whiteboard.

- One team member will ask another to model with them. This modeling session will take approximately 5 to 10 minutes. Where team members gather together to share whiteboard/paper.

- They explore issues until they don't find the main cause of the problem. Just in time, if one team member identifies the issue which he/she wants to resolve then he/she will take quick help of other team members.

- Other group members then explore the issue and then everyone continues on as before. It is also called as stand-up modeling or customer QA sessions.

Test Driven Development (TDD).

- It promotes confirmatory testing of your application code and detailed specification.

- Both acceptance test (detailed requirements) and developer tests (unit test) are inputs for TDD.

- TDD makes the code simpler and clear. It allows the developer to maintain less documentation.

Reviews

- This is optional. It includes code inspections and model reviews.

- This can be done for each iteration or for the whole project.

- This is a good option to give feedback for the project.

Test Driven Development (TDD) Vs. Agile Model Driven Development (AMDD)

TDD	AMDD
TDD shortens the programming feedback loop	AMDD shortens modeling feedback loop.
TDD is detailed specification	AMDD works for bigger issues.
TDD promotes the development of high-quality code	AMDD promotes high-quality communication with stakeholders and developers.
TDD speaks to programmers	AMDD talks to business analyst, stakeholders, and data professionals.
TDD non-visually oriented	AMDD visually oriented.
TDD has limited scope to software works	AMDD has a broad scope including stakeholders. It involves working towards a common understanding.
Both support evolutionary development	----------------------

Example of TDD

Here in this example, we will define a class password. For this class, we will try to satisfy following conditions.

A condition for Password acceptance:

- The password should be between 5 to 10 characters.

First, we write the code that fulfills all the above requirements.

```
package Prac;

import org.testng.Assert;
import org.testng.annotations.Test;

public class TestPassword {                    Needed for TestNG
  @Test
  public void TestPasswordLength() {
    PasswordValidator pv = new PasswordValidator();
    Assert.assertEquals(true, pv.isValid("Abc123"));
  }
}
```

We can not run test because this class is not created yet

This is main validation test

Scenario 1: To run the test, we create class PasswordValidator ();

```
package Prac;

public class PasswordValidator {
 public boolean isValid(String Password)
 {
     if (Password.length()>=5 && Password.length()<=10)
     {
         return true;
     }
     else
         return false;
 }
}
```

This is main condition checking length of password. If meets return true otherwise false.

We will run above class TestPassword ();

Output is PASSED as shown below;

Output

```
<terminated> TestPassword [TestNG] C:\Program Files\Java\jre1.8.0_77\bin\javaw.exe (Jul 25, 2016, 2:10:22 PM)
[TestNG] Running:
  C:\Users\kanchan\AppData\Local\Temp\testng-eclipse--571370159\testng-customsuite.xml

PASSED: TestPasswordLength                                    Result of test as Passed

===========================================
    Default test
    Tests run: 1, Failures: 0, Skips: 0
===========================================


===========================================
Default suite
Total tests run: 1, Failures: 0, Skips: 0
===========================================

[TestNG] Time taken by org.testng.reporters.EmailableReporter2@1b40d5f0: 202 ms
[TestNG] Time taken by org.testng.reporters.XMLReporter@28f67ac7: 63 ms
[TestNG] Time taken by org.testng.reporters.jq.Main@546a03af: 78 ms
[TestNG] Time taken by org.testng.reporters.JUnitReportReporter@5a01ccaa: 2 ms
[TestNG] Time taken by [FailedReporter passed=0 failed=0 skipped=0]: 1 ms
[TestNG] Time taken by org.testng.reporters.SuiteHTMLReporter@2b80d80f: 10 ms
```

Scenario 2: Here we can see in method TestPasswordLength() there is no need of creating an instance of class PasswordValidator. Instance means creating an object of class to refer the members (variables/methods) of that class.

```
package Prac;

import org.testng.Assert;                        We will remove it.

public class TestPassword {
 @Test
 public void TestPasswordLength() {

     PasswordValidator pv = new PasswordValidator();

     Assert.assertEquals(true, pv.isValid("Abc123"));

 }
}
```

We will remove class PasswordValidator pv = new PasswordValidator () from the code. We can call the isValid () method directly by PasswordValidator. IsValid ("Abc123").

So we Refactor (change code) as below:

```
package Prac;

import org.testng.Assert;
import org.testng.annotations.Test;

public class TestPassword {
  @Test
  public void TestPasswordLength() {

      Assert.assertEquals(true, PasswordValidator.isValid("Abc123"));

  }
}
```

Re factor code as there is no need of creating instance of class PasswordValidator().

Scenario 3: After refactoring the output shows failed status this is because we have removed the instance. So there is no reference to non –static method isValid ().

```
[TestNG] Running:
  C:\Users\kanchan\AppData\Local\Temp\testng-eclipse--157192639\testng-customsuite.xml

FAILED: TestPasswordLength
java.lang.Error: Unresolved compilation problem:
    Cannot make a static reference to the non-static method isValid(String) from the type PasswordValidator

    at Prac.TestPassword.TestPasswordLength(TestPassword.java:10)
    at sun.reflect.NativeMethodAccessorImpl.invoke0(Native Method)
    at sun.reflect.NativeMethodAccessorImpl.invoke(Unknown Source)
    at sun.reflect.DelegatingMethodAccessorImpl.invoke(Unknown Source)
    at java.lang.reflect.Method.invoke(Unknown Source)
    at org.testng.internal.MethodInvocationHelper.invokeMethod(Method
    at org.testng.internal.Invoker.invokeMethod(Invoker.java:639)
    at org.testng.internal.Invoker.invokeTestMethod(Invoker.java:821)
```

If we removed instance creation statement compiler will give error. As we do not create instance it becomes non static method and there is no any reference to this method. Test results in Fail. To remove this error we have to make isValid() method of class PasswordValidator as static.

So we need to change this method by adding "static" word before Boolean as public static boolean isValid (String password). Refactoring Class PasswordValidator () to remove above error to pass the test.

```
package Prac;

public class PasswordValidator {
  public static boolean isValid(String Password)
  {
      if (Password.length()>=5 && Password.length()<=10)
      {
          return true;
      }
      else
          return false;
  }
}
```

Re factor : Added static word to pass test.

Output

After making changes to class PassValidator () if we run the test then the output will be PASSED as shown below.

```
<terminated> TestPassword [TestNG] C:\Program Files\Java\jre1.8.0_77\bin\javaw.exe (Jul 25, 2016, 3:02:16 PM)
[TestNG] Running:
  C:\Users\kanchan\AppData\Local\Temp\testng-eclipse--1385484104\testng-customsuite.xml

PASSED: TestPasswordLength

===============================================
    Default test
    Tests run: 1, Failures: 0, Skips: 0
===============================================


===============================================
Default suite
Total tests run: 1, Failures: 0, Skips: 0
===============================================

[TestNG] Time taken by org.testng.reporters.EmailableReporter2@1b40d5f0: 19 ms
[TestNG] Time taken by org.testng.reporters.XMLReporter@28f67ac7: 10 ms
[TestNG] Time taken by org.testng.reporters.jq.Main@546a03af: 34 ms
```

Test results passed as we changed code in class PasswordValidator().

Benefits of TDD

- Early bug notification.

  Developers test their code but in the database world, this often consists of manual tests or one-off scripts. Using TDD you build up, over time, a suite of automated tests that you and any other developer can rerun at will.

- Better Designed, cleaner and more extensible code.

  o It helps to understand how the code will be used and how it interacts with other modules.

  o It results in better design decision and more maintainable code.

  o TDD allows writing smaller code having single responsibility rather than monolithic procedures with multiple responsibilities. This makes the code simpler to understand.

  o TDD also forces to write only production code to pass tests based on user requirements.

- Confidence to Refactor.

  o If you refactor code, there can be possibilities of breaks in the code. So having a set of automated tests you can fix those breaks before release. Proper warning will be given if breaks found when automated tests are used.

    o Using TDD, should results in faster, more extensible code with fewer bugs that can be updated with minimal risks.

- Good for teamwork.

  In the absence of any team member, other team members can easily pick up and work on the code. It also aids knowledge sharing, thereby making the team more effective overall.

- Good for Developers.

  Though developers have to spend more time in writing TDD test cases, it takes a lot less time for debugging and developing new features. You will write cleaner, less complicated code.

Agile Software Development

Agile SDLC model is a combination of iterative and incremental process models with focus on process adaptability and customer satisfaction by rapid delivery of working software product. Agile Methods break the product into small incremental builds. These builds are provided in iterations. Each iteration typically lasts from about one to three weeks. Every iteration involves cross-functional teams working simultaneously on various areas like –

- Planning.
- Requirements Analysis.

- Design.
- Coding.
- Unit Testing.
- Acceptance Testing.

At the end of the iteration, a working product is displayed to the customer and important stakeholders.

Agile model believes that every project needs to be handled differently and the existing methods need to be tailored to best suit the project requirements. In Agile, the tasks are divided to time boxes small time frames to deliver specific features for a release.

Iterative approach is taken and working software build is delivered after each iteration. Each build is incremental in terms of features; the final build holds all the features required by the customer.

The Agile thought process had started early in the software development and started becoming popular with time due to its flexibility and adaptability.

The most popular Agile methods include Rational Unified Process, Scrum, Crystal Clear, Extreme Programming, Adaptive Software Development, Feature Driven Development, and Dynamic Systems Development Method (DSDM). These are now collectively referred to as Agile Methodologies, after the Agile Manifesto was published in 2001.

Here is a graphical illustration of the Agile Model –

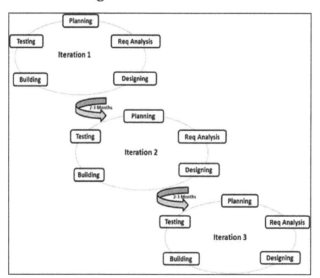

Following are the Agile Manifesto principles:

- Individuals and interactions: In Agile development, self-organization and motivation are important, as are interactions like co-location and pair programming.

- Working software: Demo working software is considered the best means of communication with the customers to understand their requirements, instead of just depending on documentation.

- Customer collaboration: As the requirements cannot be gathered completely in the beginning of the project due to various factors, continuous customer interaction is very important to get proper product requirements.

- Responding to change: Agile Development is focused on quick responses to change and continuous development.

Agile Vs Traditional SDLC Models

Agile is based on the adaptive software development methods, whereas the traditional SDLC models like the waterfall model is based on a predictive approach. Predictive teams in the traditional SDLC models usually work with detailed planning and have a complete forecast of the exact tasks and features to be delivered in the next few months or during the product life cycle.

Predictive methods entirely depend on the requirement analysis and planning done in the beginning of cycle. Any changes to be incorporated go through a strict change control management and prioritization.

Agile uses an adaptive approach where there is no detailed planning and there is clarity on future tasks only in respect of what features need to be developed. There is feature driven development and the team adapts to the changing product requirements dynamically. The product is tested very frequently, through the release iterations, minimizing the risk of any major failures in future.

Customer Interaction is the backbone of this Agile methodology, and open communication with minimum documentation are the typical features of Agile development environment. The agile teams work in close collaboration with each other and are most often located in the same geographical location.

Agile Model - Pros and Cons

Agile methods are being widely accepted in the software world recently. However, this method may not always be suitable for all products. Here are some pros and cons of the Agile model.

The advantages of the Agile Model are as follows:

- Is a very realistic approach to software development.

- Promotes teamwork and cross training.

- Functionality can be developed rapidly and demonstrated.

- Resource requirements are minimum.

- Suitable for fixed or changing requirements

- Delivers early partial working solutions.

- Good model for environments that change steadily.

- Minimal rules, documentation easily employed.

- Enables concurrent development and delivery within an overall planned context.

- Little or no planning required.

- Easy to manage.

- Gives flexibility to developers.

The disadvantages of the Agile Model are as follows –

- Not suitable for handling complex dependencies.

- More risk of sustainability, maintainability and extensibility.

- An overall plan, an agile leader and agile PM practice is a must without which it will not work.

- Strict delivery management dictates the scope, functionality to be delivered, and adjustments to meet the deadlines.

- Depends heavily on customer interaction, so if customer is not clear, team can be driven in the wrong direction.

- There is a very high individual dependency, since there is minimum documentation generated.

- Transfer of technology to new team members may be quite challenging due to lack of documentation.

Pair Programming

As the name implies, pair programming is where two developers work using only one machine. Each one has a keyboard and a mouse. One programmer acts as the driver who codes while the other will serve as the observer who will check the code being written, proofread and spell check it, while also figuring out where to go next. These roles can be switched at any time: the driver will then become the observer and vice versa.

It's also commonly called "pairing," "programming in pairs," and "paired programming."

Pair Programming Advantages

There are several compelling reasons you should consider this strategy:

- Two heads are better than one: If the driver encounters a hitch with the code, there will be two of them who'll solve the problem.

- More efficient: Common thinking is that it slows down the project completion time because you are effectively putting two programmers to develop a single program, instead of having them work independently on two different programs. But studies have shown that two programmers working on the same program are only 15% slower than when these programmers work independently, rather than the presupposed 50% slow down.

- Fewer coding mistakes: Because there is another programmer looking over your work, it results in better code. In fact, an earlier study shows that it results in 15% fewer bugs than code written by solo programmers. Plus, it allows the driver to remain focus on the code being written while the other attends to external matters or interruption.

- An effective way to share knowledge: Code Fellows talks about how it could help programmers learn from their peers in this blog post. It would allow programmers to get instant face-to-face instruction, which is much better than online tutorials and faster than looking for resources on the Internet. Plus, you can learn things better from your partner, especially in areas that may be unfamiliar to you. Developers can also pick up best practices and better techniques from more advanced programmers. It can also facilitate mentoring relationships between two programmers.

- Develops your staff's interpersonal skills: Collaborating on a single project helps your team to appreciate the value of communication and teamwork.

- Fewer mistakes are introduced into your code because a lot of errors are caught as they are being typed. This level of continuous code reviews gives rise to fewer bugs in your code.

- You have shorter and tighter code.

- Two people can solve the problems that crop up along the way faster and quicker.

- Your developers learn more about things that are specific to the applications that they are working on as well as software development in general, best practices, and other areas.

- You have more people who know how the new program works. This means that if one of the pair leaves the company, it will not kill the project.

- Your team develops better interpersonal and social skills. Team members can learn to communicate with each other, work together, and share information.

- Your team members are more satisfied.

Programming is better than code Reviews in Terms of Pair

Code reviews are a process wherein another programmer takes a look at your code to find something that needs improvement or find defects in it. It combines testing with quality control to ensure that everything in your code is good. This helps you ensure that your code is improved.

However, it is challenging to find somebody to review your code because people may not want to look at another's code and understand their reasoning just for the sake of checking its quality. Most of the time, code reviews happen when somebody else tries to add some functionality to your code, or fixes bugs. But by then, you, as the original programmer, might not even be around to appreciate the code review.

With pairing, it is like having somebody review your code instantly and regularly. It is a higher form of code reviews. Two people have to be there and understand the program being written. And if one sees problems with the other's code, then it can be instantly corrected. You also have fewer chances of having bugs written into your code. Code reviews are not as proactive as you have to wait until the code is completed — bugs and all — before somebody could take a look at and correct it.

Challenges of Pairing

The common problems observed when it comes to pair programming include the following:

- The pair should be equally engaged and be participative for the duration of the task. Otherwise, there would be no benefits.

- People who have not tried it may think that it will double the cost because you are putting two programmers on one project. However, this is a misconception that needs to be clarified. On top of the fact that pairing, done right, will only result in 15% slowdowns in terms of the individual output, it actually speeds up the coding process and ensures better quality code, which lessens the chances that the program would have to be redone.

- Pair programming should also be a programming out loud process, where the pair is verbally detailing what it is doing.

- It's not something that you can force your team to do. It's highly social and interactive, so you should be able to detect pairs that may have problems with each other, such as clashing personalities or even problems with personal hygiene.

Ways to Effectively Pair your Programmers

The best way to approach pairing is to partner two programmers and have them share a computer. Make them work together to architect, code and then test their codes in a genuine sense of a partnership. While the ideal setup would include two programmers who are equally skilled (expert – expert or novice – novice), you can also use pair programming for training and educational purposes (expert – novice).

The pair should be able to decide how to split the work, and it is advisable that they should switch roles often.

References

- Software-development-models-iterative-and-incremental-development: technologyconversations.com, Retrieved 31 March 2020

- What-is-a-software-development-process, analysis-and-design: selectbs.com, Retrieved 24 June 2020

- 6-stages-of-software-development-process-141: synapseindia.com, Retrieved 22 March 2020

- Pair-programming-advantages: stackify.com, Retrieved 14 July 2020

- Aspect-oriented-software-development-aosd-205: techopedia.com, Retrieved 30 June 2020

- Software-development: techtarget.com, Retrieved 10 April 2020

- Software-release-life-cycle: professionalqa.com, Retrieved 14 July 2020

4

Software User Interface

User interface can be defined as the means through which the user communicates and controls the software application or hardware device. The process of building this method to facilitate user-system communication is known as user interface design. User interfaces are designed with ease of use and accessibility as a priority. The chapter sheds light on user interface and its design process.

User Interface

Example of a tangible user interface.

The user interface (UI), in the industrial design field of human–computer interaction, is the space where interactions between humans and machines occur. The goal of this interaction is to allow effective operation and control of the machine from the human end, whilst the machine simultaneously feeds back information that aids the operators' decision-making process. Examples of this broad concept of user interfaces include the interactive aspects of computer operating systems, hand tools, heavy machinery operator controls, and process controls. The design considerations applicable when creating user interfaces are related to or involve such disciplines as ergonomics and psychology.

Generally, the goal of user interface design is to produce a user interface which makes it easy (self-explanatory), efficient, and enjoyable (user-friendly) to operate a machine in the way which produces the desired result. This generally means that the operator needs to provide minimal input to achieve the desired output, and also that the machine minimizes undesired outputs to the human.

With the increased use of personal computers and the relative decline in societal aware-ness of heavy machinery, the term user interface is generally assumed to mean the graphical user interface, while industrial control panel and machinery control design discussions more commonly refer to human-machine interfaces.

Other terms for user interface are man–machine interface (MMI) and when the ma-chine in question is a computer human–computer interface.

Overview

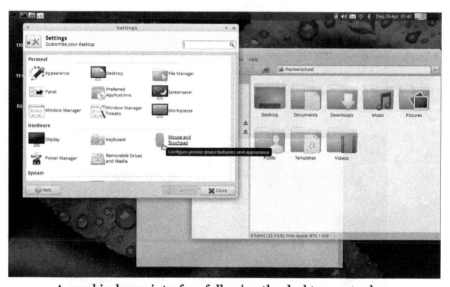

A graphical user interface following the desktop metaphor.

The user interface or *human–machine interface* is the part of the machine that han-dles the human–machine interaction. Membrane switches, rubber keypads and touch-screens are examples of the physical part of the Human Machine Interface which we can see and touch.

In complex systems, the human–machine interface is typically computerized. The term *human–computer interface* refers to this kind of system. In the context of computing the term typically extends as well to the software dedicated to control the physical ele-ments used for human-computer interaction.

The engineering of the human–machine interfaces is enhanced by considering ergo-nomics (human factors). The corresponding disciplines are human factors engineering (HFE) and usability engineering (UE), which is part of systems engineering.

Tools used for incorporating human factors in the interface design are developed based on knowledge of computer science, such as computer graphics, operating sys-tems, programming languages. Nowadays, we use the expression graphical user in-terface for human–machine interface on computers, as nearly all of them are now using graphics.

Terminology

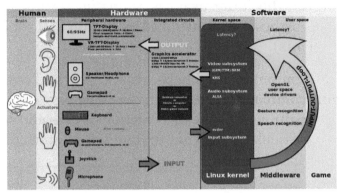

A human–machine interface usually involves peripheral hardware for the INPUT and for the OUTPUT. Often, there is an additional component implemented in software, like e.g. a graphical user interface.

There is a difference between a user interface and an operator interface or a human–machine interface (HMI).

- The term "user interface" is often used in the context of (personal) computer systems and electronic devices.

    o Where a network of equipment or computers are interlinked through an MES (Manufacturing Execution System)-or Host to display information.

    o A human-machine interface (HMI) is typically local to one machine or piece of equipment, and is the interface method between the human and the equipment/machine. An operator interface is the interface method by which multiple equipment that are linked by a host control system is accessed or controlled.

    o The system may expose several user interfaces to serve different kinds of users. For example, a computerized library database might provide two user interfaces, one for library patrons (limited set of functions, optimized for ease of use) and the other for library personnel (wide set of functions, optimized for efficiency).

- The user interface of a mechanical system, a vehicle or an industrial installation is sometimes referred to as the human–machine interface (HMI). HMI is a modification of the original term MMI (man-machine interface). In practice, the abbreviation MMI is still frequently used although some may claim that MMI stands for something different now. Another abbreviation is HCI, but is more commonly used for human–computer interaction. Other terms used are operator interface console (OIC) and operator interface terminal (OIT). However it is abbreviated, the terms refer to the 'layer' that separates a human that is operating a machine from the machine itself. Without a clean and usable interface, humans would not be able to interact with information systems.

In science fiction, HMI is sometimes used to refer to what is better described as direct neural interface. However, this latter usage is seeing increasing application in the real-life use of (medical) prostheses—the artificial extension that replaces a missing body part (e.g., cochlear implants).

In some circumstances, computers might observe the user and react according to their actions without specific commands. A means of tracking parts of the body is required, and sensors noting the position of the head, direction of gaze and so on have been used experimentally. This is particularly relevant to immersive interfaces.

History

The history of user interfaces can be divided into the following phases according to the dominant type of user interface:

1945–1968: Batch Interface

IBM 029

In the batch era, computing power was extremely scarce and expensive. User interfaces were rudimentary. Users had to accommodate computers rather than the other way around; user interfaces were considered overhead, and software was designed to keep the processor at maximum utilization with as little overhead as possible.

The input side of the user interfaces for batch machines were mainly punched cards or equivalent media like paper tape. The output side added line printers to these media. With the limited exception of the system operator's console, human beings did not interact with batch machines in real time at all.

Submitting a job to a batch machine involved, first, preparing a deck of punched cards describing a program and a dataset. Punching the program cards wasn't done on the computer itself, but on keypunches, specialized typewriter-like machines that were notoriously balky, unforgiving, and prone to mechanical failure. The software interface was similarly unforgiving, with very strict syntaxes meant to be parsed by the smallest possible compilers and interpreters.

Holes are punched in the card according to a prearranged code transferring the facts from the
census questionnaire into statistics.

Once the cards were punched, one would drop them in a job queue and wait. Eventually. operators would feed the deck to the computer, perhaps mounting magnetic tapes to
supply another dataset or helper software. The job would generate a printout, containing final results or (all too often) an abort notice with an attached error log. Successful
runs might also write a result on magnetic tape or generate some data cards to be used
in later computation.

The turnaround time for a single job often spanned entire days. If one were very lucky, it
might be hours; real-time response was unheard of. But there were worse fates than the
card queue; some computers actually required an even more tedious and error-prone
process of toggling in programs in binary code using console switches. The very earliest
machines actually had to be partly rewired to incorporate program logic into themselves, using devices known as plugboards.

Early batch systems gave the currently running job the entire computer; program decks
and tapes had to include what we would now think of as operating system code to talk
to I/O devices and do whatever other housekeeping was needed. Midway through the
batch period, after 1957, various groups began to experiment with so-called "load-and-
go" systems. These used a monitor program which was always resident on the computer. Programs could call the monitor for services. Another function of the monitor was
to do better error checking on submitted jobs, catching errors earlier and more intelligently and generating more useful feedback to the users. Thus, monitors represented a
first step towards both operating systems and explicitly designed user interfaces.

1969–present: Command-line user Interface

Command-line interfaces (CLIs) evolved from batch monitors connected to the system
console. Their interaction model was a series of request-response transactions, with
requests expressed as textual commands in a specialized vocabulary. Latency was far
lower than for batch systems, dropping from days or hours to seconds. Accordingly,
command-line systems allowed the user to change his or her mind about later stages of
the transaction in response to real-time or near-real-time feedback on earlier results.

Software could be exploratory and interactive in ways not possible before. But these interfaces still placed a relatively heavy mnemonic load on the user, requiring a serious investment of effort and learning time to master.

Teletype Model 33 ASR.

The earliest command-line systems combined teleprinters with computers, adapting a mature technology that had proven effective for mediating the transfer of information over wires between human beings. Teleprinters had originally been invented as devices for automatic telegraph transmission and reception; they had a history going back to 1902 and had already become well-established in newsrooms and elsewhere by 1920. In reusing them, economy was certainly a consideration, but psychology and the Rule of Least Surprise mattered as well; teleprinters provided a point of interface with the system that was familiar to many engineers and users.

DEC VT100 terminal.

The widespread adoption of video-display terminals (VDTs) in the mid-1970s ushered in the second phase of command-line systems. These cut latency further, because characters could be thrown on the phosphor dots of a screen more quickly than a printer head or carriage can move. They helped quell conservative resistance to interactive programming by cutting ink and paper consumables out of the cost picture, and were to the first TV generation of the late 1950s and 60s even more iconic and comfortable than teleprinters had been to the computer pioneers of the 1940s.

Just as importantly, the existence of an accessible screen — a two-dimensional display of text that could be rapidly and reversibly modified — made it economical for software designers to deploy interfaces that could be described as visual rather than textual. The pioneering applications of this kind were computer games and text editors; close descendants of some of the earliest specimens, such as rogue(6), and vi(1), are still a live part of Unix tradition.

1985: SAA user Interface or Text-Based user Interface

In 1985, with the beginning of Microsoft Windows and other graphical user interfaces, IBM created what is called the Systems Application Architecture (SAA) standard which include the Common User Access (CUA) derivative. CUA successfully created what we know and use today in Windows, and most of the more recent DOS or Windows Console Applications will use that standard as well.

This defined that a pulldown menu system should be at the top of the screen, status bar at the bottom, shortcut keys should stay the same for all common functionality (F2 to Open for example would work in all applications that followed the SAA standard). This greatly helped the speed at which users could learn an application so it caught on quick and became an industry standard.

1968–present: Graphical user Interface

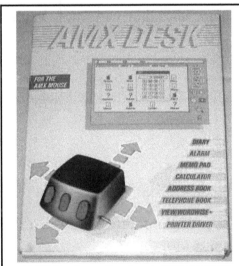

AMX Desk made a basic WIMP GUI.

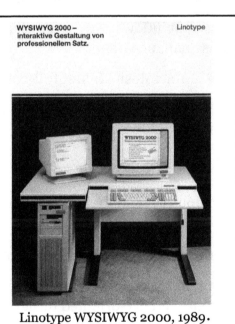

Linotype WYSIWYG 2000, 1989.

- 1968 – Douglas Engelbart demonstrated NLS, a system which uses a mouse, pointers, hypertext, and multiple windows.

- 1970 – Researchers at Xerox Palo Alto Research Center (many from SRI) develop WIMP paradigm (Windows, Icons, Menus, Pointers)

- 1973 – Xerox Alto: commercial failure due to expense, poor user interface, and lack of programs.

- 1979 – Steve Jobs and other Apple engineers visit Xerox. Pirates of Silicon Valley dramatizes the events, but Apple had already been working on the GUI before the visit.

- 1981 – Xerox Star: focus on WYSIWYG. Commercial failure (25K sold) due to cost ($16K each), performance (minutes to save a file, couple of hours to recover from crash), and poor marketing.

- 1984 – Apple Macintosh popularizes the GUI. Super Bowl commercial shown once, most expensive ever made at that time.

- 1984 – MIT's X Window System: hardware-independent platform and networking protocol for developing GUIs on UNIX-like systems.

- 1985 – Windows 1.0 – provided GUI interface to MS-DOS. No overlapping windows (tiled instead).

- 1985 – Microsoft and IBM start work on OS/2 meant to eventually replace MS-DOS and Windows.

- 1986 – Apple threatens to sue Digital Research because their GUI desktop looked too much like Apple's Mac.

- 1987 – Windows 2.0 – Overlapping and resizable windows, keyboard and mouse enhancements.

- 1987 – Macintosh II: first full-color Mac.

- 1988 – OS/2 1.10 Standard Edition (SE) has GUI written by Microsoft, looks a lot like Windows 2.

Interface Design

Primary methods used in the interface design include prototyping and simulation.

Typical human–machine interface design consists of the following stages: interaction specification, interface software specification and prototyping:

- Common practices for interaction specification include user-centered design, persona, activity-oriented design, scenario-based design, resiliency design.

- Common practices for interface software specification include use cases, constrain enforcement by interaction protocols (intended to avoid use errors).

- Common practices for prototyping are based on interactive design based on libraries of interface elements (controls, decoration, etc.).

Quality

All great interfaces share eight qualities or characteristics:

1. Clarity: The interface avoids ambiguity by making everything clear through language, flow, hierarchy and metaphors for visual elements.

2. Concision: It's easy to make the interface clear by over-clarifying and labeling everything, but this leads to interface bloat, where there is just too much stuff on the screen at the same time. If too many things are on the screen, finding what you're looking for is difficult, and so the interface becomes tedious to use. The real challenge in making a great interface is to make it concise and clear at the same time.

3. Familiarity: Even if someone uses an interface for the first time, certain elements can still be familiar. Real-life metaphors can be used to communicate meaning.

4. Responsiveness: A good interface should not feel sluggish. This means that the interface should provide good feedback to the user about what's happening and whether the user's input is being successfully processed.

5. Consistency: Keeping your interface consistent across your application is important because it allows users to recognize usage patterns.

6. Aesthetics: While you don't need to make an interface attractive for it to do its job, making something look good will make the time your users spend using your application more enjoyable; and happier users can only be a good thing.

7. Efficiency: Time is money, and a great interface should make the user more productive through shortcuts and good design.

8. Forgiveness: A good interface should not punish users for their mistakes but should instead provide the means to remedy them.

Principle of Least Astonishment

The principle of least astonishment (POLA) is a general principle in the design of all kinds of interfaces. It is based on the idea that human beings can only pay full attention to one thing at one time, leading to the conclusion that novelty should be minimized.

Habit Formation

If an interface is used persistently, the user will unavoidably develop habits for using the interface. The designer's role can thus be characterized as ensuring the user forms good habits. If the designer is experienced with other interfaces, they will similarly develop habits, and often make unconscious assumptions regarding how the user will interact with the interface.

Types

HP Series 100 HP-150 Touchscreen.

- Direct manipulation interface is the name of a general class of user interfaces that allow users to manipulate objects presented to them, using actions that correspond at least loosely to the physical world.

- Graphical user interfaces (GUI) accept input via devices such as a computer keyboard and mouse and provide articulated graphical output on the computer monitor. There are at least two different principles widely used in GUI design: Object-oriented user interfaces (OOUIs) and application oriented interfaces.

- Web-based user interfaces or web user interfaces (WUI) that accept input and provide output by generating web pages which are transmitted via the Internet and viewed by the user using a web browser program. Newer implementations utilize PHP, Java, JavaScript, AJAX, Apache Flex, .NET Framework, or similar technologies to provide real-time control in a separate program, eliminating the need to refresh a traditional HTML based web browser. Administrative web interfaces for web-servers, servers and networked computers are often called control panels.

- Touchscreens are displays that accept input by touch of fingers or a stylus. Used in a growing amount of mobile devices and many types of point of sale, industrial processes and machines, self-service machines etc.

- Command line interfaces, where the user provides the input by typing a command string with the computer keyboard and the system provides output by printing text on the computer monitor. Used by programmers and system administrators, in engineering and scientific environments, and by technically advanced personal computer users.

- Touch user interface are graphical user interfaces using a touchpad or touch-screen display as a combined input and output device. They supplement or replace other forms of output with haptic feedback methods. Used in computerized simulators etc.

- Hardware interfaces are the physical, spatial interfaces found on products in the real world from toasters, to car dashboards, to airplane cockpits. They are generally a mixture of knobs, buttons, sliders, switches, and touchscreens.

- Attentive user interfaces manage the user attention deciding when to interrupt the user, the kind of warnings, and the level of detail of the messages presented to the user.

- Batch interfaces are non-interactive user interfaces, where the user specifies all the details of the *batch job* in advance to batch processing, and receives the output when all the processing is done. The computer does not prompt for further input after the processing has started.

- Conversational interfaces enable users to command the computer with plain text English (e.g., via text messages, or chatbots) or voice commands, instead of graphic elements. These interfaces often emulate human-to-human conversations.

- Conversational interface agents attempt to personify the computer interface in the form of an animated person, robot, or other character (such as Microsoft's Clippy the paperclip), and present interactions in a conversational form.

- Crossing-based interfaces are graphical user interfaces in which the primary task consists in crossing boundaries instead of pointing.

- Gesture interfaces are graphical user interfaces which accept input in a form of hand gestures, or mouse gestures sketched with a computer mouse or a stylus.

- Holographic user interfaces provide input to electronic or electro-mechanical devices by passing a finger through reproduced holographic images of what would otherwise be tactile controls of those devices, floating freely in the air, detected by a wave source and without tactile interaction.

- Intelligent user interfaces are human-machine interfaces that aim to improve the efficiency, effectiveness, and naturalness of human-machine interaction by representing, reasoning, and acting on models of the user, domain, task, discourse, and media (e.g., graphics, natural language, gesture).

- Motion tracking interfaces monitor the user's body motions and translate them into commands, currently being developed by Apple.

- Multi-screen interfaces, employ multiple displays to provide a more flexible interaction. This is often employed in computer game interaction in both the commercial arcades and more recently the handheld markets.

- Non-command user interfaces, which observe the user to infer his / her needs and intentions, without requiring that he / she formulate explicit commands.

- Object-oriented user interfaces (OOUI) are based on object-oriented programming metaphors, allowing users to manipulate simulated objects and their properties.

- Reflexive user interfaces where the users control and redefine the entire system via the user interface alone, for instance to change its command verbs. Typically this is only possible with very rich graphic user interfaces.

- Search interface is how the search box of a site is displayed, as well as the visual representation of the search results.

- Tangible user interfaces, which place a greater emphasis on touch and physical environment or its element.

- Task-focused interfaces are user interfaces which address the information overload problem of the desktop metaphor by making tasks, not files, the primary unit of interaction.

- Text-based user interfaces are user interfaces which output a text. TUIs can either contain a command-line interface or a text-based WIMP environment.

- Voice user interfaces, which accept input and provide output by generating voice prompts. The user input is made by pressing keys or buttons, or responding verbally to the interface.

- Natural-language interfaces – Used for search engines and on webpages. User types in a question and waits for a response.

- Zero-input interfaces get inputs from a set of sensors instead of querying the user with input dialogs.

- Zooming user interfaces are graphical user interfaces in which information objects are represented at different levels of scale and detail, and where the user can change the scale of the viewed area in order.

Types of user interfaces

User interfaces can be classified into the following three categories:

- Command language based interfaces.

- Menu-based interfaces.

- Direct manipulation interfaces.

Command Language-based Interface

A command language-based interface – as the name itself suggests, is based on designing a command language which the user can use to issue the commands. The user is expected to frame the appropriate commands in the language and type them in appropriately whenever required. A simple command language-based interface might simply assign unique names to the different commands. However, a more sophisticated command language-based interface may allow users to compose complex commands by using a set of primitive commands. Such a facility to compose commands dramatically reduces the number of command names one would have to remember. Thus, a command language-based interface can be made concise requiring minimal typing by the user. Command language-based interfaces allow fast interaction with the computer and simplify the input of complex commands.

Menu-based Interface

An important advantage of a menu-based interface over a command language-based interface is that a menu-based interface does not require the users to remember the exact syntax of the commands. A menu-based interface is based on recognition of the command names, rather than recollection. Further, in a menu-based interface the typing effort is minimal as most interactions are carried out through menu selections using a pointing device. This factor is an important consideration for the occasional user who cannot type fast.

However, experienced users find a menu-based user interface to be slower than a command language-based interface because an experienced user can type fast and can get speed advantage by composing different primitive commands to express complex commands. Composing commands in a menu-based interface is not possible. This is because of the fact that actions involving logical connectives (and, or, etc.) are awkward to specify in a menu-based system. Also, if the number of choices is large, it is difficult to select from the menu. In fact, a major challenge in the design of a menu-based interface is to structure large number of menu choices into manageable forms.

Direct Manipulation Interfaces

Direct manipulation interfaces present the interface to the user in the form of visual models (i.e. icons or objects). For this reason, direct manipulation interfaces are sometimes called as iconic interface. In this type of interface, the user issues commands by performing actions on the visual representations of the objects, e.g. pull an icon representing a file into an icon representing a trash box, for deleting the file. Important advantages of iconic interfaces include the fact that the icons can be recognized by the users very easily, and that icons are language-independent. However, direct manipulation interfaces can be considered slow for experienced users. Also, it is difficult to give complex commands using a direct manipulation interface. For example, if one has to drag an icon representing the file to a trash box icon for deleting a file, then in order to delete all the files in the directory one has to perform this operation individually for all files – which could be very easily done by issuing a command like delete *.*.

Menu-based Interfaces

When the menu choices are large, they can be structured as the following way:

Scrolling Menu

When a full choice list can not be displayed within the menu area, scrolling of the menu items is required. This would enable the user to view and select the menu items that cannot be accommodated on the screen. However, in a scrolling menu all the commands should be highly correlated, so that the user can easily locate a command that he needs. This is important since the user cannot see all the commands at any one time. An example situation where a scrolling menu is frequently used is font size selection in a document processor. Here, the user knows that the command list contains only the font sizes that are arranged in some order and he can scroll up and down to find the size he is looking for. However, if the commands do not have any definite ordering relation, then the user would have to in the worst case, scroll through all the commands to find the exact command he is looking for, making this organization inefficient.

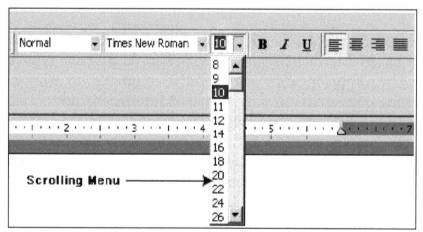

Font size selection using scrolling menu.

Walking Menu

Walking menu is very commonly used to structure a large collection of menu items. In this technique, when a menu item is selected, it causes further menu items to be displayed adjacent to it in a sub-menu. An example of a walking menu is shown in figure. A walking menu can successfully be used to structure commands only if there are tens rather than hundreds of choices since each adjacently displayed menu does take up screen space and the total screen area is after limited.

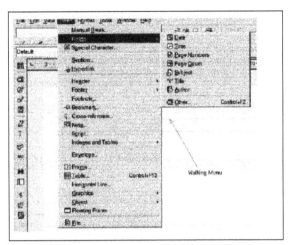

Example of walking menu.

Hierarchical Menu

In this technique, the menu items are organized in a hierarchy or tree structure. Selecting a menu item causes the current menu display to be replaced by an appropriate sub-menu. Thus in this case, one can consider the menu and its various sub-menus to form a hierarchical tree-like structure. Walking menu can be considered to be a form of hierarchical menu which is practicable when the tree is shallow. Hierarchical menu can be used to manage large number of choices, but the users are likely to face navigational problems because they might lose track of where they are in the menu tree. This probably is the main reason why this type of interface is very rarely used.

Characteristics of Command Language-based Interface

Characteristics of command language-based interface have been discussed earlier.

Disadvantages of Command Language-based Interface

Command language-based interfaces suffer from several drawbacks. Usually, command language-based interfaces are difficult to learn and require the user to memorize the set of primitive commands. Also, most users make errors while formulating commands in the command language and also while typing them in. Further, in a command language-based interface, all interactions with the system is through a key-board and can not take advantage of effective interaction devices such as a mouse. Obviously, for casual and inexperienced users, command language-based interfaces are not suitable.

Issues in Designing a Command Language-based Interface

Two overbearing command design issues are to reduce the number of primitive commands that a user has to remember and to minimize the total typing required while issuing commands. These can be elaborated as follows:

- The designer has to decide what mnemonics are to be used for the different commands. The designer should try to develop meaningful mnemonics and yet be concise to minimize the amount of typing required. For example, the shortest mnemonic should be assigned to the most frequently used commands.

- The designer has to decide whether the users will be allowed to redefine the command names to suit their own preferences. Letting a user define his own mnemonics for various commands is a useful feature, but it increases the complexity of user interface development.

- The designer has to decide whether it should be possible to compose primitive commands to form more complex commands. A sophisticated command composition facility would require the syntax and semantics of the various command composition options to be clearly and unambiguously specified. The ability to combine commands is a powerful facility in the hands of experienced users, but quite unnecessary for inexperienced users.

Types of Menus and their Features

Three main types of menus are scrolling menu, walking menu, and hierarchical menu. The features of scrolling menu, walking menu, and hierarchical menu have been discussed earlier.

Iconic Interface

Direct manipulation interfaces present the interface to the user in the form of visual models (i.e. icons or objects). For this reason, direct manipulation interfaces are sometimes called iconic interfaces. In this type of interface, the user issues commands by performing actions on the visual representations of the objects, e.g. pull an icon representing a file into an icon representing a trash box, for deleting the file.

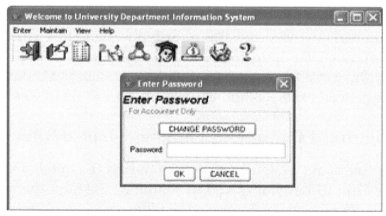

Example of an iconic interface.

Figure shows an iconic interface. Here, the user is presented with a set of icons at the top of the frame for performing various activities. On clicking on any of the icons, either the user is prompted with a sub menu or the desired activity is performed.

Component-based GUI Development

A development style based on widgets (window objects) is called component- based (or widget-based) GUI development style. There are several important advantages of using a widget-based design style. One of the most important reasons to use widgets as building blocks is because they help users learn an interface fast. In this style of development, the user interfaces for different applications are built from the same basic components. Therefore, the user can extend his knowledge of the behavior of the standard components from one application to the other. Also, the component-based user interface development style reduces the application programmer's work significantly as he is more of a user interface component integrator than a programmer in the traditional sense.

Need for Component-based GUI Development

The current style of user interface development is component-based. It recognizes that every user interface can easily be built from a handful of predefined components such as menus, dialog boxes, forms, etc. Besides the standard components, and the facilities to create good interfaces from them, one of the basic support available to the user interface developers is the window system. The window system lets the application programmer create and manipulate windows without having to write the basic windowing functions.

Command-line Interface

Screenshot of a sample bash session in GNOME Terminal 3, Fedora 15.

Screenshot of Windows PowerShell 1.0, running on Windows Vista.

A command-line user interface (CLI), also known as a console user interface, and character user interface (CUI), is a means of interacting with a computer program where the user (or client) issues commands to the program in the form of successive lines of text (command lines). A program which handles the interface is called a command language interpreter or shell.

The CLI was the primary means of interaction with most computer systems until the introduction of the video display terminal in the mid-1960s, and continued to be used throughout the 1970s and 1980s on OpenVMS, Unix systems and personal computer systems including MS-DOS, CP/M and Apple DOS. The interface is usually implemented with a command line shell, which is a program that accepts commands as text input and converts commands into appropriate operating system functions.

Command-line interfaces to computer operating systems are less widely used by casual computer users, who favor graphical user interfaces or menu-driven interaction.

Alternatives to the command line include, but are not limited to text user interface menus, keyboard shortcuts, and various other desktop metaphors centered on the pointer (usually controlled with a mouse). Examples of this include the Windows versions 1, 2, 3, 3.1, and 3.11 (an OS shell that runs in DOS), DosShell, and Mouse Systems PowerPanel.

Command-line interfaces are often preferred by more advanced computer users, as they often provide a more concise and powerful means to control a program or operating system.

Programs with command-line interfaces are generally easier to automate via scripting.

Command line interfaces for software other than operating systems include a number of programming languages such as Tcl/Tk, PHP and others, as well as utilities such as the compression utilities WinZip and UltimateZip, and some FTP and ssh/telnet clients.

Advantages

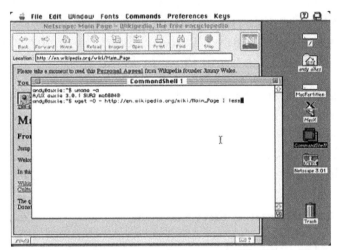

Screenshot of Apple Computer's CommandShell in A/UX 3.0.1.

- Requires fewer resources.
- Concise access to options.
- *Expert*-friendly.
- Easier to automate via scripting or batch files.
- Commands can be logged to review or repeat.
- Easy to add special sub-options.
- Shorter to show multi-step actions.

Disadvantages

- Requires help guide for commands.
- Commands can foster complex options.
- Not visually rich, results might scroll off-screen.
- *Beginner*-unfriendly.

Operating System Command-line Interfaces

Operating system (OS) command line interfaces are usually distinct programs supplied with the operating system.

A program that implements such a text interface is often called a command-line interpreter, command processor or shell.

Examples of command-line interpreters include DEC's DIGITAL Command Language (DCL) in OpenVMS and RSX-11, the various Unix shells (sh, ksh, csh, tcsh, bash, etc.), the historical CP/M CCP, and MS-DOS/IBM-DOS/DR-DOS's COMMAND.COM, as well as the OS/2 and the Windows CMD.EXE programs, the latter groups being based heavily on DEC's RSX-11 and RSTS CLIs. Under most operating systems, it is possible to replace the default shell program with alternatives; examples include 4DOS for DOS, 4OS2 for OS/2, and 4NT or Take Command for Windows.

Although the term 'shell' is often used to describe a command-line interpreter, strictly speaking a 'shell' can be any program that constitutes the user-interface, including fully graphically oriented ones. For example, the default Windows GUI is a shell program named EXPLORER.EXE, as defined in the SHELL=EXPLORER.EXE line in the WIN. INI configuration file. These programs are shells, but not CLIs.

Application Command-line Interfaces

Application programs (as opposed to operating systems) may also have command line interfaces.

An application program may support none, any, or all of these three major types of command line interface mechanisms:

- Parameters: Most operating systems support a means to pass additional information to a program when it is launched. When a program is launched from an OS command line shell, additional text provided along with the program name is passed to the launched program.

- Interactive command line sessions: After launch, a program may provide an operator with an independent means to enter commands in the form of text.

- OS inter-process communication: Most operating systems support means of inter-process communication (for example; standard streams or named pipes). Command lines from client processes may be redirected to a CLI program by one of these methods.

CLI Software

Some applications support only a CLI, presenting a CLI prompt to the user and acting upon command lines as they are entered. Some examples of CLI-only applications are:

- DEBUG.

- Diskpart.

- Ed.

- Edlin.

- Fdisk.

- Ping.

Hybrid Software

Some computer programs support both a CLI and a GUI. In some cases, a GUI is simply a wrapper around a separate CLI executable file. In other cases, a program may provide a CLI as an optional alternative to its GUI. CLIs and GUIs often support different functionality. For example, all features of MATLAB, a numerical analysis computer program, are available via the CLI, whereas the MATLAB GUI exposes only a subset of features.

The early Sierra games, like the first three King's Quest games (1984–1986), used commands from an internal command line to move the character around in the graphic window.

History

The command-line interface evolved from a form of dialog once conducted by humans over teleprinter (TTY) machines, in which human operators remotely exchanged information, usually one line of text at a time. Early computer systems often used teleprinter machines as the means of interaction with a human operator. The computer became one end of the human-to-human teleprinter model. So instead of a human communicating with another human over a teleprinter, a human communicated with a computer.

In time, the actual mechanical teleprinter was replaced by a "glass tty" (keyboard and screen, but emulating the teleprinter), and then by a "smart" terminal (where a microprocessor in the terminal could address all of the screen, rather than only print successive lines). As the microcomputer revolution replaced the traditional – minicomputer + terminals – time sharing architecture, hardware terminals were replaced by terminal emulators — PC software that interpreted terminal signals sent through the PC›s serial ports. These were typically used to interface an organization's new PC's with their existing mini- or mainframe computers, or to connect PC to PC. Some of these PCs were running Bulletin Board System software.

Early operating system CLIs were implemented as part of resident monitor programs, and could not easily be replaced. The concept of implementing the shell as a replaceable component is usually attributed to Multics.

Early microcomputers themselves were based on a command-line interface such as CP/M, MS-DOS or AppleSoft BASIC. Throughout the 1980s and 1990s—especially after the introduction of the Apple Macintosh and Microsoft Windows—command line interfaces were replaced in popular usage by the Graphical User Interface. The command line remains in use, however, by system administrators and other advanced users for system administration, computer programming, and batch processing.

In November 2006, Microsoft released version 1.0 of Windows PowerShell (formerly codenamed *Monad*), which combined features of traditional Unix shells with their proprietary object-oriented .NET Framework. MinGW and Cygwin are open-source packages for Windows that offer a Unix-like CLI. Microsoft provides MKS Inc.'s ksh implementation *MKS Korn shell* for Windows through their Services for UNIX add-on.

Since 2001, the Macintosh operating system is based on a variation of Unix called Darwin. On these computers, users can access a Unix-like command-line interface called Terminal found in the Applications Utilities folder. This terminal uses bash by default.

Screenshot of the MATLAB 7.4 command-line interface and GUI.

Usage

A CLI is used whenever a large vocabulary of commands or queries, coupled with a wide (or arbitrary) range of options, can be entered more rapidly as text than with a pure GUI. This is typically the case with operating system command shells. CLIs are also used by systems with insufficient resources to support a graphical user interface. Some computer language systems (such as Python, Forth, LISP, Rexx, and many dialects of BASIC) provide an interactive command-line mode to allow for rapid evaluation of code.

CLIs are often used by programmers and system administrators, in engineering and scientific environments, and by technically advanced personal computer users. CLIs are also popular among people with visual disability, since the commands and responses can be displayed using Refreshable Braille displays.

Anatomy of a Shell CLI

The general pattern of an OS command line interface is:

Prompt command param1 param2 param3 ... paramN

- Prompt - generated by the program to provide context for the client.

- Command — provided by the client. Commands are usually one of three classes:

    1. Internal — recognized and processed by the command line interpreter itself and not dependent upon any external executable file.

    2. Included — A separate executable file generally considered part of the operating environment and always included with the OS.

    3. External — External executable files not part of the basic OS, but added by other parties for specific purposes and applications.

- param1 ...paramN — Optional parameters provided by the client. The format and meaning of the parameters depends upon the command issued. In the case of Included or External commands, the values of the parameters are delivered to the program (specified by the Command) as it is launched by the OS. Parameters may be either Arguments or Options.

In this example, the delimiters between command line elements are whitespace characters and the end-of-line delimiter is the newline delimiter. This is a widely used (but not universal) convention for command-line interfaces.

A CLI can generally be considered as consisting of syntax and semantics. The *syntax* is the grammar that all commands must follow. In the case of operating systems (OS), MS-DOS and Unix each define their own set of rules that all commands must follow. In the case of embedded systems, each vendor, such as Nortel, Juniper Networks or Cisco Systems, defines their own proprietary set of rules that all commands within their CLI conform to. These rules also dictate how a user navigates through the system of commands. The *semantics* define what sort of operations are possible, on what sort of data these operations can be performed, and how the grammar represents these operations and data—the symbolic meaning in the syntax.

Two different CLIs may agree on either syntax or semantics, but it is only when they agree on both that they can be considered sufficiently similar to allow users to use both CLIs without needing to learn anything, as well as to enable re-use of scripts.

A simple CLI will display a prompt, accept a "command line" typed by the user terminated by the Enter key, then execute the specified command and provide textual display of results or error messages. Advanced CLIs will validate, interpret and parameter-expand the command line before executing the specified command, and optionally capture or redirect its output.

Unlike a button or menu item in a GUI, a command line is typically self-documenting, stating exactly what the user wants done. In addition, command lines usually include many defaults that can be changed to customize the results. Useful command lines can be saved by assigning a character string or alias to represent the full command, or several commands can be grouped to perform a more complex sequence – for instance, compile the program, install it, and run it — creating a single entity, called a command procedure or script which itself can be treated as a command. These advantages mean that a user must figure out a complex command or series of commands only once, because they can be saved, to be used again.

The commands given to a CLI shell are often in one of the following forms:

- *doSomething how toFiles*

- *doSomething how sourceFile destinationFile*

- *doSomething how < inputFile > outputFile*

- *doSomething how | doSomething how | doSomething how > outputFile*

Where *doSomething* is, in effect, a verb, *how* an adverb (for example, should the command be executed "verbosely" or "quietly") and *toFiles* an object or objects (typically one or more files) on which the command should act. The > in the third example is a redirection operator, telling the command-line interpreter to send the output of the command not to its own standard output (the screen) but to the named file. This will overwrite the file. Using >> will redirect the output and append it to the file. Another redirection operator is the vertical bar (|), which creates a pipeline where the output of one command becomes the input to the next command.

CLI and Resource Protection

One can modify the set of available commands by modifying which paths appear in the PATH environment variable. Under Unix, commands also need be marked as executable files. The directories in the path variable are searched in the order they are given. By re-ordering the path, one can run e.g. \OS2\MDOS\E.EXE instead of \OS2\E.EXE, when the default is the opposite. Renaming of the executables also works: people often rename their favourite editor to EDIT, for example.

The command line allows one to restrict available commands, such as access to advanced internal commands. The Windows CMD.EXE does this. Often, shareware programs will limit the range of commands, including printing a command 'your administrator has disabled running batch files' from the prompt.

Some CLIs, such as those in network routers, have a hierarchy of modes, with a different set of commands supported in each mode. The set of commands are grouped by association with security, system, interface, etc. In these systems the user might traverse through a series of sub-modes. For example, if the CLI had two modes called *interface* and *system*, the user might use the command *interface* to enter the interface mode. At this point, commands from the system mode may not be accessible and the user exits the interface mode and enters the system mode.

Command Prompt

A command prompt (or just *prompt*) is a sequence of (one or more) characters used in a command-line interface to indicate readiness to accept commands. It literally prompts the user to take action. A prompt usually ends with one of the characters $, %, #, :, > and often includes other information, such as the path of the current working directory and the hostname.

On many Unix and derivative systems, the prompt commonly ends in $ or % if the user is a normal user, but in # if the user is a superuser ("root" in Unix terminology).

End-users can often modify prompts. Depending on the environment, they may include colors, special characters, and other elements (like variables and functions for the current time, user, shell number or working directory) in order, for instance, to make the prompt more informative or visually pleasing, to distinguish sessions on various machines, or to indicate the current level of nesting of commands. On some systems, special tokens in the definition of the prompt can be used to cause external programs to be called by the command-line interpreter while displaying the prompt.

In DOS's COMMAND.COM and in Windows NT's cmd.exe users can modify the prompt by issuing a `prompt` command or by directly changing the value of the corresponding %PROMPT% environment variable. The default of most modern systems, the C:\> style is obtained, for instance, with `prompt $P$G`. The default of older DOS systems, C> is obtained by just prompt, although on some systems this produces the newer C:\> style, unless used on floppy drives A: or B:; on those systems `prompt $N$G` can be used to override the automatic default and explicitly switch to the older style.

Many Unix systems feature the $PS1 variable (Prompt String 1), although other variables also may affect the prompt (depending on the shell used). In the bash shell, a prompt of the form:

```
[time] user@host: work_dir $
```

could be set by issuing the command

```
export PS1='[\t] \u@\H: \W $'
```

In zsh the $RPROMPT variable controls an optional "prompt" on the right-hand side of the display. It is not a real prompt in that the location of text entry does not change. It is used to display information on the same line as the prompt, but right-justified.

In RISC OS the command prompt is a * symbol, and thus (OS)CLI commands are often referred to as "star commands". One can also access the same commands from other command lines (such as the BBC BASIC command line), by preceding the command with a *.

Arguments

An MS DOS command line, illustrating parsing into command and arguments.

A command-line argument or parameter is an item of information provided to a program when it is started. A program can have many command-line arguments that identify sources or destinations of information, or that alter the operation of the program.

When a command processor is active a program is typically invoked by typing its name followed by command-line arguments (if any). For example, in Unix and Unix-like environments, an example of a command-line argument is:

```
rm file.s
```

"file.s" is a command-line argument which tells the program rm to remove the file "file.s".

Some programming languages, such as C, C++ and Java, allow a program to interpret the command-line arguments by handling them as string parameters in the main function. Other languages, such as Python, expose these arguments as global variables.

In Unix-like operating systems, a single hyphen-minus by itself is usually a special value specifying that a program should handle data coming from the standard input or send data to the standard output.

Command-line Option

A command-line option or simply option (also known as a flag or switch) modifies the operation of a command; the effect is determined by the command's program. Options follow the command name on the command line, separated by spaces. A space before the first option is not always required, for example Dir/? and DIR /? have the same effect in DOS (list the DIR command's options) whereas dir --help (in many versions of Unix) *does* require the option to be preceded by at least one space (and is case-sensitive).

The format of options varies widely between operating systems. In most cases the syntax is by convention rather than an operating system requirement; the entire command line is simply a string passed to a program, which can process it in any way the programmer wants, so long as the interpreter can tell where the command name ends and its arguments and options begin.

A few representative samples of command-line options, all relating to listing files in a directory, to illustrate some conventions:

Operating system	Com-mand	Valid alternative	Notes
OpenVMS	directory/ owner	Dir /Owner	instruct the *directory* command to also display the ownership of the files. *Note the Directory command name is not case sensitive, and can be abbreviated to as few letters as required to remain unique.*
DOS	dir/Q/O:S d*	diR /q d* /o:s	display ownership of files whose names begin with "D", sorted by size, smallest first. *Note spaces around argument d* are required.*
Unix-like systems	ls -lS D*	ls -S -l D*	display in long format files and directories beginning with "D" (but not "d"), sorted by size (largest first). *Note spaces are required around all arguments and options, but some can be run together, e.g. -lS is the same as -l -S.*
Data General RDOS CLI	list/e/s 04-26-80/b	List /S/E 4-26-80/B	list every attribute for files created before 26 April 1980. *Note the /B at the end of the date argument is a **local switch**, that modifies the meaning of that argument, while /S and /E are **global switches**, i.e. apply to the whole command.*

Abbreviating Commands

In Multics, command-line options and subsystem keywords may be abbreviated. This idea appears to derive from the PL/I programming language, with its shortened keywords (e.g., STRG for STRINGRANGE and DCL for DECLARE). For example, in the Multics "forum" subsystem, the *-long_subject* parameter can be abbreviated *-lgsj*. It is also common for Multics commands to be abbreviated, typically corresponding to the initial letters of the words that are strung together with underscores to form command names, such as the use of *did* for *delete_iacl_dir*.

In some other systems abbreviations are automatic, such as permitting enough of the first characters of a command name to uniquely identify it (such as SU as an abbreviation for SUPERUSER) while others may have some specific abbreviations pre-programmed (e.g. MD for MKDIR in COMMAND.COM) or user-defined via batch scripts and aliases (e.g. alias md mkdir in tcsh).

Option Conventions in DOS, Windows, OS/2

On DOS, OS/2 and Windows, different programs called from their COMMAND.COM or CMD.EXE (or internal their commands) may use different syntax within the same operating system. For example:

- Options may be indicated by either of the "switch characters": -, /, or either may be allowed.

- They may or may not be case-sensitive.

- Sometimes options and their arguments are run together, sometimes separated by whitespace, and sometimes by a character, typically : or =; thus `Prog -fFilename`, `Prog -f Filename`, `Prog -f:Filename`, `Prog -f=-Filename`.

- Some programs allow single-character options to be combined; others do not. The switch `-fA` may mean the same as `-f -A`, or it may be incorrect, or it may even be a valid but different parameter.

In DOS, OS/2 and Windows, the forward slash (/) is most prevalent, although the hyphen-minus is also sometimes used. In many versions of DOS (MS-DOS/PC DOS 2.xx and higher, all versions of DR-DOS since 5.0, as well as PTS-DOS, Embedded DOS, FreeDOS and RxDOS) the switch character (sometimes abbreviated switchar or switchchar) to be used is defined by a value returned from a system call (INT 21h/AH=37h). The default character returned by this API is /, but can be changed to a hyphen-minus on the above-mentioned systems, except for Datalight ROM-DOS and MS-DOS/PC DOS 5.0 and higher, which always return / from this call (unless one of many available TSRs to reenable the SwitChar feature is loaded). In some of these systems (MS-DOS/PC DOS 2.xx, DOS Plus 2.1, DR-DOS 7.02 and higher, PTS-DOS, Embedded DOS, FreeDOS and RxDOS), the setting can also be pre-configured by a SWITCHAR directive in CONFIG.SYS. Embedded DOS provides a SWITCH command for the same purpose, whereas 4DOS allows the setting to be changed via `SETDOS /W:n`. Under DR-DOS, if the setting has been changed from /, the first directory separator \ in the display of the PROMPT parameter `$G` will change to a forward slash / (which is also a valid directory separator in DOS, FlexOS, 4680 OS, 4690 OS, OS/2 and Windows) thereby serving as a visual clue to indicate the change. Some versions of DR-DOS COMMAND.COM also support a PROMPT token `$/` to display the current setting. COMMAND.COM since DR-DOS 7.02 and 4DOS also provide a pseudo-environment variable named `%/%` to allow portable batchjobs to be written. Several external DR-DOS commands additionally support an environment variable `%SWITCHAR%` to override the system setting.

However, many programs are hardwired to use / only, rather than retrieving the switch setting before parsing command line arguments. A very small number, mainly ports from Unix-like systems, are programmed to accept "-" even if the switch character is not set to it (for example netstat and ping, supplied with Windows, will accept the /? option to list available options, and yet the list will specify the "-" convention).

Option Conventions in Unix-like Systems

In Unix-like systems, the ASCII hyphen-minus begins options; the new (and GNU) convention is to use *two* hyphens then a word (e.g. `--create`) to identify the option's use while the old convention (and still available as an option for frequently-used options) is to use one hyphen then one letter (e.g. -c); if one hyphen is followed by two or more letters it may mean two options are being specified, or it may mean the second and subsequent letters are a parameter (such as filename or date) for the first option.

Two hyphen-minus characters without following letters (--) may indicate that the remaining arguments should not be treated as options, which is useful for example if a file name itself begins with a hyphen, or if further arguments are meant for an inner command (e.g. sudo). Double hyphen-minuses are also sometimes used to prefix "long options" where more descriptive option names are used. This is a common feature of GNU software. The *getopt* function and program, and the *getopts* command are usually used for parsing command-line options.

Unix command names, arguments and options are case-sensitive (except in a few examples, mainly where popular commands from other operating systems have been ported to Unix).

Options Conventions in other Systems

FlexOS, 4680 OS and 4690 OS use - .

CP/M typically used [.

Conversational Monitor System (CMS) uses a single left parenthesis to separate options at the end of the command from the other arguments. For example, in the following command the options indicate that the target file should be replaced if it exists, and the date and time of the source file should be retained on the copy: `COPY source file a target file b (REPLACE OLDDATE)`.

Data General's CLI under their RDOS, AOS, etc. operating systems, as well as the version of CLI that came with their Business Basic, uses only / as the switch character, is case-insensitive, and allows "local switches" on some arguments to control the way they are interpreted, such as `MAC/U LIB/S A B C $LPT/L` has the global option "U" to the macro assembler command to appemd user symbols, but two local switches, one to specify LIB should be skipped on pass 2 and the other to direct listing to the printer, $LPT.

Built-in usage Help

One of the criticisms of a CLI is the lack of cues to the user as to the available actions. In contrast, GUIs usually inform the user of available actions with menus, icons, or other visual cues. To overcome this limitation, many CLI programs display a brief summary of its valid parameters, typically when invoked with no arguments or one of `?,  -?, -h, -H, /?, /h, /H, -help, or --help`.

However, entering a program name without parameters in the hope that it will display usage help can be hazardous, as some programs and scripts execute without further notice.

Although desirable at least for the help parameter, programs may not support all option lead-in characters exemplified above. Under DOS, where the default command line option character can be changed from / to -, programs may query the SwitChar API in order to determine the current setting. So, if a program is not hard-wired to support them all, a user may need to know the current setting even to be able to reliably request help. If the SwitChar has been changed to - and therefore the / character is accepted as alternative path delimiter also at the DOS command line, programs may misinterpret options like /h or /H as paths rather than help parameters. However, if given as first or only parameter, most DOS programs will, by convention, accept it as request for help regardless of the current SwitChar setting.

In some cases, different levels of help can be selected for a program. Some programs supporting this allow to give a verbosity level as an optional argument to the help parameter (as in /H:1, /H:2, etc.) or they give just a short help on help parameters with question mark and a longer help screen for the other help options.

Depending on the program, additional or more specific help on accepted parameters is sometimes available by either providing the parameter in question as an argument to the help parameter or vice versa (as in /H:W or in /W:? (assuming /W would be another parameter supported by the program)).

In a similar fashion to the help parameter, but much less common, some programs provide additional information about themselves (like mode, status, version, author, license or contact information) when invoked with an "about" parameter like -!, /!, -about, or --about.

Since the ? and ! characters typically also serve other purposes at the command line, they may not be available in all scenarios, therefore, they should not be the only options to access the corresponding help information.

If more detailed help is necessary than provided by a program's built-in internal help, many systems support a dedicated external "HELP command" command (or similar), which accepts a command name as calling parameter and will invoke an external help system.

In the DR-DOS family, typing /? or /H at the COMMAND.COM prompt instead of a command itself will display a dynamically generated list of available internal commands; 4DOS and NDOS support the same feature by typing ? at the prompt (which is also accepted by newer versions of DR-DOS COMMAND.COM); internal commands can be individually disabled or reenabled via SETDOS /I. In addition to this, some newer versions of DR-DOS COMMAND.COM also accept a ?% command to display a list of available built-in pseudo-environment variables. Besides their purpose as quick help reference this can be used in batchjobs to query the facilities of the underlying command line processor.

Command Description Syntax

Built-in usage help and man pages commonly employ a small syntax to describe the valid command form:

- Angle brackets for *required* parameters: `ping <hostname>`.

- Square brackets for *optional* parameters: `mkdir [-p] <dirname>`.

- Ellipses for *repeated* items: `cp <source1> [source2...] <dest>`.

- Vertical bars for *choice* of items: `netstat {-t|-u}`.

Notice that these characters have different meanings than when used directly in the shell. Angle brackets may be omitted when confusing the parameter name with a literal string is not likely.

The Space Character

In many areas of computing, but particularly in the command line, the space character can cause problems as it has two distinct and incompatible functions: as part of a command or parameter, or as a parameter or name separator. Ambiguity can be prevented either by prohibiting embedded spaces in file and directory names in the first place (for example, by substituting them with underscores _), or by enclosing a name with embedded spaces between quote characters or using an escape character before the space, usually a backslash (\). For example:

```
Long path/Long program name Parameter one Parameter two ...
```

is ambiguous (is "program name" part of the program name, or two parameters?); however;

```
Long_path/Long_program_name   Parameter_one   Parameter_two
...,

LongPath/LongProgramName ParameterOne ParameterTwo ...,

"Long path/Long program name" "Parameter one" "Parameter
two" ...
```

and

```
Long\ path/Long\ program\ name Parameter\ one Parameter\
two ...
```

are not ambiguous. Unix-based operating systems minimize the use of embedded spaces to minimize the need for quotes. In Microsoft Windows, one often has to use quotes because embedded spaces (such as in directory names) are common.

Command-line Interpreter

"Although most users think of the shell as an interactive command interpreter, it is really a programming language in which each statement runs a command. Because it must satisfy both the interactive and programming aspects of command execution, it is a strange language, shaped as much by history as by design."

— Brian Kernighan & Rob Pike

The terms command-line interpreter, command line shell, command language interpreter, or identical abbreviation CLI, are applied to computer programs designed to interpret a sequence of lines of text which may be entered by a user, read from a file or another kind of data stream. The context of interpretation is usually one of a given operating system or programming language.

Command-line interpreters allow users to issue various commands in a very efficient (and often terse) way. This requires the user to know the names of the commands and their parameters, and the syntax of the language that is interpreted.

The Unix #! mechanism and OS/2 EXTPROC command facilitate the passing of batch files to external processors. One can use these mechanisms to write specific command processors for dedicated uses, and process external data files which reside in batch files.

Many graphical interfaces, such as the OS/2 Presentation Manager and early versions of Microsoft Windows use command-lines to call helper programs to open documents and programs. The commands are stored in the graphical shell or in files like the registry or the OS/2 `os2user.ini` file.

Early History

The earliest computers did not support interactive input/output devices, often relying on sense switches and lights to communicate with the computer operator. This was adequate for batch systems that ran one program at a time, often with the programmer acting as operator. This also had the advantage of low overhead, since lights and switches could be tested and set with one machine instruction. Later a single system console was added to allow the operator to communicate with the system.

From the 1960s onwards, user interaction with computers was primarily by means of command-line interfaces, initially on machines like the Teletype Model 33 ASR, but then on early CRT-based computer terminals such as the VT52.

All of these devices were purely text based, with no ability to display graphic or pictures. For business application programs, text-based menus were used, but for more general interaction the command line was the interface.

Around 1964 Louis Pouzin introduced the concept and the name *shell* in Multics, building on earlier, simpler facilities in the Compatible Time-Sharing System (CTSS).

From the early 1970s the Unix operating system adapted the concept of a powerful command-line environment, and introduced the ability to *pipe* the output of one command in as input to another. Unix also had the capability to save and re-run strings of commands as "shell scripts" which acted like custom commands.

The command-line was also the main interface for the early home computers such as the Commodore PET, Apple II and BBC Micro – almost always in the form of a BASIC interpreter. When more powerful business oriented microcomputers arrived with CP/M and later MS-DOS computers such as the IBM PC, the command-line began to borrow some of the syntax and features of the Unix shells such as globbing and piping of output.

The command-line was first seriously challenged by the PARC GUI approach used in the 1983 Apple Lisa and the 1984 Apple Macintosh. A few computer users used GUIs such as GEOS and Windows 3.1 but the majority of IBM PC users did not replace their command.com shell with a GUI until Windows 95 was released in 1995.

Modern usage as an Operating System Shell

While most non-expert computer users now use a GUI almost exclusively, more advanced users have access to powerful command-line environments:

- The default VAX/VMS command shell, using the DCL language, has been ported to Windows systems at least three times, including PC-DCL and Acceler8 DCL Lite. MS-DOS 6.22 has been ported to Linux type systems, Unix command shells have been ported to VMS and MS-DOS/Windows 95 and Windows NT types of operating systems. Command.com and Windows NT cmd.exe have been ported to Windows CE and presumably works on Microsoft Windows NT Embedded 4.0.

- Windows Resource Kit and Windows Services for Unix include Korn and the Bourne shells along with a Perl interpreter (Services of Unix contains Active State ActivePerl in later versions and Interix for versions 1 and 2 and a shell compiled by Microsoft).

- IBM OS/2 has the cmd.exe processor. This copies the command.com commands, with extensions to REXX.

- Cmd.exe and Command.com are part of the Windows NT stream operating systems.

- Yet another Cmd.exe is a stripped-down shell for Windows CE 3.0.

- An MS-DOS type interpreter called PocketDOS has been ported to Windows CE machines; the most recent release is almost identical to MS-DOS 6.22 and can also run Windows 1, 2, and 3.0, QBasic and other development tools, 4NT and

4DOS. The latest release includes several shells, namely MS-DOS 6.22, PC-DOS 7, DR DOS 3, and others.

- PocketConsole is a Windows NT 4.0 shell for Windows CE that is much like 4NT.

- Windows users have a CLI environment named Windows Command Prompt, which might use the CScript interface to alternate programs. PowerShell provides a command-line interface, but its applets are not written in Shell script. Implementations of the Unix shell are also available as part of the POSIX sub-system, Cygwin, MKS Toolkit, UWIN, Hamilton C shell and other software packages. Available shells for these interoperability tools include csh, ksh, sh, bash, rsh, tclsh and less commonly zsh, ysh, psh.

- Command.com (4DOS), Windows NT cmd.exe (4NT, TCC), and OS/2 cmd.exe (4OS2) and others based on them are enhanced shells which can be a replacement for the native shell or a means of enhancement of the default shell.

- Implementations of PHP have a shell for interactive use called php-cli.

- Standard Tcl/Tk has two interactive shells, Tclsh and Wish, the latter being the GUI version.

- Python, Ruby, Lua, XLNT, and other interpreters also have command shells for interactive use.

- FreeBSD uses tcsh as its default interactive shell for the superuser.

- Apple macOS and many Linux distributions have the Bash implementation of the Unix shell. Early versions of macOS used tcsh as the default shell.

- Embedded Linux (and other embedded Unix-like) devices often use the Ash implementation of the Unix shell, as part of Busybox.

- Android uses the mksh shell, which replaces a shell derived from ash that was used in older Android versions, supplemented with commands from the separate *toolbox* binary.

- Routers with Cisco IOS, Junos and many others are commonly configured from the command line.

Scripting

Most command-line interpreters support scripting, to various extents. (They are, after all, interpreters of an interpreted programming language, albeit in many cases the language is unique to the particular command-line interpreter.) They will interpret scripts (variously termed shell scripts or batch files) written in the language that they interpret. Some command-line interpreters also incorporate the interpreter engines of other languages, such as REXX, in addition to their own, allowing the executing of scripts, in those languages, directly within the command-line interpreter itself.

Conversely, scripting programming languages, in particular those with an eval function (such as REXX, Perl, Python, Ruby or Jython), can be used to implement command-line interpreters and filters. For a few operating systems, most notably DOS, such a command interpreter provides a more flexible command line interface than the one supplied. In other cases, such a command interpreter can present a highly customised user interface employing the user interface and input/output facilities of the language.

Other Command-line Interfaces

The command line provides an interface between programs as well as the user. In this sense, a command line is an alternative to a dialog box. Editors and data-bases present a command line, in which alternate command processors might run. On the other hand, one might have options on the command line which opens a dialog box. The latest version of 'Take Command' has this feature. DBase used a dialog box to construct command lines, which could be further edited before use.

Programs like Basic, Diskpart, Edlin, and QBasic all provide command-line interfaces, some of which use the system shell. Basic is modeled on the default interface for 8-bit Intel computers. Calculators can be run as command-line or dialog interfaces.

Emacs provides a command line interface in the form of its minibuffer. Commands and arguments can be entered using Emacs standard text editing support, and output is displayed in another buffer.

There are a number of pre-mouse games, like *Adventure* or *King's Quest 1-3*, which relied on the user typing commands at the bottom of the screen. One controls the character by typing commands like 'get ring' or 'look'. The program returns a text which describes how the character sees it, or makes the action happen. The text adventure *The Hitchhiker's Guide to the Galaxy*, a piece of interactive fiction based on Douglas Adam's book of the same name, is a teletype-style command-line game.

The most notable of these interfaces is the standard streams interface, which allows the output of one command to be passed to the input of another. Text files can serve either purpose as well. This provides the interfaces of piping, filters and redirection. Under Unix, devices are files too, so the normal type of file for the shell used for stdin,stdout and stderr is a tty device file.

Another command-line interface allows a shell program to launch helper programs, either to launch documents or start a program. The command is processed internally by the shell, and then passed on to another program to launch the document. The graphical interface of Windows and OS/2 rely heavily on command-lines passed through to other programs – console or graphical, which then usually process the command line without presenting a user-console.

Programs like the OS/2 E editor and some other IBM editors, can process command-lines normally meant for the shell, the output being placed directly in the document window.

A web browser's URL input field can be used as a command line. It can be used to "launch" web apps, access browser configuration, as well as perform a search. Google, which has been called "the command line of the internet" will perform a domain-specific search when it detects search parameters in a known format. This functionality is present whether the search is triggered from a browser field or one on Google's web site.

Direct Manipulation Interface

In computer science, direct manipulation is a human–computer interaction style which involves continuous representation of objects of interest and rapid, reversible, and incremental actions and feedback. As opposed to other interaction styles, for example, a command language, the intention of direct manipulation is to allow a user to manipulate objects presented to them, using actions that correspond at least loosely to manipulation of physical objects. An example of direct-manipulation is resizing a graphical shape, such as a rectangle, by dragging its corners or edges with a mouse.

Having real-world metaphors for objects and actions can make it easier for a user to learn and use an interface (some might say that the interface is more natural or intuitive), and rapid, incremental feedback allows a user to make fewer errors and complete tasks in less time, because they can see the results of an action before completing the action, thus evaluating the output and compensating for mistakes.

The term was introduced by Ben Shneiderman in 1982 within the context of office applications and the desktop metaphor. Individuals in academia and computer scientists doing research on future user interfaces often put as much or even more stress on tactile control and feedback, or sonic control and feedback than on the visual feedback given by most GUIs. As a result, the term has been more widespread in these environments.

In Contrast to WIMP/GUI Interfaces

Direct manipulation is closely associated with interfaces that use windows, icons, menus, and a pointing device (WIMP GUI) as these almost always incorporate direct manipulation to at least some degree. However, direct manipulation should not be confused with these other terms, as it does not imply the use of windows or even graphical output. For example, direct manipulation concepts can be applied to interfaces for blind or vision-impaired users, using a combination of tactile and sonic devices and software.

Compromises to the degree to which an interface implements direct manipulation are frequently seen. For example, most versions of windowing interfaces allow users to reposition a window by dragging it with the mouse. In early systems, redrawing the window while dragging was not feasible due to computational limitations. Instead, a rectangular outline of the window was drawn while dragging. The complete window contents were redrawn once the user released the mouse button.

In Computer Graphics

Because of the difficulty of visualizing and manipulating various aspects of computer graphics, including geometry creation and editing, animation, layout of objects and cameras, light placement, and other effects, direct manipulation is an extremely important part of 3D computer graphics. There are standard direct manipulation widgets as well as many unique widgets that are developed either as a better solution to an old problem or as a solution for a new and/or unique problem. The widgets attempt to allow the user to modify an object in any possible direction while also providing easy guides or constraints to allow the user to easily modify an object in the most common directions, while also attempting to be as intuitive as to the function of the widget as possible. The three most ubiquitous transformation widgets are mostly standardized and are:

- The translation widget, which usually consists of three arrows aligned with the orthogonal axes centered on the object to be translated. Dragging the center of the widget translates the object directly underneath the mouse pointer in the plane parallel to the camera plane, while dragging any of the three arrows translates the object along the appropriate axis. The axes may be aligned with the world-space axes, the object-space axes, or some other space.

- The rotation widget, which usually consists of three circles aligned with the three orthogonal axes, and one circle aligned with the camera plane. Dragging any of the circles rotates the object around the appropriate axis, while dragging elsewhere will freely rotate the object (virtual trackball rotation).

- The scale widget, which usually consists of three short lines aligned with the orthogonal axes terminating in boxes, and one box in the center of the widget. Dragging any of the three axis-aligned boxes effects a non-uniform scale along solely that axis, while dragging the center box effects a uniform scale on all three axes at once.

Depending on the specific common uses of an object, different kinds of widgets may be used. For example, a light in computer graphics is, like any other object, also defined by a transformation (translation and rotation), but it is sometimes positioned and directed simply with its endpoint positions because it may be more intuitive to define the position of the light source and then define the light's target, rather than rotating it around the coordinate axes in order to point it at a known position.

Other widgets may be unique for a particular tool, such as edge controls to change the cone of a spotlight, points and handles to define the position and tangent vector for a spline control point, circles of variable size to define a blur filter width or paintbrush size, IK targets for hands and feet, or color wheels and swatches for quickly choosing colors. Complex widgets may even incorporate some from scientific visualization to efficiently present relevant data (such as vector fields for particle effects or false color images to display vertex maps).

Direct manipulation, as well as user interface design in general, for 3D computer graphics tasks, is still an active area of invention and innovation, as the process of generating CG images is generally not considered to be intuitive or easy in comparison to the difficulty of what the user wants to do, especially for complex tasks. The user interface for word processing, for example, is easy to learn for new users and is sufficient for most word processing purposes, so it is a mostly solved and standardized UI, while the user interfaces for 3D computer graphics are usually either difficult to learn and use and not sufficiently powerful for complex tasks, or sufficiently powerful but difficult to learn and use, so direct manipulation and user interfaces will vary wildly from application to application.

Graphical user Interface

The Xerox Alto was the first device to use a graphical user interface.

Example of GUI in macOS Sierra.

The graphical user interface, is a type of user interface that allows users to interact with electronic devices through graphical icons and visual indicators such as secondary notation, instead of text-based user interfaces, typed command labels or text navigation. GUIs were introduced in reaction to the perceived steep learning curve of command-line interfaces (CLIs), which require commands to be typed on a computer keyboard.

The actions in a GUI are usually performed through direct manipulation of the graphical elements. Beyond computers, GUIs are used in many handheld mobile devices such as MP3 players, portable media players, gaming devices, smartphones and smaller household, office and industrial controls. The term *GUI* tends not to be applied to other lower-display resolution types of interfaces, such as video games (where *heads-up display* (HUD) is preferred), or not including flat screens, like volumetric displays because the term is restricted to the scope of two-dimensional display screens able to describe generic information, in the tradition of the computer science research at the Xerox Palo Alto Research Center (PARC).

User Interface and Interaction Design

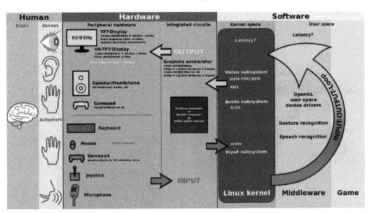

The graphical user interface is presented (displayed) on the computer screen. It is the result of processed user input and usually the main interface for human-machine interaction. The touch user interfaces popular on small mobile devices are an overlay of the visual output to the visual input.

Designing the visual composition and temporal behavior of a GUI is an important part of software application programming in the area of human–computer interaction. Its goal is to enhance the efficiency and ease of use for the underlying logical design of a stored program, a design discipline named *usability*. Methods of user-centered design are used to ensure that the visual language introduced in the design is well-tailored to the tasks.

The visible graphical interface features of an application are sometimes referred to as *chrome* or *GUI* (pronounced *gooey*). Typically, users interact with information by manipulating visual widgets that allow for interactions appropriate to the kind of data they hold. The widgets of a well-designed interface are selected to support the actions necessary to achieve the goals of users. A model–view–controller allows a flexible structure in which the interface is independent from and indirectly linked to application functions, so the GUI can be customized easily. This allows users to select or design a different *skin* at will, and eases the designer's work to change the interface as user needs evolve. Good user interface design relates to users more, and to system architecture less.

Large widgets, such as windows, usually provide a frame or container for the main presentation content such as a web page, email message or drawing. Smaller ones usually act as a user-input tool.

A GUI may be designed for the requirements of a vertical market as application-specific graphical user interfaces. Examples include automated teller machines (ATM), point of sale (POS) touchscreens at restaurants, self-service checkouts used in a retail store, airline self-ticketing and check-in, information kiosks in a public space, like a train station or a museum, and monitors or control screens in an embedded industrial application which employ a real-time operating system (RTOS).

By the 1990s, cell phones and handheld game systems also employed application specific touchscreen GUIs. Newer automobiles use GUIs in their navigation systems and multimedia centers, or navigation multimedia center combinations.

Examples

- Sample graphical desktop environments

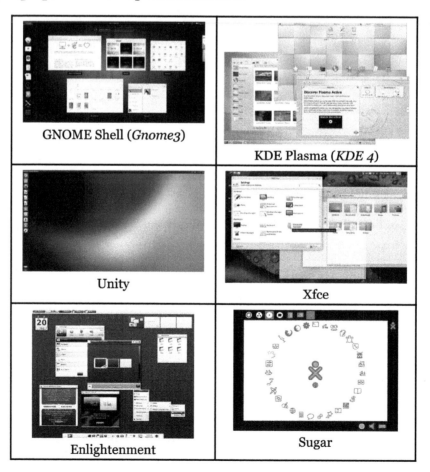

GNOME Shell (*Gnome3*)

KDE Plasma (*KDE 4*)

Unity

Xfce

Enlightenment

Sugar

Components

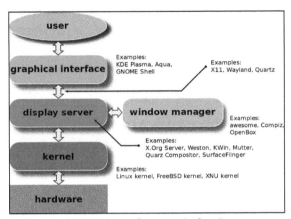

Layers of a GUI based on a windowing system.

A GUI uses a combination of technologies and devices to provide a platform that users can interact with, for the tasks of gathering and producing information.

A series of elements conforming a visual language have evolved to represent information stored in computers. This makes it easier for people with few computer skills to work with and use computer software. The most common combination of such elements in GUIs is the *windows, icons, menus, pointer* (WIMP) paradigm, especially in personal computers.

The WIMP style of interaction uses a virtual input device to represent the position of a pointing device, most often a mouse, and presents information organized in windows and represented with icons. Available commands are compiled together in menus, and actions are performed making gestures with the pointing device. A window manager facilitates the interactions between windows, applications, and the windowing system. The windowing system handles hardware devices such as pointing devices, graphics hardware, and positioning of the pointer.

In personal computers, all these elements are modeled through a desktop metaphor to produce a simulation called a desktop environment in which the display represents a desktop, on which documents and folders of documents can be placed. Window managers and other software combine to simulate the desktop environment with varying degrees of realism.

Post-WIMP Interfaces

Smaller mobile devices such as personal digital assistants (PDAs) and smartphones typically use the WIMP elements with different unifying metaphors, due to constraints in space and available input devices. Applications for which WIMP is not well suited may use newer interaction techniques, collectively termed *post-WIMP* user interfaces.

As of 2011, some touchscreen-based operating systems such as Apple's iOS (iPhone) and Android use the class of GUIs named post-WIMP. These support styles of interaction using more than one finger in contact with a display, which allows actions such as pinching and rotating, which are unsupported by one pointer and mouse.

Interaction

Human interface devices, for the efficient interaction with a GUI include a computer keyboard, especially used together with keyboard shortcuts, pointing devices for the cursor (or rather pointer) control: mouse, pointing stick, touchpad, trackball, joystick, virtual keyboards, and head-up displays (translucent information devices at the eye level).

There are also actions performed by programs that affect the GUI. For example, there are components like inotify or D-Bus to facilitate communication between computer programs.

History

Early Efforts

Ivan Sutherland developed Sketchpad in 1963, widely held as the first graphical computer-aided design program. It used a light pen to creating and manipulate objects in engineering drawings in realtime with coordinated graphics. In the late 1960s, researchers at the Stanford Research Institute, led by Douglas Engelbart, developed the On-Line System (NLS), which used text-based hyperlinks manipulated with a then new device: the mouse. In the 1970s, Engelbart's ideas were further refined and extended to graphics by researchers at Xerox PARC and specifically Alan Kay, who went beyond text-based hyperlinks and used a GUI as the main interface for the Xerox Alto computer, released in 1973. Most modern general-purpose GUIs are derived from this system.

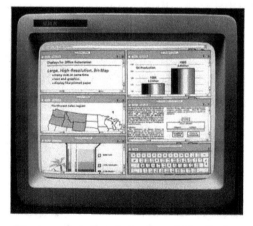

The Xerox Star 8010 workstation introduced the first commercial GUI.

The Xerox PARC user interface consisted of graphical elements such as windows, menus, radio buttons, and check boxes. The concept of icons was later introduced by David

Canfield Smith, who had written a thesis on the subject under the guidance of Kay. The PARC user interface employs a pointing device along with a keyboard. These aspects can be emphasized by using the alternative term and acronym for *windows, icons, menus, pointing device* (WIMP). This effort culminated in the 1973 Xerox Alto, the first computer with a GUI, though the system never reached commercial production.

The first commercially available computer with a GUI was the 1979 PERQ workstation, manufactured by Three Rivers Computer Corporation. In 1981, Xerox eventually commercialized the Alto in the form of a new and enhanced system – the Xerox 8010 Information System – more commonly known as the Xerox Star. These early systems spurred many other GUI efforts, including the Apple Lisa (which presented the concept of menu bar and window controls) in 1983, the Apple Macintosh 128K in 1984, and the Atari ST with Digital Research's GEM, and Commodore Amiga in 1985. Visi On was released in 1983 for the IBM PC compatible computers, but was never popular due to its high hardware demands. Nevertheless, it was a crucial influence on the contemporary development of Microsoft Windows.

Apple, Digital Research, IBM and Microsoft used many of Xerox's ideas to develop products, and IBM's Common User Access specifications formed the basis of the user interfaces used in Microsoft Windows, IBM OS/2 Presentation Manager, and the Unix Motif toolkit and window manager. These ideas evolved to create the interface found in current versions of Microsoft Windows, and in various desktop environments for Unix-like operating systems, such as macOS and Linux. Thus most current GUIs have largely common idioms.

Macintosh 128K, the first Macintosh (1984).

Popularization

GUIs were a hot topic in the early 1980s. The Apple Lisa was released in 1983, and various windowing systems existed for DOS operating systems (including PC GEM and PC/GEOS). Individual applications for many platforms presented their own GUI variants. Despite the GUIs advantages, many reviewers questioned the value of the entire concept, citing hardware limits, and problems in finding compatible software.

In 1984, Apple released a television commercial which introduced the Apple Macintosh during the telecast of Super Bowl XVIII by CBS, with allusions to George Orwell's noted novel, *Nineteen Eighty-Four*. The goal of the commercial was to make people think about computers, identifying the user-friendly interface as a personal computer which departed from prior business-oriented systems, and becoming a signature representation of Apple products.

Accompanied by an extensive marketing campaign, Windows 95 was a major success in the marketplace at launch and shortly became the most popular desktop operating system.

In 2007, with the iPhone and later in 2010 with the introduction of the iPad, Apple popularized the post-WIMP style of interaction for multi-touch screens, and those devices were considered to be milestones in the development of mobile devices.

The GUIs familiar to most people as of the mid-2010s are Microsoft Windows, macOS, and the X Window System interfaces for desktop and laptop computers, and Android, Apple's iOS, Symbian, BlackBerry OS, Windows Phone/Windows 10 Mobile, Palm OS-WebOS, and Firefox OS for handheld (smartphone) devices.

Comparison to Other Interfaces

Command-line Interfaces

A modern CLI

Since the commands available in command line interfaces can be many, complex operations can be performed using a short sequence of words and symbols. This allows greater efficiency and productivity once many commands are learned, but reaching this level takes some time because the command words may not be easily discoverable or mnemonic. Also, using the command line can become slow and error-prone when users must enter long commands comprising many parameters or several different filenames at once. However, *windows, icons, menus, pointer* (WIMP) interfaces present users with many widgets that represent and can trigger some of the system's available commands.

GUIs can be made quite hard when dialogs are buried deep in a system, or moved about to different places during redesigns. Also, icons and dialog boxes are usually harder for users to script.

WIMPs extensively use modes, as the meaning of all keys and clicks on specific positions on the screen are redefined all the time. Command line interfaces use modes only in limited forms, such as for current directory and environment variables.

Most modern operating systems provide both a GUI and some level of a CLI, although the GUIs usually receive more attention. The GUI is usually WIMP-based, although occasionally other metaphors surface, such as those used in Microsoft Bob, 3dwm, or File System Visualizer (FSV).

GUI Wrappers

Graphical user interface (GUI) wrappers circumvent the command-line interface versions (CLI) of (typically) Linux and Unix-like software applications and their text-based user interfaces or typed command labels. While command-line or text-based application allow users to run a program non-interactively, GUI wrappers atop them avoid the steep learning curve of the command-line, which requires commands to be typed on the keyboard. By starting a GUI wrapper, users can intuitively interact with, start, stop, and change its working parameters, through graphical icons and visual indicators of a desktop environment, for example. Applications may also provide both interfaces, and when they do the GUI is usually a WIMP wrapper around the command-line version. This is especially common with applications designed for Unix-like operating systems. The latter used to be implemented first because it allowed the developers to focus exclusively on their product's functionality without bothering about interface details such as designing icons and placing buttons. Designing programs this way also allows users to run the program in a shell script.

Three-dimensional user Interfaces

For typical computer displays, *three-dimensional* is a misnomer—their displays are two-dimensional. Semantically, however, most graphical user interfaces use three dimensions. With height and width, they offer a third dimension of layering or stacking screen elements over one another. This may be represented visually on screen through an illusionary transparent effect, which offers the advantage that information in background windows may still be read, if not interacted with. Or the environment may simply hide the background information, possibly making the distinction apparent by drawing a drop shadow effect over it.

Some environments use the methods of 3D graphics to project virtual three dimensional user interface objects onto the screen. These are often shown in use in science fiction films. As the processing power of computer graphics hardware increases, this becomes less of an obstacle to a smooth user experience.

Three-dimensional graphics are currently mostly used in computer games, art, and computer-aided design (CAD). A three-dimensional computing environment can also be useful in other uses, like molecular graphics and aircraft design.

Several attempts have been made to create a multi-user three-dimensional environment, including the Croquet Project and Sun's Project Looking Glass.

Technologies

The use of three-dimensional graphics has become increasingly common in mainstream operating systems, from creating attractive interfaces, termed eye candy, to functional purposes only possible using three dimensions. For example, user switching is represented by rotating a cube which faces are each user's workspace, and window management is represented via a Rolodex-style flipping mechanism in Windows Vista. In both cases, the operating system transforms windows on-the-fly while continuing to update the content of those windows.

Interfaces for the X Window System have also implemented advanced three-dimensional user interfaces through compositing window managers such as Beryl, Compiz and KWin using the AIGLX or XGL architectures, allowing use of OpenGL to animate user interactions with the desktop.

Another branch in the three-dimensional desktop environment is the three-dimensional GUIs that take the desktop metaphor a step further, like the BumpTop, where users can manipulate documents and windows as if they were physical documents, with realistic movement and physics.

The zooming user interface (ZUI) is a related technology that promises to deliver the representation benefits of 3D environments without their usability drawbacks of orientation problems and hidden objects. It is a logical advance on the GUI, blending some three-dimensional movement with two-dimensional or *2.5D* vector objects. In 2006, Hillcrest Labs introduced the first zooming user interface for television, literature and films before they were technically feasible or in common use. For example; the 1993 American film *Jurassic Park* features Silicon Graphics' three-dimensional file manager File System Navigator, a real-life file manager for Unix operating systems. The film Minority Report has scenes of police officers using specialized 3d data systems. In prose fiction, three-dimensional user interfaces have been portrayed as immersible environments like William Gibson's Cyberspace or Neal Stephenson's Metaverse. Many futuristic imaginings of user interfaces rely heavily on object-oriented user interface (OOUI) style and especially object-oriented graphical user interface (OOGUI) style.

Touch user Interface

A touch user interface (TUI) is a computer-pointing technology based upon the sense of touch (haptics). Whereas a graphical user interface (GUI) relies upon the sense of sight, a TUI enables not only the sense of touch to innervate and activate computer-based functions, it also allows the user, particularly those with visual impairments, an added level of interaction based upon tactile or Braille input.

Technology

Generally, the TUI requires pressure or presence with a switch located outside of the printed paper. Electronic paper endeavors, the TUI requires the printed pages to act as a template or overlay to a switch array. By interacting with the switch through touch or presence, an action is innervated. The switching sensor cross-references with a database. The database retains the correct pathway to retrieve the associated digital content or launch the appropriate application.

TUI icons may be used to indicate to the reader of the printed page what action will occur upon interacting with a particular position on the printed page.

Turning pages and interacting with new pages that may have the same touch points as previous or subsequent pages, a z-axis may be used to indicate the plane of activity. Z-axis can be offset around the boundary of the page. When the unique z-axis is interacted with, x,y-axis can have identical touch points as other pages. For example, 1,1,1 indicates a z-axis of 1 (page 1) and the x,y-axis is 1,1. However, turning the page and pressing a new z-axis, say page 2, and then the same x,y-axis content position as page 1, gains the following coordinate structure: 2,1,1.

An integrated circuit (IC) is located either within the printed material or within an enclosure that cradles the printed material. This IC receives a signal when a switch is innervated. The firmware located within the IC communicates via Universal Serial Bus (USB) either connected to a cable, or using a wireless protocol adapter to a reference database that can reside on media within a computer or appliance. Upon receipt of the coordinate structure from the firmware, the database correlates the position with a pre-determined link or pathway to digital content or execution command for an application. After correlating the link with the pathway, a signal is sent to retrieve and render the terminal of the path.

Implications for use

Those with special requirements can use touch with fingers or pointer to gain access to the digital environment. Typing, currently a traditional method for accessing the digital world, can be replaced for users who are missing fingers or are not capable of typing. Touching a link on printed paper takes advantage of the ubiquitous presence of printed paper while it removes barriers of entry to the digital world. Further, removing the need to type pathways removes errors from the entry process, potentially protecting companies and organizations that have potential users going to a cybersquatting site due to a misspelling. Typing is also time consuming. A touch interface provides a reduction in time to get where the reader wants to go in the digital world.

The coupling of printed advertising with online advertising is promising. A reader can touch a printed advertisement and connect directly to the online experience provided by the advertiser. This can include initiating a Voice over Internet Protocol (VoIP), Instant Messaging (IM), or Electronic Mail (e-mail) by simply touching the page. Further, electronic commerce (e-commerce) transactions can be initiated and completed with the TUI. This type of interaction can also exist in the Television Commerce (tcommerce) space with a magazine, catalog, or television guide.

The TUI technology applied to the printed world serves to converge the printed world with the digital world. This provides an alternative to the either print or digital paradigm shift currently experienced by today's users. It also serves to facilitate the vast majority of the world's peoples to a linguistic and culturally non-specific experience that can provide an on-ramp to the digital world.

Educational Mandate

In the United States, legislation took effect in December 2006, that requires educational publishers in the K-12 education industry to provide a National Instructional Materials Accessibility Standard (NIMAS). In essence, educational publishers must provide an inclusive experience to those students who are blind. If they are unable to provide this experience, they are required to provide the digital content source files to a clearing house that will convert the materials into an accessible experience for the student. The TUI has the promise of enabling the publishers to maintain control of their content while providing an inclusive, tactile, or Braille experience to students who are visually impaired. Further, using a Braille approach may serve to help enhance Braille literacy while meeting the mandates of NIMAS.

Characteristics of a user Interface

It is very important to identify the characteristics desired of a good user interface. Because unless we are aware of these, it is very much difficult to design a good user interface. A few important characteristics of a good user interface are the following:

- Speed of learning: A good user interface should be easy to learn. Speed of learning is hampered by complex syntax and semantics of the command issue procedures. A good user interface should not require its users to memorize commands. Neither should the user be asked to remember information from one screen to another while performing various tasks using the interface. Besides, the following three issues are crucial to enhance the speed of learning:

- Use of Metaphors and intuitive command names: Speed of learning an interface is greatly facilitated if these are based on some day-to-day real-life examples or some physical objects with which the users are familiar. The abstractions of real-life objects or concepts used in user interface design are called metaphors. If the user interface of a text editor uses concepts similar to the tools used by a writer for text editing such as cutting lines and paragraphs and pasting it at other places, users can immediately relate to it. Another popular metaphor is a shopping cart. Everyone knows how a shopping cart is used to make choices while purchasing items in a supermarket. If a user interface uses the shopping cart metaphor for designing the interaction style for a situation where similar types of choices have to be made, then the users can easily understand and learn to use the interface. Yet another example of a metaphor is the trashcan. To delete a file, the user may drag it to the trashcan. Also, learning is facilitated by intuitive command names and symbolic command issue procedures.

- Consistency: Once a user learns about a command, he should be able to use the similar commands in different circumstances for carrying out similar actions. This makes it easier to learn the interface since the user can extend his knowledge about one part of the interface to the other parts. For example, in a word processor, "Control-b" is the short-cut key to embolden the selected text. The same short-cut should be used on the other parts of the interface, for example, to embolden text in graphic objects also - circle, rectangle, polygon, etc. Thus, the different commands supported by an interface should be consistent.

- Component-based interface: Users can learn an interface faster if the interaction style of the interface is very similar to the interface of other applications with which the user is already familiar. This can be achieved if the interfaces of different applications are developed using some standard user interface components. This, in fact, is the theme of the component-based user interface. Examples of standard user interface components are: radio button, check box, text field, slider, progress bar, etc.

The speed of learning characteristic of a user interface can be determined by measuring the training time and practice that users require before they can effectively use the software.

- Speed of use: Speed of use of a user interface is determined by the time and user effort necessary to initiate and execute different commands. This characteristic of the interface is some times referred to as productivity support of the interface. It indicates how fast the users can perform their intended tasks. The time and user effort necessary to initiate and execute different commands should be minimal. This can be achieved through careful design of the interface. For example, an interface that requires users to type in lengthy commands or involves mouse movements to different areas of the screen that are wide apart for issuing commands can slow down the operating speed of users. The most frequently used commands should have the smallest length or be available at the top of the menu to minimize the mouse movements necessary to issue commands.

- Speed of recall: Once users learn how to use an interface, the speed with which they can recall the command issue procedure should be maximized. This characteristic is very important for intermittent users. Speed of recall is improved if the interface is based on some metaphors, symbolic command issue procedures, and intuitive command names.

- Error prevention: A good user interface should minimize the scope of committing errors while initiating different commands. The error rate of an interface can be easily determined by monitoring the errors committed by average users while using the interface. This monitoring can be automated by instrumenting the user interface code with monitoring code which can record the frequency and types of user error and later display the statistics of various kinds of errors committed by different users.

Moreover, errors can be prevented by asking the users to confirm any potentially destructive actions specified by them, for example, deleting a group of files.

Consistency of names, issue procedures, and behavior of similar commands and the simplicity of the command issue procedures minimize error possibilities. Also, the interface should prevent the user from entering wrong values.

- Attractiveness: A good user interface should be attractive to use. An attractive user interface catches user attention and fancy. In this respect, graphics-based user interfaces have a definite advantage over text-based interfaces.

- Consistency: The commands supported by a user interface should be consistent. The basic purpose of consistency is to allow users to generalize the knowledge about aspects of the interface from one part to another. Thus, consistency facilitates speed of learning, speed of recall, and also helps in reduction of error rate.

- Feedback: A good user interface must provide feedback to various user actions. Especially, if any user request takes more than few seconds to process, the user should be informed about the state of the processing of his request. In the absence of any response from the computer for a long time, a novice user might even start recovery/shutdown procedures in panic. If required, the user should be periodically informed about the progress made in processing his command.

For example, if the user specifies a file copy/file download operation, a progress bar can be displayed to display the status. This will help the user to monitor the status of the action initiated.

- Support for multiple skill levels: A good user interface should support multiple levels of sophistication of command issue procedure for different categories of users. This is necessary because users with different levels of experience in using an application prefer different types of user interfaces. Experienced users are more concerned about the efficiency of the command issue procedure, whereas novice users pay importance to usability aspects. Very cryptic and complex commands discourage a novice, whereas elaborate command sequences make the command issue procedure very slow and therefore put off experienced users. When someone uses an application for the first time, his primary concern is speed of learning. After using an application for extended periods of time, he becomes familiar with the operation of the software. As a user becomes more and more familiar with an interface, his focus shifts from usability aspects to speed of command issue aspects. Experienced users look for options such as "hot-keys", "macros", etc. Thus, the skill level of users improves as they keep using a software product and they look for commands to suit their skill levels.

- Error recovery (undo facility): While issuing commands, even the expert users can commit errors. Therefore, a good user interface should allow a user to undo a mistake committed by him while using the interface. Users are put to inconvenience, if they cannot recover from the errors they commit while using the software.

- User guidance and on-line help: Users seek guidance and on-line help when they either forget a command or are unaware of some features of the software. Whenever users need guidance or seek help from the system, they should be provided with the appropriate guidance and help.

User Guidance and Online Help

Users may seek help about the operation of the software any time while using the software. This is provided by the on-line help system. This is different from the guidance and error messages which are flashed automatically without the user asking for them. The guidance messages prompt the user regarding the options he has regarding the next command, and the status of the last command, etc.

On-line Help System. Users expect the on-line help messages to be tailored to the context in which they invoke the "help system". Therefore, a good on-line help system should keep track of what a user is doing while invoking the help system and provide the output message in a context- dependent way. Also, the help messages should be tailored to the user's experience level. Further, a good on-line help system should take advantage of any graphics and animation characteristics of the screen and should not just be a copy of the user's manual. Figure gives a snapshot of a typical on-line help provided by a user interface.

—

178 Fundamentals of Software Engineering

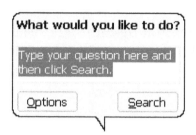

Example of an on-line help interface.

Guidance Messages: The guidance messages should be carefully designed to prompt the user about the next actions he might purse, the current status of the system, the progress made so far in processing his last command, etc. A good guidance system should have different levels of sophistication for different categories of users. For example, a user using a command language interface might need a different type of guidance compared to a user using a menu or iconic interface. Also, users should have an option to turn off detailed messages.

Mode-based Interface Vs. Modeless Interface

A mode is a state or collection of states in which only a subset of all user interaction tasks can be performed. In a modeless interface, the same set of commands can be invoked at any time during the running of the software. Thus, a modeless interface has only a single mode and all the commands are available all the time during the operation of the software. On the other hand, in a mode-based interface, different set of commands can be invoked depending on the mode in which the system is, i.e. the mode at any instant is determined by the sequence of commands already issued by the user.

A mode-based interface can be represented using a state transition diagram, where each node of the state transition diagram would represent a mode. Each state of the state transition diagram can be annotated with the commands that are meaningful in that state.

An example of mode-based interface.

Figure shows the interface of a word processing program. The top-level menu provides the user with a gamut of operations like file open, close, save, etc. When the user chooses the open option, another frame is popped up which limits the user to select a name from one of the folders.

Graphical user Interface Vs. Text-based user Interface

The following comparisons are based on various characteristics of a GUI with those of a text-based user interface.

- In a GUI multiple windows with different information can simultaneously be displayed on the user screen. This is perhaps one of the biggest advantages of GUI over text- based interfaces since the user has the flexibility to simultaneously interact with several related items at any time and can have access to different system information displayed in different windows.

- Iconic information representation and symbolic information manipulation is possible in a GUI. Symbolic information manipulation such as dragging an icon representing a file to a trash can be deleting is intuitively very appealing and the user can instantly remember it.

- A GUI usually supports command selection using an attractive and user-friendly menu selection system.

- In a GUI, a pointing device such as a mouse or a light pen can be used for issuing commands. The use of a pointing device increases the efficacy issue procedure.

- On the flip side, a GUI requires special terminals with graphics capabilities for running and also requires special input devices such a mouse. On the other hand, a text-based user interface can be implemented even on a cheap alphanumeric display terminal. Graphics terminals are usually much more expensive than alphanumeric terminals. However, display terminals with graphics capability with bit-mapped high-resolution displays and significant amount of local processing power have become affordable and over the years have replaced text-based terminals on all desktops. Therefore, the emphasis of this lesson is on GUI design rather than text- based user interface design.

User Interface Design

User interface design (UI) or user interface engineering is the design of user interfaces for machines and software, such as computers, home appliances, mobile devices, and other electronic devices, with the focus on maximizing usability and the user experience. The goal of user interface design is to make the user's interaction as simple and efficient as possible, in terms of accomplishing user goals (user-centered design).

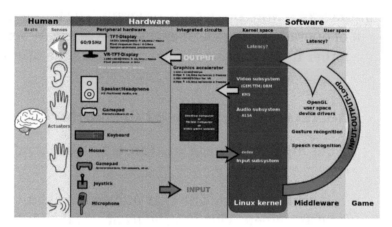

The graphical user interface is presented (displayed) on the computer screen. It is the result of processed user input and usually the primary interface for human-machine interaction. The touch user interfaces popular on small mobile devices are an overlay of the visual output to the visual input.

Good user interface design facilitates finishing the task at hand without drawing unnecessary attention to itself. Graphic design and typography are utilized to support its usability, influencing how the user performs certain interactions and improving the aesthetic appeal of the design; design aesthetics may enhance or detract from the ability of users to use the functions of the interface. The design process must balance technical functionality and visual elements (e.g., mental model) to create a system that is not only operational but also usable and adaptable to changing user needs.

Interface design is involved in a wide range of projects from computer systems, to cars, to commercial planes; all of these projects involve much of the same basic human interactions yet also require some unique skills and knowledge. As a result, designers tend to specialize in certain types of projects and have skills centered on their expertise, whether that be software design, user research, web design, or industrial design.

Processes

User interface design requires a good understanding of user needs. There are several phases and processes in the user interface design, some of which are more demanded upon than others, depending on the project. (Note: for the remainder of this section, the word *system* is used to denote any project whether it is a website, application, or device.)

- Functionality requirements gathering – assembling a list of the functionality required by the system to accomplish the goals of the project and the potential needs of the users.

- User and task analysis – a form of field research, it's the analysis of the potential users of the system by studying how they perform the tasks that the design must support, and conducting interviews to elucidate their goals. Typical questions involve:

  o What would the user want the system to do?

- o How would the system fit in with the user's normal workflow or daily activities?

- o How technically savvy is the user and what similar systems does the user already use?

- o What interface look & feel styles appeal to the user?

- Information architecture – development of the process and/or information flow of the system (i.e. for phone tree systems, this would be an option tree flowchart and for web sites this would be a site flow that shows the hierarchy of the pages).

- Prototyping – development of wire-frames, either in the form of paper prototypes or simple interactive screens. These prototypes are stripped of all look & feel elements and most content in order to concentrate on the interface.

- Usability inspection – letting an evaluator inspect a user interface. This is generally considered to be cheaper to implement than usability testing, and can be used early on in the development process since it can be used to evaluate prototypes or specifications for the system, which usually cannot be tested on users. Some common usability inspection methods include cognitive walkthrough, which focuses the simplicity to accomplish tasks with the system for new users, heuristic evaluation, in which a set of heuristics are used to identify usability problems in the UI design, and pluralistic walkthrough, in which a selected group of people step through a task scenario and discuss usability issues.

- Usability testing – testing of the prototypes on an actual user—often using a technique called think aloud protocol where you ask the user to talk about their thoughts during the experience. User interface design testing allows the designer to understand the reception of the design from the viewer's standpoint, and thus facilitates creating successful applications.

- Graphical user interface design – actual look and feel design of the final graphical user interface (GUI). It may be based on the findings developed during the user research, and refined to fix any usability problems found through the results of testing.Depending on the type of interface being created, this process typically involves some computer programming in order to validate forms, establish links or perform a desired action.

- Software Maintenance - After the deployment of a new interface, occasional maintenance may be required to fix software bugs, change features, or completely upgrade the system. Once a decision is made to upgrade the interface, the legacy system will undergo another version of the design process, and will begin to repeat the stages of the interface life cycle.

Requirements

The dynamic characteristics of a system are described in terms of the dialogue requirements contained in seven principles of part 10 of the ergonomics standard, the ISO 9241. This standard establishes a framework of ergonomic "principles" for the dialogue techniques with high-level definitions and illustrative applications and examples of the principles. The principles of the dialogue represent the dynamic aspects of the interface and can be mostly regarded as the "feel" of the interface. The seven dialogue principles are:

- Suitability for the task: the dialogue is suitable for a task when it supports the user in the effective and efficient completion of the task.

- Self-descriptiveness: the dialogue is self-descriptive when each dialogue step is immediately comprehensible through feedback from the system or is explained to the user on request.

- Controllability: the dialogue is controllable when the user is able to initiate and control the direction and pace of the interaction until the point at which the goal has been met.

- Conformity with user expectations: the dialogue conforms with user expectations when it is consistent and corresponds to the user characteristics, such as task knowledge, education, experience, and to commonly accepted conventions.

- Error tolerance: the dialogue is error tolerant if despite evident errors in input, the intended result may be achieved with either no or minimal action by the user.

- Suitability for individualization: the dialogue is capable of individualization when the interface software can be modified to suit the task needs, individual preferences, and skills of the user.

- Suitability for learning: the dialogue is suitable for learning when it supports and guides the user in learning to use the system.

The concept of usability is defined of the ISO 9241 standard by effectiveness, efficiency, and satisfaction of the user. Part 11 gives the following definition of usability:

- Usability is measured by the extent to which the intended goals of use of the overall system are achieved (effectiveness).

- The resources that have to be expended to achieve the intended goals (efficiency).

- The extent to which the user finds the overall system acceptable (satisfaction).

Effectiveness, efficiency, and satisfaction can be seen as quality factors of usability. To evaluate these factors, they need to be decomposed into sub-factors, and finally, into usability measures.

The information presentation is described in Part 12 of the ISO 9241 standard for the organization of information (arrangement, alignment, grouping, labels, location), for the display of graphical objects, and for the coding of information (abbreviation, color, size, shape, visual cues) by seven attributes. The "attributes of presented information" represent the static aspects of the interface and can be generally regarded as the "look" of the interface. The attributes are detailed in the recommendations given in the standard. Each of the recommendations supports one or more of the seven attributes. The seven presentation attributes are:

- Clarity: the information content is conveyed quickly and accurately.

- Discriminability: the displayed information can be distinguished accurately.

- Conciseness: users are not overloaded with extraneous information.

- Consistency: a unique design, conformity with user's expectation.

- Detectability: the user's attention is directed towards information required.

- Legibility: information is easy to read.

- Comprehensibility: the meaning is clearly understandable, unambiguous, interpretable, and recognizable.

The user guidance in Part 13 of the ISO 9241 standard describes that the user guidance information should be readily distinguishable from other displayed information and should be specific for the current context of use. User guidance can be given by the following five means:

- Prompts indicating explicitly (specific prompts) or implicitly (generic prompts) that the system is available for input.

- Feedback informing about the user's input timely, perceptible, and non-intrusive.

- Status information indicating the continuing state of the application, the system's hardware and software components, and the user's activities.

- Error management including error prevention, error correction, user support for error management, and error messages.

- On-line help for system-initiated and user initiated requests with specific information for the current context of use.

Research

User interface design has been a topic of considerable research, including on its aesthetics. Standards have been developed as far back as the 1980s for defining the usability of software products. One of the structural bases has become the IFIP user interface reference model. The model proposes four dimensions to structure the user interface:

- The input/output dimension (the look).

- The dialogue dimension (the feel).

- The technical or functional dimension (the access to tools and services).

- The organizational dimension (the communication and co-operation support).

This model has greatly influenced the development of the international standard ISO 9241 describing the interface design requirements for usability. The desire to understand application-specific UI issues early in software development, even as an application was being developed, led to research on GUI rapid prototyping tools that might offer convincing simulations of how an actual application might behave in production use. Some of this research has shown that a wide variety of programming tasks for GUI-based software can, in fact, be specified through means other than writing program code.

Research in recent years is strongly motivated by the increasing variety of devices that can, by virtue of Moore's law, host very complex interfaces.

Research has also been conducted on generating user interfaces automatically, to match a user's level of ability for different levels of interaction.

At the moment, in addition to traditional prototypes, the literature proposes new solutions, such as an experimental mixed prototype based on a configurable physical prototype that allow to achieve a complete sense of touch, thanks to the physical mock-up, and a realistic visual experience, thanks to the superimposition of the virtual interface on the physical prototype with Augmented Reality techniques.

References

- Raskin, Jef (2000). The human interface : new directions for designing interactive systems (1. printing. ed.). Reading, Mass. [u.a.]: Addison Wesley. ISBN 0-201-37937-6

- "The role of context in perceptions of the aesthetics of web pages over time". International Journal of Human–Computer Studies. 2009-01-05. Retrieved 2009-04-02

- Washington Post (August 24, 1995). "With Windows 95's Debut, Microsoft Scales Heights of Hype". Washington Post. Retrieved November 8, 2013

- Sweet, David (October 2001). "9 - Constructing A Responsive User Interface". KDE 2.0 Development. Sams Publishing. Retrieved 13 June 2014

- "Introduction Section". Recent advances in business administration. [S.l.]: Wseas. 2010. p. 190. ISBN 978-960-474-161-8. Other terms used are operator interface console (OIC) and operator interface terminal (OIT)

- Greg Wilson (2006). "Off with Their HUDs!: Rethinking the Heads-Up Display in Console Game Design". Gamasutra. Retrieved February 14, 2006

- John W. Satzinger; Lorne Olfman (March 1998). "User interface consistency across end-user applications: the effects on mental models". Journal of Management Information Systems. Managing virtual workplaces and teleworking with information technology. Armonk, NY. 14 (4): 167–193

- Citi, Luca (2009). "Development of a neural interface for the control of a robotic hand" (PDF). Scuola Superiore Sant'Anna, Pisa, Italy: IMT Institute for Advanced Studies Lucca: 5. Retrieved 7 June 2014

Applied Software Engineering

Software Engineering is used in a wide variety of fields. The development of artificial intelligence is one such area where the potential of software engineering is evident. Computational neuroscience and augmented reality are two other areas where software engineering has displayed promising possibilities. This chapter comprehensively summarizes all these applications of software engineering.

Artificial Intelligence

Artificial intelligence (AI) is intelligence exhibited by machines. In computer science, an ideal "intelligent" machine is a flexible rational agent that perceives its environment and takes actions that maximize its chance of success at some goal. Colloquially, the term "artificial intelligence" is applied when a machine mimics "cognitive" functions that humans associate with other human minds, such as "learning" and "problem solving". As machines become increasingly capable, facilities once thought to require intelligence are removed from the definition. For example, optical character recognition is no longer perceived as an exemplar of "artificial intelligence" having become a routine technology. Capabilities still classified as AI include advanced Chess and Go systems and self-driving cars.

AI research is divided into subfields that focus on specific problems or on specific approaches or on the use of a particular tool or towards satisfying particular applications.

The central problems (or goals) of AI research include reasoning, knowledge, planning, learning, natural language processing (communication), perception and the ability to move and manipulate objects. General intelligence is among the field's long-term goals. Approaches include statistical methods, computational intelligence, soft computing (e.g. machine learning), and traditional symbolic AI. Many tools are used in AI, including versions of search and mathematical optimization, logic, methods based on probability and economics. The AI field draws upon computer science, mathematics, psychology, linguistics, philosophy, neuroscience and artificial psychology.

The field was founded on the claim that human intelligence "can be so precisely described that a machine can be made to simulate it." This raises philosophical arguments about the nature of the mind and the ethics of creating artificial beings endowed with human-like intelligence, issues which have been explored by myth, fiction and philosophy since antiquity. Attempts to create artificial intelligence has experienced many setbacks, including the ALPAC report of 1966, the abandonment of perceptrons in 1970, the Lighthill Report of 1973 and the collapse of the Lisp machine market in 1987. In the twenty-first century AI techniques became an essential part of the technology industry, helping to solve many challenging problems in computer science.

History

While the concept of artificial beings (some of which are capable of thought) appeared as storytelling devices in antiquity, the idea of actually trying to build a machine to perform useful reasoning may have begun with Ramon Lull (c. 1300 CE). The first known calculating machine was built around 1623 by scientist Wilhelm Schickard. Gottfried Leibniz then built a crude variant, intended to perform operations on concepts rather than numbers. Since the 19th century, artificial beings are common in fiction, as in Mary Shelley's *Frankenstein* or Karel Čapek's *R.U.R. (Rossum's Universal Robots)*.

Mechanical or "formal" reasoning began with philosophers and mathematicians in antiquity. In the 19th century, George Boole refined those ideas into propositional logic and Gottlob Frege developed a notational system for mechanical reasoning (a *"predicate calculus"*). Around the 1940s, Alan Turing's theory of computation suggested that a machine, by shuffling symbols as simple as "0" and "1", could simulate any conceivable act of mathematical deduction. This insight, that digital computers can simulate any process of formal reasoning, is known as the Church–Turing thesis. Along with concurrent discoveries in neurology, information theory and cybernetics, this led researchers to consider the possibility of building an electronic brain. The first work that is now generally recognized as AI was McCullough and Pitts' 1943 formal design for Turing-complete "artificial neurons".

The field of AI research was founded at a conference at Dartmouth College in 1956. The attendees, including John McCarthy, Marvin Minsky, Allen Newell, Arthur Samuel and Herbert Simon, became the leaders of AI research. They and their students wrote programs that were, to most people, simply astonishing: computers were winning at checkers, solving word problems in algebra, proving logical theorems and speaking English. By the middle of the 1960s, research in the U.S. was heavily funded by the Department of Defense and laboratories had been established around the world. AI's founders were optimistic about the future: Herbert Simon predicted that "machines will be capable, within twenty years, of doing any work a man can do". Marvin Minsky agreed, writing that "within a generation ... the problem of creating 'artificial intelligence' will substantially be solved".

They failed to recognize the difficulty of some of the remaining tasks. Progress slowed and in 1974, in response to the criticism of Sir James Lighthill and ongoing pressure from the US Congress to fund more productive projects, both the U.S. and British governments cut off exploratory research in AI. The next few years would later be called an "AI winter", a period when funding for AI projects was hard to find.

In the early 1980s, AI research was revived by the commercial success of expert systems, a form of AI program that simulated the knowledge and analytical skills of human experts. By 1985 the market for AI had reached over a billion dollars. At the same time, Japan's fifth generation computer project inspired the U.S and British governments to restore funding for academic research. However, beginning with the collapse of the Lisp Machine market in 1987, AI once again fell into disrepute, and a second, longer-lasting hiatus began.

In the late 1990s and early 21st century, AI began to be used for logistics, data mining, medical diagnosis and other areas. The success was due to increasing computational power, greater emphasis on solving specific problems, new ties between AI and other fields and a commitment by researchers to mathematical methods and scientific standards. Deep Blue became the first computer chess-playing system to beat a reigning world chess champion, Garry Kasparov on 11 May 1997.

Advanced statistical techniques (loosely known as deep learning), access to large amounts of data and faster computers enabled advances in machine learning and perception. By the mid 2010s, machine learning applications were used throughout the world. In a *Jeopardy!* quiz show exhibition match, IBM's question answering system, Watson, defeated the two greatest Jeopardy champions, Brad Rutter and Ken Jennings, by a significant margin. The Kinect, which provides a 3D body–motion interface for the Xbox 360 and the Xbox One use algorithms that emerged from lengthy AI research as do intelligent personal assistants in smartphones. In March 2016, AlphaGo won 4 out of 5 games of Go in a match with Go champion Lee Sedol, becoming the first computer Go-playing system to beat a professional Go player without handicaps.

Research

Goals

The general problem of simulating (or creating) intelligence has been broken down into sub-problems. These consist of particular traits or capabilities that researchers expect an intelligent system to display. The traits described below have received the most attention.

Deduction, Reasoning, Problem Solving

Early researchers developed algorithms that imitated step-by-step reasoning that humans use when they solve puzzles or make logical deductions (reason). By the late 1980s and 1990s, AI research had developed methods for dealing with uncertain or incomplete information, employing concepts from probability and economics.

For difficult problems, algorithms can require enormous computational resources—most experience a "combinatorial explosion": the amount of memory or computer time required becomes astronomical for problems of a certain size. The search for more efficient problem-solving algorithms is a high priority.

Human beings ordinarily use fast, intuitive judgments rather than step-by-step deduction that early AI research was able to model. AI has progressed using "sub-symbolic" problem solving: embodied agent approaches emphasize the importance of sensorimotor skills to higher reasoning; neural net research attempts to simulate the structures inside the brain that give rise to this skill; statistical approaches to AI mimic the human ability to guess.

Knowledge Representation

Knowledge representation and knowledge engineering are central to AI research. Many of the problems machines are expected to solve will require extensive knowledge about the world. Among the things that AI needs to represent are: objects, properties, categories and relations between objects; situations, events, states and time; causes and effects; knowledge about knowledge (what we know about what other people know); and many other, less well researched domains. A representation of "what exists" is an ontology: the set of objects, relations, concepts and so on that the machine knows about. The most general are called upper ontologies, which attempt to provide a foundation for all other knowledge.

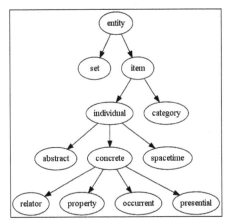

An ontology represents knowledge as a set of concepts within a domain and the relationships between those concepts.

Among the most difficult problems in knowledge representation are:

Default reasoning and the qualification problem:

> Many of the things people know take the form of "working assumptions." For example, if a bird comes up in conversation, people typically picture an animal that is fist sized, sings, and flies. None of these things are true about all birds. John McCarthy identified this problem in 1969 as the qualification problem: for any commonsense rule that AI researchers care to represent, there tend to be a huge number of exceptions. Almost nothing is simply true or false in the way that abstract logic requires. AI research has explored a number of solutions to this problem.

The breadth of commonsense knowledge:

> The number of atomic facts that the average person knows is astronomical. Research projects that attempt to build a complete knowledge base of commonsense knowledge (e.g., Cyc) require enormous amounts of laborious ontological engineering—they must be built, by hand, one complicated concept at a time. A major goal is to have the computer understand enough concepts to be able to learn by reading from sources like the Internet, and thus be able to add to its own ontology.

The subsymbolic form of some commonsense knowledge:

> Much of what people know is not represented as "facts" or "statements" that they could express verbally. For example, a chess master will avoid a particular chess position because it "feels too exposed" or an art critic can take one look at a statue and instantly realize that it is a fake. These are intuitions or tendencies that are represented in the brain non-consciously and sub-symbolically. Knowledge like this informs, supports and provides a context for symbolic, conscious knowledge. As with the related problem of sub-symbolic reasoning, it is hoped that situated AI, computational intelligence, or statistical AI will provide ways to represent this kind of knowledge.

Planning

Intelligent agents must be able to set goals and achieve them. They need a way to visualize the future (they must have a representation of the state of the world and be able to make predictions about how their actions will change it) and be able to make choices that maximize the utility (or "value") of the available choices.

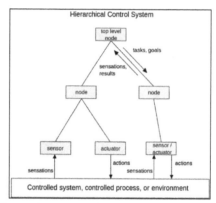

A hierarchical control system is a form of control system in which a set of devices and governing software is arranged in a hierarchy.

In classical planning problems, the agent can assume that it is the only thing acting on the world and it can be certain what the consequences of its actions may be. However, if the agent is not the only actor, it must periodically ascertain whether the world matches its predictions and it must change its plan as this becomes necessary, requiring the agent to reason under uncertainty.

Multi-agent planning uses the cooperation and competition of many agents to achieve a given goal. Emergent behavior such as this is used by evolutionary algorithms and swarm intelligence.

Learning

Machine learning is the study of computer algorithms that improve automatically through experience and has been central to AI research since the field's inception.

Unsupervised learning is the ability to find patterns in a stream of input. Supervised learning includes both classification and numerical regression. Classification is used to determine what category something belongs in, after seeing a number of examples of things from several categories. Regression is the attempt to produce a function that describes the relationship between inputs and outputs and predicts how the outputs should change as the inputs change. In reinforcement learning the agent is rewarded for good responses and punished for bad ones. The agent uses this sequence of rewards and punishments to form a strategy for operating in its problem space. These three types of learning can be analyzed in terms of decision theory, using concepts like utility. The mathematical analysis of machine learning algorithms and their performance is a branch of theoretical computer science known as computational learning theory.

Within developmental robotics, developmental learning approaches were elaborated for lifelong cumulative acquisition of repertoires of novel skills by a robot, through autonomous self-exploration and social interaction with human teachers, and using guidance mechanisms such as active learning, maturation, motor synergies, and imitation.

Natural Language Processing (Communication)

Natural language processing gives machines the ability to read and understand the languages that humans speak. A sufficiently powerful natural language processing system would enable natural language user interfaces and the acquisition of knowledge directly from human-written sources, such as newswire texts. Some straightforward applications of natural language processing include information retrieval, text mining, question answering and machine translation.

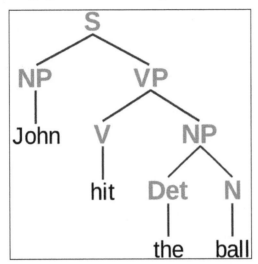

A parse tree represents the syntactic structure of a sentence according to some formal grammar.

A common method of processing and extracting meaning from natural language is through semantic indexing. Increases in processing speeds and the drop in the cost of data storage makes indexing large volumes of abstractions of the user's input much more efficient.

Perception

Machine perception is the ability to use input from sensors (such as cameras, microphones, tactile sensors, sonar and others more exotic) to deduce aspects of the world. Computer vision is the ability to analyze visual input. A few selected subproblems are speech recognition, facial recognition and object recognition.

Motion and manipulation

The field of robotics is closely related to AI. Intelligence is required for robots to be able to handle such tasks as object manipulation and navigation, with sub-problems of localization (knowing where you are, or finding out where other things are), mapping (learning what is around you, building a map of the environment), and motion planning (figuring out how to get there) or path planning (going from one point in space to another point, which may involve compliant motion – where the robot moves while maintaining physical contact with an object).

Long-term Goals

Among the long-term goals in the research pertaining to artificial intelligence are: (1) Social intelligence, (2) Creativity, and (3) General intelligence.

Social Intelligence

Affective computing is the study and development of systems and devices that can recognize, interpret, process, and simulate human affects. It is an interdisciplinary field spanning computer sciences, psychology, and cognitive science. While the origins of the field may be traced as far back as to early philosophical inquiries into emotion, the more modern branch of computer science originated with Rosalind Picard's 1995 paper on affective computing. A motivation for the research is the ability to simulate empathy. The machine should interpret the emotional state of humans and adapt its behaviour to them, giving an appropriate response for those emotions.

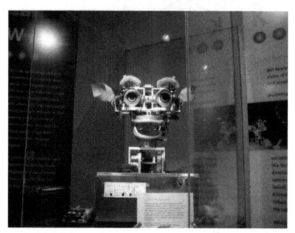

Kismet, a robot with rudimentary social skills.

Emotion and social skills play two roles for an intelligent agent. First, it must be able to predict the actions of others, by understanding their motives and emotional states. (This involves elements of game theory, decision theory, as well as the ability to model human emotions and the perceptual skills to detect emotions.) Also, in an effort to facilitate human-computer interaction, an intelligent machine might want to be able to *display* emotions—even if it does not actually experience them itself—in order to appear sensitive to the emotional dynamics of human interaction.

Creativity

A sub-field of AI addresses creativity both theoretically (from a philosophical and psychological perspective) and practically (via specific implementations of systems that generate outputs that can be considered creative, or systems that identify and assess creativity). Related areas of computational research are Artificial intuition and Artificial thinking.

General Intelligence

Many researchers think that their work will eventually be incorporated into a machine with *general* intelligence (known as strong AI), combining all the skills above and exceeding human abilities at most or all of them. A few believe that anthropomorphic features like artificial consciousness or an artificial brain may be required for such a project.

Many of the problems above may require general intelligence to be considered solved. For example, even a straightforward, specific task like machine translation requires that the machine read and write in both languages (NLP), follow the author's argument (reason), know what is being talked about (knowledge), and faithfully reproduce the author's intention (social intelligence). A problem like machine translation is considered "AI-complete". In order to solve this particular problem, one must solve all the problems.

Approaches

There is no established unifying theory or paradigm that guides AI research. Researchers disagree about many issues. A few of the most long standing questions that have remained unanswered are these: should artificial intelligence simulate natural intelligence by studying psychology or neurology? Or is human biology as irrelevant to AI research as bird biology is to aeronautical engineering? Can intelligent behavior be described using simple, elegant principles (such as logic or optimization)? Or does it necessarily require solving a large number of completely unrelated problems? Can intelligence be reproduced using high-level symbols, similar to words and ideas? Or does it require "sub-symbolic" processing? John Haugeland, who coined the term GOFAI (Good Old-Fashioned Artificial Intelligence), also proposed that AI should more properly be referred to as synthetic intelligence, a term which has since been adopted by some non-GOFAI researchers.

Cybernetics and Brain Simulation

In the 1940s and 1950s, a number of researchers explored the connection between neurology, information theory, and cybernetics. Some of them built machines that used electronic networks to exhibit rudimentary intelligence, such as W. Grey Walter's turtles and the Johns Hopkins Beast. Many of these researchers gathered for meetings of the Teleological Society at Princeton University and the Ratio Club in England. By 1960, this approach was largely abandoned, although elements of it would be revived in the 1980s.

Symbolic

When access to digital computers became possible in the middle 1950s, AI research began to explore the possibility that human intelligence could be reduced to symbol manipulation. The research was centered in three institutions: Carnegie Mellon University, Stanford and MIT, and each one developed its own style of research. John Haugeland named these approaches to AI "good old fashioned AI" or "GOFAI". During the 1960s, symbolic approaches had achieved great success at simulating high-level thinking in small demonstration programs. Approaches based on cybernetics or neural networks were abandoned or pushed into the background. Researchers in the 1960s and the 1970s were convinced that symbolic approaches would eventually succeed in creating a machine with artificial general intelligence and considered this the goal of their field.

Cognitive simulation:

> Economist Herbert Simon and Allen Newell studied human problem-solving skills and attempted to formalize them, and their work laid the foundations of the field of artificial intelligence, as well as cognitive science, operations research and management science. Their research team used the results of psychological experiments to develop programs that simulated the techniques that people used to solve problems. This tradition, centered at Carnegie Mellon University would eventually culminate in the development of the Soar architecture in the middle 1980s.

Logic-based:

> Unlike Newell and Simon, John McCarthy felt that machines did not need to simulate human thought, but should instead try to find the essence of abstract reasoning and problem solving, regardless of whether people used the same algorithms. His laboratory at Stanford (SAIL) focused on using formal logic to solve a wide variety of problems, including knowledge representation, planning and learning. Logic was also the focus of the work at the University of Edinburgh and elsewhere in Europe which led to the development of the programming language Prolog and the science of logic programming.

"Anti-logic" or "scruffy":

> Researchers at MIT (such as Marvin Minsky and Seymour Papert) found that solving difficult problems in vision and natural language processing required ad-hoc solutions – they argued that there was no simple and general principle (like logic) that would capture all the aspects of intelligent behavior. Roger Schank described their "anti-logic" approaches as "scruffy" (as opposed to the "neat" paradigms at CMU and Stanford). Commonsense knowledge bases (such as Doug Lenat's Cyc) are an example of "scruffy" AI, since they must be built by hand, one complicated concept at a time.

Knowledge-based:

> When computers with large memories became available around 1970, researchers from all three traditions began to build knowledge into AI applications. This "knowledge revolution" led to the development and deployment of expert systems (introduced by Edward Feigenbaum), the first truly successful form of AI software. The knowledge revolution was also driven by the realization that enormous amounts of knowledge would be required by many simple AI applications.

Sub-symbolic

By the 1980s progress in symbolic AI seemed to stall and many believed that symbolic systems would never be able to imitate all the processes of human cognition, especially perception, robotics, learning and pattern recognition. A number of researchers began to look into "sub-symbolic" approaches to specific AI problems. Sub-symbolic methods manage to approach intelligence without specific representations of knowledge.

Bottom-up, embodied, situated, behavior-based or nouvelle AI:

> Researchers from the related field of robotics, such as Rodney Brooks, rejected symbolic AI and focused on the basic engineering problems that would allow robots to move and survive. Their work revived the non-symbolic viewpoint of the early cybernetics researchers of the 1950s and reintroduced the use of control theory in AI. This coincided with the development of the embodied mind thesis in the related field of cognitive science: the idea that aspects of the body (such as movement, perception and visualization) are required for higher intelligence.

Computational intelligence and soft computing:

> Interest in neural networks and "connectionism" was revived by David Rumelhart and others

in the middle 1980s. Neural networks are an example of soft computing --- they are solutions to problems which cannot be solved with complete logical certainty, and where an approximate solution is often enough. Other soft computing approaches to AI include fuzzy systems, evolutionary computation and many statistical tools. The application of soft computing to AI is studied collectively by the emerging discipline of computational intelligence.

Statistical

In the 1990s, AI researchers developed sophisticated mathematical tools to solve specific subproblems. These tools are truly scientific, in the sense that their results are both measurable and verifiable, and they have been responsible for many of AI's recent successes. The shared mathematical language has also permitted a high level of collaboration with more established fields (like mathematics, economics or operations research). Stuart Russell and Peter Norvig describe this movement as nothing less than a "revolution" and "the victory of the neats." Critics argue that these techniques (with few exceptions) are too focused on particular problems and have failed to address the long-term goal of general intelligence. There is an ongoing debate about the relevance and validity of statistical approaches in AI, exemplified in part by exchanges between Peter Norvig and Noam Chomsky.

Integrating the Approaches

Intelligent agent paradigm:

> An intelligent agent is a system that perceives its environment and takes actions which maximize its chances of success. The simplest intelligent agents are programs that solve specific problems. More complicated agents include human beings and organizations of human beings (such as firms). The paradigm gives researchers license to study isolated problems and find solutions that are both verifiable and useful, without agreeing on one single approach. An agent that solves a specific problem can use any approach that works – some agents are symbolic and logical, some are sub-symbolic neural networks and others may use new approaches. The paradigm also gives researchers a common language to communicate with other fields—such as decision theory and economics—that also use concepts of abstract agents. The intelligent agent paradigm became widely accepted during the 1990s.

Agent architectures and cognitive architectures:

> Researchers have designed systems to build intelligent systems out of interacting intelligent agents in a multi-agent system. A system with both symbolic and sub-symbolic components is a hybrid intelligent system, and the study of such systems is artificial intelligence systems integration. A hierarchical control system provides a bridge between sub-symbolic AI at its lowest, reactive levels and traditional symbolic AI at its highest levels, where relaxed time constraints permit planning and world modelling. Rodney Brooks' subsumption architecture was an early proposal for such a hierarchical system.

Tools

In the course of 50 years of research, AI has developed a large number of tools to solve the most difficult problems in computer science. A few of the most general of these methods are discussed.

Search and Optimization

Many problems in AI can be solved in theory by intelligently searching through many possible solutions: Reasoning can be reduced to performing a search. For example, logical proof can be viewed as searching for a path that leads from premises to conclusions, where each step is the application of an inference rule. Planning algorithms search through trees of goals and subgoals, attempting to find a path to a target goal, a process called means-ends analysis. Robotics algorithms for moving limbs and grasping objects use local searches in configuration space. Many learning algorithms use search algorithms based on optimization.

Simple exhaustive searches are rarely sufficient for most real world problems: the search space (the number of places to search) quickly grows to astronomical numbers. The result is a search that is too slow or never completes. The solution, for many problems, is to use "heuristics" or "rules of thumb" that eliminate choices that are unlikely to lead to the goal (called "pruning the search tree"). Heuristics supply the program with a "best guess" for the path on which the solution lies. Heuristics limit the search for solutions into a smaller sample size.

A very different kind of search came to prominence in the 1990s, based on the mathematical theory of optimization. For many problems, it is possible to begin the search with some form of a guess and then refine the guess incrementally until no more refinements can be made. These algorithms can be visualized as blind hill climbing: we begin the search at a random point on the landscape, and then, by jumps or steps, we keep moving our guess uphill, until we reach the top. Other optimization algorithms are simulated annealing, beam search and random optimization.

Evolutionary computation uses a form of optimization search. For example, they may begin with a population of organisms (the guesses) and then allow them to mutate and recombine, selecting only the fittest to survive each generation (refining the guesses). Forms of evolutionary computation include swarm intelligence algorithms (such as ant colony or particle swarm optimization) and evolutionary algorithms (such as genetic algorithms, gene expression programming, and genetic programming).

Logic

Logic is used for knowledge representation and problem solving, but it can be applied to other problems as well. For example, the satplan algorithm uses logic for planning and inductive logic programming is a method for learning.

Several different forms of logic are used in AI research. Propositional or sentential logic is the logic of statements which can be true or false. First-order logic also allows the use of quantifiers and predicates, and can express facts about objects, their properties, and their relations with each other. Fuzzy logic, is a version of first-order logic which allows the truth of a statement to be represented as a value between 0 and 1, rather than simply True (1) or False (0). Fuzzy systems can be used for uncertain reasoning and have been widely used in modern industrial and consumer product control systems. Subjective logic models uncertainty in a different and more explicit manner than fuzzy-logic: a given binomial opinion satisfies belief + disbelief + uncertainty = 1 within a Beta distribution. By this method, ignorance can be distinguished from probabilistic statements that an agent makes with high confidence.

Default logics, non-monotonic logics and circumscription are forms of logic designed to help with default reasoning and the qualification problem. Several extensions of logic have been designed to handle specific domains of knowledge, such as: description logics; situation calculus, event calculus and fluent calculus (for representing events and time); causal calculus; belief calculus; and modal logics.

Probabilistic Methods for Uncertain Reasoning

Many problems in AI (in reasoning, planning, learning, perception and robotics) require the agent to operate with incomplete or uncertain information. AI researchers have devised a number of powerful tools to solve these problems using methods from probability theory and economics.

Bayesian networks are a very general tool that can be used for a large number of problems: reasoning (using the Bayesian inference algorithm), learning (using the expectation-maximization algorithm), planning (using decision networks) and perception (using dynamic Bayesian networks). Probabilistic algorithms can also be used for filtering, prediction, smoothing and finding explanations for streams of data, helping perception systems to analyze processes that occur over time (e.g., hidden Markov models or Kalman filters).

A key concept from the science of economics is "utility": a measure of how valuable something is to an intelligent agent. Precise mathematical tools have been developed that analyze how an agent can make choices and plan, using decision theory, decision analysis, and information value theory. These tools include models such as Markov decision processes, dynamic decision networks, game theory and mechanism design.

Classifiers and Statistical Learning Methods

The simplest AI applications can be divided into two types: classifiers ("if shiny then diamond") and controllers ("if shiny then pick up"). Controllers do, however, also classify conditions before inferring actions, and therefore classification forms a central part of many AI systems. Classifiers are functions that use pattern matching to determine a closest match. They can be tuned according to examples, making them very attractive for use in AI. These examples are known as observations or patterns. In supervised learning, each pattern belongs to a certain predefined class. A class can be seen as a decision that has to be made. All the observations combined with their class labels are known as a data set. When a new observation is received, that observation is classified based on previous experience.

A classifier can be trained in various ways; there are many statistical and machine learning approaches. The most widely used classifiers are the neural network, kernel methods such as the support vector machine, k-nearest neighbor algorithm, Gaussian mixture model, naive Bayes classifier, and decision tree. The performance of these classifiers have been compared over a wide range of tasks. Classifier performance depends greatly on the characteristics of the data to be classified. There is no single classifier that works best on all given problems; this is also referred to as the "no free lunch" theorem. Determining a suitable classifier for a given problem is still more an art than science.

Neural Networks

The study of non-learning artificial neural networks began in the decade before the field of AI research was founded, in the work of Walter Pitts and Warren McCullough. Frank Rosenblatt invented the perceptron, a learning network with a single layer, similar to the old concept of linear regression. Early pioneers also include Alexey Grigorevich Ivakhnenko, Teuvo Kohonen, Stephen Grossberg, Kunihiko Fukushima, Christoph von der Malsburg, David Willshaw, Shun-Ichi Amari, Bernard Widrow, John Hopfield, and others.

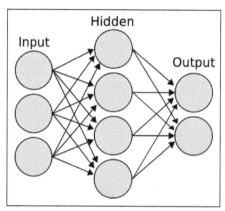

A neural network is an interconnected group of nodes, akin to the vast network of neurons in the human brain.

The main categories of networks are acyclic or feedforward neural networks (where the signal passes in only one direction) and recurrent neural networks (which allow feedback and short-term memories of previous input events). Among the most popular feedforward networks are perceptrons, multi-layer perceptrons and radial basis networks. Neural networks can be applied to the problem of intelligent control (for robotics) or learning, using such techniques as Hebbian learning, GMDH or competitive learning.

Today, neural networks are often trained by the backpropagation algorithm, which had been around since 1970 as the reverse mode of automatic differentiation published by Seppo Linnainmaa, and was introduced to neural networks by Paul Werbos.

Hierarchical temporal memory is an approach that models some of the structural and algorithmic properties of the neocortex.

Deep Feedforward Neural Networks

Deep learning in artificial neural networks with many layers has transformed many important subfields of artificial intelligence, including computer vision, speech recognition, natural language processing and others.

According to a survey, the expression "Deep Learning" was introduced to the Machine Learning community by Rina Dechter in 1986 and gained traction after Igor Aizenberg and colleagues introduced it to Artificial Neural Networks in 2000. The first functional Deep Learning networks were published by Alexey Grigorevich Ivakhnenko and V. G. Lapa in 1965. These networks are trained one layer at a time. Ivakhnenko's 1971 paper describes the learning of a deep feedforward multilayer perceptron with eight layers, already much deeper than many later networks. In 2006, a publication by Geoffrey Hinton and Ruslan Salakhutdinov introduced another way of pre-training many-layered feedforward neural networks (FNNs) one layer at a time, treating each layer in turn as an unsupervised restricted Boltzmann machine, then using supervised backpropagation for fine-tuning. Similar to shallow artificial neural networks, deep neural networks can model complex non-linear relationships. Over the last few years, advances in both machine learning algorithms and computer hardware have led to more efficient methods for training deep neural networks that contain many layers of non-linear hidden units and a very large output layer.

Deep learning often uses convolutional neural networks (CNNs), whose origins can be traced back to the Neocognitron introduced by Kunihiko Fukushima in 1980. In 1989, Yann LeCun and colleagues applied backpropagation to such an architecture. In the early 2000s, in an industrial application CNNs already processed an estimated 10% to 20% of all the checks written in the US. Since 2011, fast implementations of CNNs on GPUs have won many visual pattern recognition competitions.

Deep feedforward neural networks were used in conjunction with reinforcement learning by AlphaGo, Google Deepmind's program that was the first to beat a professional human player.

Deep Recurrent Neural Networks

Early on, deep learning was also applied to sequence learning with recurrent neural networks (RNNs) which are general computers and can run arbitrary programs to process arbitrary sequences of inputs. The depth of an RNN is unlimited and depends on the length of its input sequence. RNNs can be trained by gradient descent but suffer from the vanishing gradient problem. In 1992, it was shown that unsupervised pre-training of a stack of recurrent neural networks can speed up subsequent supervised learning of deep sequential problems.

Numerous researchers now use variants of a deep learning recurrent NN called the Long short term memory (LSTM) network published by Hochreiter & Schmidhuber in 1997. LSTM is often trained by Connectionist Temporal Classification (CTC). At Google, Microsoft and Baidu this approach has revolutionised speech recognition. For example, in 2015, Google's speech recognition experienced a dramatic performance jump of 49% through CTC-trained LSTM, which is now available through Google Voice to billions of smartphone users. Google also used LSTM to improve machine translation, Language Modeling and Multilingual Language Processing. LSTM combined with CNNs also improved automatic image captioning and a plethora of other applications.

Control Theory

Control theory, the grandchild of cybernetics, has many important applications, especially in robotics.

Languages

AI researchers have developed several specialized languages for AI research, including Lisp and Prolog.

Evaluating Progress

In 1950, Alan Turing proposed a general procedure to test the intelligence of an agent now known as the Turing test. This procedure allows almost all the major problems of artificial intelligence to be tested. However, it is a very difficult challenge and at present all agents fail.

Artificial intelligence can also be evaluated on specific problems such as small problems in chemistry, hand-writing recognition and game-playing. Such tests have been termed subject matter expert Turing tests. Smaller problems provide more achievable goals and there are an ever-increasing number of positive results.

One classification for outcomes of an AI test is:

1. Optimal: it is not possible to perform better.

2. Strong super-human: performs better than all humans.

3. Super-human: performs better than most humans.

4. Sub-human: performs worse than most humans.

For example, performance at draughts (i.e. checkers) is optimal, performance at chess is super-human and nearing strong super-human and per-formance at many everyday tasks (such as recognizing a face or crossing a room without bumping into something) is sub-human.

A quite different approach measures machine intelligence through tests which are developed from *mathematical* definitions of intelligence. Examples of these kinds of tests start in the late nineties devising intelligence tests using notions from Kolmogorov complexity and data compression. Two major advantages of mathematical definitions are their applicability to nonhuman intelligences and their absence of a requirement for human testers.

A derivative of the Turing test is the Completely Automated Public Turing test to tell Computers and Humans Apart (CAPTCHA). As the name implies, this helps to determine that a user is an actual person and not a computer posing as a human. In contrast to the standard Turing test, CAPTCHA administered by a machine and targeted to a human as opposed to being administered by a human and targeted to a machine. A computer asks a user to complete a simple test then generates a grade for that test. Computers are unable to solve the problem, so correct solutions are deemed to be the result of a person taking the test. A common type of CAPTCHA is the test that requires the typing of distorted letters, numbers or symbols that appear in an image undecipherable by a computer.

Applications

An automated online assistant providing customer service on a web page – one of many very primitive applications of artificial intelligence.

AI is relevant to any intellectual task. Modern artificial intelligence techniques are pervasive and are too numerous to list here. Frequently, when a technique reaches mainstream use, it is no longer considered artificial intelligence; this phenomenon is described as the AI effect.

High-profile examples of AI include autonomous vehicles (such as drones and self-driving cars), medical diagnosis, creating art (such as poetry), proving mathemetical theorems, playing games (such as Chess or Go), search engines (such as Google search), online assistants (such as Siri), image recognition in photographs, spam filtering, and targeting online advertisements.

Competitions and Prizes

There are a number of competitions and prizes to promote research in artificial intelligence. The main areas promoted are: general machine intelligence, conversational behavior, data-mining, robotic cars, robot soccer and games.

Platforms

A platform (or "computing platform") is defined as "some sort of hardware architecture or software framework (including application frameworks), that allows software to run." As Rodney Brooks pointed out many years ago, it is not just the artificial intelligence software that defines the AI features of the platform, but rather the actual platform itself that affects the AI that results, i.e., there needs to be work in AI problems on real-world platforms rather than in isolation.

A wide variety of platforms has allowed different aspects of AI to develop, ranging from expert systems such as Cyc to deep-learning frameworks to robot platforms such as the Roomba with open interface. Recent advances in deep artificial neural networks and distributed computing have led to a proliferation of software libraries, including Deeplearning4j, TensorFlow, Theano and Torch.

Philosophy and Ethics

There are three philosophical questions related to AI:

1. Is artificial general intelligence possible? Can a machine solve any problem that a human being can solve using intelligence? Or are there hard limits to what a machine can accomplish?

2. Are intelligent machines dangerous? How can we ensure that machines behave ethically and that they are used ethically?

3. Can a machine have a mind, consciousness and mental states in exactly the same sense that human beings do? Can a machine be sentient, and thus deserve certain rights? Can a machine intentionally cause harm?

The Limits of Artificial General Intelligence

Can a machine be intelligent? Can it "think"?

Turing's "polite convention":

> We need not decide if a machine can "think"; we need only decide if a machine can act as

intelligently as a human being. This approach to the philosophical problems associated with artificial intelligence forms the basis of the Turing test.

The Dartmouth proposal:

"Every aspect of learning or any other feature of intelligence can be so precisely described that a machine can be made to simulate it." This conjecture was printed in the proposal for the Dartmouth Conference of 1956, and represents the position of most working AI researchers.

Newell and Simon's physical symbol system hypothesis:

"A physical symbol system has the necessary and sufficient means of general intelligent action." Newell and Simon argue that intelligence consists of formal operations on symbols. Hubert Dreyfus argued that, on the contrary, human expertise depends on unconscious instinct rather than conscious symbol manipulation and on having a "feel" for the situation rather than explicit symbolic knowledge.

Gödelian arguments:

Gödel himself, John Lucas (in 1961) and Roger Penrose (in a more detailed argument from 1989 onwards) argued that humans are not reducible to Turing machines. The detailed arguments are complex, but in essence they derive from Kurt Gödel's 1931 proof in his first incompleteness theorem that it is always possible to create statements that a formal system could not prove. A human being, however, can (with some thought) see the truth of these "Gödel statements". Any Turing program designed to search for these statements can have its methods reduced to a formal system, and so will always have a "Gödel statement" derivable from its program which it can never discover. However, if humans are indeed capable of understanding mathematical truth, it doesn't seem possible that we could be limited in the same way. This is quite a general result, if accepted, since it can be shown that hardware neural nets, and computers based on random processes (e.g. annealing approaches) and quantum computers based on entangled qubits (so long as they involve no new physics) can all be reduced to Turing machines. All they do is reduce the complexity of the tasks, not permit new types of problems to be solved. Roger Penrose speculates that there may be new physics involved in our brain, perhaps at the intersection of gravity and quantum mechanics at the Planck scale. This argument, if accepted does not rule out the possibility of true artificial intelligence, but means it has to be biological in basis or based on new physical principles. The argument has been followed up by many counter arguments, and then Roger Penrose has replied to those with counter counter examples, and it is now an intricate complex debate.

The artificial brain argument:

The brain can be simulated by machines and because brains are intelligent, simulated brains must also be intelligent; thus machines can be intelligent. Hans Moravec, Ray Kurzweil and others have argued that it is technologically feasible to copy the brain directly into hardware and software, and that such a simulation will be essentially identical to the original.

The AI effect:

> Machines are *already* intelligent, but observers have failed to recognize it. When Deep Blue beat Garry Kasparov in chess, the machine was acting intelligently. However, onlookers commonly discount the behavior of an artificial intelligence program by arguing that it is not "real" intelligence after all; thus "real" intelligence is whatever intelligent behavior people can do that machines still can not. This is known as the AI Effect: "AI is whatever hasn't been done yet."

Intelligent Behaviour and Machine Ethics

As a minimum, an AI system must be able to reproduce aspects of human intelligence. This raises the issue of how ethically the machine should behave towards both humans and other AI agents. This issue was addressed by Wendell Wallach in his book titled *Moral Machines* in which he introduced the concept of artificial moral agents (AMA). For Wallach, AMAs have become a part of the research landscape of artificial intelligence as guided by its two central questions which he identifies as "Does Humanity Want Computers Making Moral Decisions" and "Can (Ro)bots Really Be Moral". For Wallach the question is not centered on the issue of *whether* machines can demonstrate the equivalent of moral behavior in contrast to the *constraints* which society may place on the development of AMAs.

Machine Ethics

The field of machine ethics is concerned with giving machines ethical principles, or a procedure for discovering a way to resolve the ethical dilemmas they might encounter, enabling them to function in an ethically responsible manner through their own ethical decision making. The field was delineated in the AAAI Fall 2005 Symposium on Machine Ethics: "Past research concerning the relationship between technology and ethics has largely focused on responsible and irresponsible use of technology by human beings, with a few people being interested in how human beings ought to treat machines. In all cases, only human beings have engaged in ethical reasoning. The time has come for adding an ethical dimension to at least some machines. Recognition of the ethical ramifications of behavior involving machines, as well as recent and potential developments in machine autonomy, necessitate this. In contrast to computer hacking, software property issues, privacy issues and other topics normally ascribed to computer ethics, machine ethics is concerned with the behavior of machines towards human users and other machines. Research in machine ethics is key to alleviating concerns with autonomous systems—it could be argued that the notion of autonomous machines without such a dimension is at the root of all fear concerning machine intelligence. Further, investigation of machine ethics could enable the discovery of problems with current ethical theories, advancing our thinking about Ethics." Machine ethics is sometimes referred to as machine morality, computational ethics or computational morality. A variety of perspectives of this nascent field can be found in the collected edition "Machine Ethics" that stems from the AAAI Fall 2005 Symposium on Machine Ethics. Some suggest that to ensure that AI-equipped machines (sometimes called "smart machines") will act ethically requires a new kind of AI. This AI would be able to monitor, supervise, and if need be, correct the first order AI.

Malevolent and Friendly AI

Political scientist Charles T. Rubin believes that AI can be neither designed nor guaranteed to be benevolent. He argues that "any sufficiently advanced benevolence may be indistinguishable from malevolence." Humans should not assume machines or robots would treat us favorably, because there is no *a priori* reason to believe that they would be sympathetic to our system of morality, which has evolved along with our particular biology (which AIs would not share). Hyper-intelligent software may not necessarily decide to support the continued existence of mankind, and would be extremely difficult to stop. This topic has also recently begun to be discussed in academic publications as a real source of risks to civilization, humans, and planet Earth.

Physicist Stephen Hawking, Microsoft founder Bill Gates and SpaceX founder Elon Musk have expressed concerns about the possibility that AI could evolve to the point that humans could not control it, with Hawking theorizing that this could "spell the end of the human race".

One proposal to deal with this is to ensure that the first generally intelligent AI is 'Friendly AI', and will then be able to control subsequently developed AIs. Some question whether this kind of check could really remain in place.

Leading AI researcher Rodney Brooks writes, "I think it is a mistake to be worrying about us developing malevolent AI anytime in the next few hundred years. I think the worry stems from a fundamental error in not distinguishing the difference between the very real recent advances in a particular aspect of AI, and the enormity and complexity of building sentient volitional intelligence."

Devaluation of Humanity

Joseph Weizenbaum wrote that AI applications can not, by definition, successfully simulate genuine human empathy and that the use of AI technology in fields such as customer service or psychotherapy was deeply misguided. Weizenbaum was also bothered that AI researchers (and some philosophers) were willing to view the human mind as nothing more than a computer program (a position now known as computationalism). To Weizenbaum these points suggest that AI research devalues human life.

Decrease in Demand for Human Labor

Martin Ford, author of *The Lights in the Tunnel: Automation, Accelerating Technology and the Economy of the Future*, and others argue that specialized artificial intelligence applications, robotics and other forms of automation will ultimately result in significant unemployment as machines begin to match and exceed the capability of workers to perform most routine and repetitive jobs. Ford predicts that many knowledge-based occupations—and in particular entry level jobs—will be increasingly susceptible to automation via expert systems, machine learning and other AI-enhanced applications. AI-based applications may also be used to amplify the capabilities of low-wage offshore workers, making it more feasible to outsource knowledge work.

Machine Consciousness, Sentience and Mind

If an AI system replicates all key aspects of human intelligence, will that system also be sentient – will it have a mind which has conscious experiences? This question is closely related to the philosophical problem as to the nature of human consciousness, generally referred to as the hard problem of consciousness.

Consciousness

Computationalism

Computationalism is the position in the philosophy of mind that the human mind or the human brain (or both) is an information processing system and that thinking is a form of computing. Computationalism argues that the relationship between mind and body is similar or identical to the relationship between software and hardware and thus may be a solution to the mind-body problem. This philosophical position was inspired by the work of AI researchers and cognitive scientists in the 1960s and was originally proposed by philosophers Jerry Fodor and Hillary Putnam.

Strong AI Hypothesis

Searle's strong AI hypothesis states that "The appropriately programmed computer with the right inputs and outputs would thereby have a mind in exactly the same sense human beings have minds." John Searle counters this assertion with his Chinese room argument, which asks us to look *inside* the computer and try to find where the "mind" might be.

Robot Rights

Mary Shelley's *Frankenstein* considers a key issue in the ethics of artificial intelligence: if a machine can be created that has intelligence, could it also *feel*? If it can feel, does it have the same rights as a human? The idea also appears in modern science fiction, such as the film *A.I.: Artificial Intelligence*, in which humanoid machines have the ability to feel emotions. This issue, now known as "robot rights", is currently being considered by, for example, California's Institute for the Future, although many critics believe that the discussion is premature. The subject is profoundly discussed in the 2010 documentary film *Plug & Pray*.

Superintelligence

Are there limits to how intelligent machines – or human-machine hybrids – can be? A superintelligence, hyperintelligence, or superhuman intelligence is a hypothetical agent that would possess intelligence far surpassing that of the brightest and most gifted human mind. "Superintelligence" may also refer to the form or degree of intelligence possessed by such an agent.

Technological Singularity

If research into Strong AI produced sufficiently intelligent software, it might be able to reprogram and improve itself. The improved software would be even better at improving itself, leading to recursive self-improvement. The new intelligence could thus increase exponentially and dramatically surpass humans. Science fiction writer Vernor Vinge named this scenario "singularity". Technological singularity is when accelerating progress in technologies will cause a runaway effect wherein artificial intelligence will exceed human intellectual capacity and control, thus radically changing or even ending civilization. Because the capabilities of such an intelligence may be impossible to comprehend, the technological singularity is an occurrence beyond which events are unpredictable or even unfathomable.

Ray Kurzweil has used Moore's law (which describes the relentless exponential improvement in digital technology) to calculate that desktop computers will have the same processing power as human brains by the year 2029, and predicts that the singularity will occur in 2045.

Transhumanism

You awake one morning to find your brain has another lobe functioning. Invisible, this auxiliary lobe answers your questions with information beyond the realm of your own memory, suggests plausible courses of action, and asks questions that help bring out relevant facts. You quickly come to rely on the new lobe so much that you stop wondering how it works. You just use it. This is the dream of artificial intelligence.

—BYTE, April 1985

Robot designer Hans Moravec, cyberneticist Kevin Warwick and inventor Ray Kurzweil have predicted that humans and machines will merge in the future into cyborgs that are more capable and powerful than either. This idea, called transhumanism, which has roots in Aldous Huxley and Robert Ettinger, has been illustrated in fiction as well, for example in the manga *Ghost in the Shell* and the science-fiction series *Dune*.

In the 1980s artist Hajime Sorayama's Sexy Robots series were painted and published in Japan depicting the actual organic human form with lifelike muscular metallic skins and later "the Gynoids" book followed that was used by or influenced movie makers including George Lucas and other creatives. Sorayama never considered these organic robots to be real part of nature but always unnatural product of the human mind, a fantasy existing in the mind even when realized in actual form.

Edward Fredkin argues that "artificial intelligence is the next stage in evolution", an idea first proposed by Samuel Butler's "Darwin among the Machines" (1863), and expanded upon by George Dyson in his book of the same name in 1998.

Existential Risk

The development of full artificial intelligence could spell the end of the human race. Once humans develop artificial intelligence, it will take off on its own and redesign itself at an ever-increasing rate. Humans, who are limited by slow biological evolution, couldn't compete and would be superseded.

—Stephen Hawking

A common concern about the development of artificial intelligence is the potential threat it could pose to mankind. This concern has recently gained attention after mentions by celebrities including Stephen Hawking, Bill Gates, and Elon Musk. A group of prominent tech titans including Peter Thiel, Amazon Web Services and Musk have committed $1billion to OpenAI a nonprofit company aimed at championing responsible AI development. The opinion of experts within the field of artificial intelligence is mixed, with sizable fractions both concerned and unconcerned by risk from eventual superhumanly-capable AI.

In his book *Superintelligence*, Nick Bostrom provides an argument that artificial intelligence will pose a threat to mankind. He argues that sufficiently intelligent AI, if it chooses actions based on achieving some goal, will exhibit convergent behavior such as acquiring resources or protecting itself from being shut down. If this AI's goals do not reflect humanity's - one example is an AI told to compute as many digits of pi as possible - it might harm humanity in order to acquire more resources or prevent itself from being shut down, ultimately to better achieve its goal.

For this danger to be realized, the hypothetical AI would have to overpower or out-think all of humanity, which a minority of experts argue is a possibility far enough in the future to not be worth researching. Other counterarguments revolve around humans being either intrinsically or convergently valuable from the perspective of an artificial intelligence.

Concern over risk from artificial intelligence has led to some high-profile donations and investments. In January 2015, Elon Musk donated ten million dollars to the Future of Life Institute to fund research on understanding AI decision making. The goal of the institute is to "grow wisdom with which we manage" the growing power of technology. Musk also funds companies developing artificial intelligence such as Google DeepMind and Vicarious to "just keep an eye on what's going on with artificial intelligence. I think there is potentially a dangerous outcome there."

Development of militarized artificial intelligence is a related concern. Currently, 50+ countries are researching battlefield robots, including the United States, China, Russia, and the United Kingdom. Many people concerned about risk from superintelligent AI also want to limit the use of artificial soldiers.

Moral Decision-making

To keep AI ethical, some have suggested teaching new technologies equipped with AI, such as driver-less cars, to render moral decisions on their own. Others argued that these technologies could learn to act ethically the way children do—by interacting with adults, in particular, with ethicists. Still others suggest these smart technologies can determine the moral preferences of those who use them (just the way one learns about consumer preferences) and then be programmed to heed these preferences.

In Fiction

The implications of artificial intelligence have been a persistent theme in science fiction. Early stories typically revolved around intelligent robots. The word "robot" itself was coined by Karel Čapek in his 1921 play *R.U.R.*, the title standing for "Rossum's Universal Robots". Later, the SF writer Isaac Asimov developed the Three Laws of Robotics which he subsequently explored in a long series of robot stories. These laws have since gained some traction in genuine AI research.

Other influential fictional intelligences include HAL, the computer in charge of the spaceship in *2001: A Space Odyssey*, released as both a film and a book in 1968 and written by Arthur C. Clarke.

AI has since become firmly rooted in popular culture and is in many films, such as *The Terminator* (1984) and *A.I. Artificial Intelligence* (2001).

Computational Neuroscience

Computational neuroscience (also theoretical neuroscience) is the study of brain function in terms of the information processing properties of the structures that make up the nervous system. It is an interdisciplinary science that links the diverse fields of neuroscience, cognitive science, and psychology with electrical engineering, computer science, mathematics, and physics.

Computational neuroscience is distinct from psychological connectionism and from learning theories of disciplines such as machine learning, neural networks, and computational learning theory in that it emphasizes descriptions of functional and biologically realistic neurons (and neural systems) and their physiology and dynamics. These models capture the essential features of the biological system at multiple spatial-temporal scales, from membrane currents, proteins, and chemical coupling to network oscillations, columnar and topographic architecture, and learning and memory.

These computational models are used to frame hypotheses that can be directly tested by biological or psychological experiments.

History

The term "computational neuroscience" was introduced by Eric L. Schwartz, who organized a conference, held in 1985 in Carmel, California, at the request of the Systems Development Foundation to provide a summary of the current status of a field which until that point was referred to by a variety of names, such as neural modeling, brain theory and neural networks. The proceedings of this definitional meeting were published in 1990 as the book *Computational Neuroscience*. The first open international meeting focused on Computational Neuroscience was organized by James M. Bower and John Miller in San Francisco, California in 1989 and has continued each year since as the annual CNS meeting The first graduate educational program in computational neuroscience was organized as the Computational and Neural Systems Ph.D. program at the California Institute of Technology in 1985.

The early historical roots of the field can be traced to the work of people such as Louis Lapicque, Hodgkin & Huxley, Hubel & Wiesel, and David Marr, to name a few. Lapicque introduced the integrate and fire model of the neuron in a seminal article published in 1907; this model is still one of the most popular models in computational neuroscience for both cellular and neural networks studies, as well as in mathematical neuroscience because of its simplicity. About 40 years later, Hodgkin & Huxley de-veloped the voltage clamp and created the first biophysical model of the action potential. Hubel & Wiesel discovered that neurons in the primary visual cortex, the first cortical area to process infor-mation coming from the retina, have oriented receptive fields and are organized in columns. David Marr's work focused on the interactions between neurons, suggesting computational approaches to the study of how functional groups of neurons within the hippocampus and neocortex interact, store, process, and transmit information. Computational modeling of biophysically realistic neu-rons and dendrites began with the work of Wilfrid Rall, with the first multicompartmental model using cable theory.

Major Topics

Research in computational neuroscience can be roughly categorized into several lines of inquiry. Most computational neuroscientists collaborate closely with experimentalists in analyzing novel data and synthesizing new models of biological phenomena.

Single-neuron Modeling

Even single neurons have complex biophysical characteristics and can perform computations (e.g.). Hodgkin and Huxley's original model only employed two voltage-sensitive currents (Voltage sensitive ion channels are glycoprotein molecules which extend through the lipid bilayer, allowing ions to traverse under certain conditions through the axolemma), the fast-acting sodium and the inward-rectifying potassium. Though successful in predicting the timing and qualitative features of the action potential, it nevertheless failed to predict a number of important features such as adaptation and shunting. Scientists now believe that there are a wide variety of voltage-sensitive currents, and the implications of the differing dynamics, modulations, and sensitivity of these currents is an important topic of computational neuroscience.

The computational functions of complex dendrites are also under intense investigation. There is a large body of literature regarding how different currents interact with geometric properties of neurons.

Some models are also tracking biochemical pathways at very small scales such as spines or synaptic clefts.

There are many software packages, such as GENESIS and NEURON, that allow rapid and systematic *in silico* modeling of realistic neurons. Blue Brain, a project founded by Henry Markram from the École Polytechnique Fédérale de Lausanne, aims to construct a biophysically detailed simulation of a cortical column on the Blue Gene supercomputer.

A problem in the field is that detailed neuron descriptions are computationally expensive and this can handicap the pursuit of realistic network investigations, where many neurons need to be simulated. So, researchers that study large neural circuits typically represent each neuron and synapse simply, ignoring much of the biological detail. This is unfortunate as there is evidence that the richness of biophysical properties on the single neuron scale can supply mechanisms that serve as the building blocks for network dynamics. Hence there is a drive to produce simplified neuron models that can retain significant biological fidelity at a low computational overhead. Algorithms have been developed to produce faithful, faster running, simplified surrogate neuron models from computationally expensive, detailed neuron models.

Development, Axonal Patterning, and Guidance

How do axons and dendrites form during development? How do axons know where to target and how to reach these targets? How do neurons migrate to the proper position in the central and peripheral systems? How do synapses form? We know from molecular biology that distinct parts of the nervous system release distinct chemical cues, from growth factors to hormones that modulate and influence the growth and development of functional connections between neurons.

Theoretical investigations into the formation and patterning of synaptic connection and morphology are still nascent. One hypothesis that has recently garnered some attention is the *minimal wiring hypothesis*, which postulates that the formation of axons and dendrites effectively minimizes resource allocation while maintaining maximal information storage.

Sensory Processing

Early models of sensory processing understood within a theoretical framework are credited to Horace Barlow. Somewhat similar to the minimal wiring hypothesis described in the preceding section, Barlow understood the processing of the early sensory systems to be a form of efficient coding, where the neurons encoded information which minimized the number of spikes. Experimental and computational work have since supported this hypothesis in one form or another.

Current research in sensory processing is divided among a biophysical modelling of different subsystems and a more theoretical modelling of perception. Current models of perception have suggested that the brain performs some form of Bayesian inference and integration of different sensory information in generating our perception of the physical world.

Memory and Synaptic Plasticity

Earlier models of memory are primarily based on the postulates of Hebbian learning. Biologically relevant models such as Hopfield net have been developed to address the properties of associative, rather than content-addressable, style of memory that occur in biological systems. These attempts are primarily focusing on the formation of medium- and long-term memory, localizing in the hippocampus. Models of working memory, relying on theories of network oscillations and persistent activity, have been built to capture some features of the prefrontal cortex in context-related memory.

One of the major problems in neurophysiological memory is how it is maintained and changed through multiple time scales. Unstable synapses are easy to train but also prone to stochastic disruption. Stable synapses forget less easily, but they are also harder to consolidate. One recent computational hypothesis involves cascades of plasticity that allow synapses to function at multiple time scales. Stereochemically detailed models of the acetylcholine receptor-based synapse with the Monte Carlo method, working at the time scale of microseconds, have been built. It is likely that computational tools will contribute greatly to our understanding of how synapses function and change in relation to external stimulus in the coming decades.

Behaviors of Networks

Biological neurons are connected to each other in a complex, recurrent fashion. These connections are, unlike most artificial neural networks, sparse and usually specific. It is not known how information is transmitted through such sparsely connected networks. It is also unknown what the computational functions of these specific connectivity patterns are, if any.

The interactions of neurons in a small network can be often reduced to simple models such as the Ising model. The statistical mechanics of such simple systems are well-characterized theoretically. There has been some recent evidence that suggests that dynamics of arbitrary neuronal networks can be reduced to pairwise interactions. It is not known, however, whether such descriptive dynamics impart any important computational function. With the emergence of two-photon microscopy and calcium imaging, we now have powerful experimental methods with which to test the new theories regarding neuronal networks.

In some cases the complex interactions between *inhibitory* and *excitatory* neurons can be simplified using mean field theory, which gives rise to the population model of neural networks. While many neurotheorists prefer such models with reduced complexity, others argue that uncovering structural functional relations depends on including as much neuronal and network structure as possible. Models of this type are typically built in large simulation platforms like GENESIS or NEURON. There have been some attempts to provide unified methods that bridge and integrate these levels of complexity.

Cognition, Discrimination, and Learning

Computational modeling of higher cognitive functions has only recently begun. Experimental data comes primarily from single-unit recording in primates. The frontal lobe and parietal lobe function as integrators of information from multiple sensory modalities. There are some tentative ideas regarding how simple mutually inhibitory functional circuits in these areas may carry out biologically relevant computation.

The brain seems to be able to discriminate and adapt particularly well in certain contexts. For instance, human beings seem to have an enormous capacity for memorizing and recognizing faces. One of the key goals of computational neuroscience is to dissect how biological systems carry out these complex computations efficiently and potentially replicate these processes in building intelligent machines.

The brain's large-scale organizational principles are illuminated by many fields, including biology, psychology, and clinical practice. Integrative neuroscience attempts to consolidate these observations through unified descriptive models and databases of behavioral measures and recordings. These are the bases for some quantitative modeling of large-scale brain activity.

The Computational Representational Understanding of Mind (CRUM) is another attempt at modeling human cognition through simulated processes like acquired rule-based systems in decision making and the manipulation of visual representations in decision making.

Consciousness

One of the ultimate goals of psychology/neuroscience is to be able to explain the everyday experience of conscious life. Francis Crick and Christof Koch made some attempts to formulate a consistent framework for future work in neural correlates of consciousness (NCC), though much of the work in this field remains speculative.

Computational Clinical Neuroscience

It is a field that brings together experts in neuroscience, neurology, psychiatry, decision sciences and computational modeling to quantitatively define and investigate problems in neurological and psychiatric diseases, and to train scientists and clinicians that wish to apply these models to diagnosis and treatment.

Augmented Reality

Samsung SARI AR SDK markerless tracker used in the *AR EdiBear* game (Android OS).

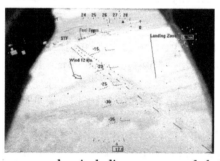

AR Tower Defense game on the Nokia N95 smartphone (Symbian OS) uses fiducial markers.

NASA X38 display showing video map overlays including runways and obstacles during flight test in 2000.

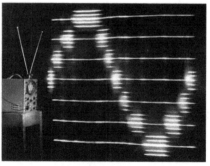

Early example of AR: Overlaying electromagnetic radio waves onto visual reality. Sequential Wave Imprinting Machine imprints visual images onto the human eye's retina or photographic film.

Augmented reality (AR) is a live direct or indirect view of a physical, real-world environment whose elements are *augmented* (or supplemented) by computer-generated sensory input such as sound, video, graphics or GPS data. It is related to a more general concept called mediated reality, in which a view of reality is modified (possibly even diminished rather than augmented) by a computer. As a result, the technology functions by enhancing one's current perception of reality. By contrast, virtual reality replaces the real world with a simulated one. Augmentation is conventionally in real-time and in semantic context with environmental elements, such as sports scores on TV during a match. With the help of advanced AR technology (e.g. adding computer vision and object recognition) the information about the surrounding real world of the user becomes interactive and digitally manipulable. Information about the environment and its objects is overlaid on the real world. This information can be virtual or real, e.g. seeing other real sensed or measured information such as electromagnetic radio waves overlaid in exact alignment with where they actually are in space.

Technology

Hardware

Hardware components for augmented reality are: processor, display, sensors and input devices. Modern mobile computing devices like smartphones and tablet computers contain these elements which often include a camera and MEMS sensors such as accelerometer, GPS, and solid state compass, making them suitable AR platforms.

Display

Various technologies are used in Augmented Reality rendering including optical projection systems, monitors, hand held devices, and display systems worn on the human body.

Head-mounted

A head-mounted display (HMD) is a display device paired to a headset such as a harness or helmet. HMDs place images of both the physical world and virtual objects over the user's field of view. Modern HMDs often employ sensors for six degrees of freedom monitoring that allow the system to align virtual information to the physical world and adjust accordingly with the user's head movements. HMDs can provide users immersive, mobile and collaborative AR experiences.

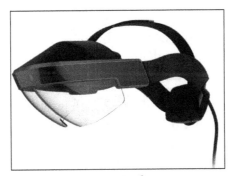

Meta 2 Headset

In January 2015, Meta launched a $23 million project led by Horizons Ventures, Tim Draper, Alexis Ohanian, BOE Optoelectronics and Garry Tan. On February 17, 2016, Meta announced their second-generation product at TED, Meta 2. The Meta 2 head-mounted display headset uses a sensory array for hand interactions and positional tracking, visual field view of 90 degrees (diagonal), and resolution display of 2560 x 1440 (20 pixels per degree), which is considered the largest field view (FOV) currently available.

Eyeglasses

AR displays can be rendered on devices resembling eyeglasses. Versions include eyewear that employ cameras to intercept the real world view and re-display its augmented view through the eye pieces and devices in which the AR imagery is projected through or reflected off the surfaces of the eyewear lens pieces.

HUD

Near eye augmented reality devices can be used as portable head-up displays as they can show data, information, and images while the user views the real world. Many definitions of augmented reality only define it as overlaying the information. This is basically what a head-up display does; however, practically speaking, augmented reality is expected to include tracking between the superimposed information, data, and images and some portion of the real world.

Microsoft HoloLens

CrowdOptic, an existing app for smartphones, applies algorithms and triangulation techniques to photo metadata including GPS position, compass heading, and a time stamp to arrive at a relative significance value for photo objects. CrowdOptic technology can be used by Google Glass users to learn where to look at a given point in time.

In January 2015, Microsoft introduced HoloLens, which is an independent smartglasses unit. Brian Blau, research director of consumer technology and markets at Gartner, said that "Out of all the head-mounted displays that I've tried in the past couple of decades, the HoloLens was the best in its class.". First impressions and opinions have been generally that HoloLens is a superior device to the Google Glass, and manages to do several things "right" in which Glass failed.

Contact Lenses

Contact lenses that display AR imaging are in development. These bionic contact lenses might contain the elements for display embedded into the lens including integrated circuitry, LEDs and an antenna for wireless communication. The first contact lens display was reported in 1999 and subsequently, 11 years later in 2010/2011 Another version of contact lenses, in development for the U.S. Military, is designed to function with AR spectacles, allowing soldiers to focus on close-to-the-eye AR images on the spectacles and distant real world objects at the same time. The futuristic short film *Sight* features contact lens-like augmented reality devices.

Virtual Retinal Display

A virtual retinal display (VRD) is a personal display device under development at the University of Washington's Human Interface Technology Laboratory. With this technology, a display is scanned directly onto the retina of a viewer's eye. The viewer sees what appears to be a conventional display floating in space in front of them.

EyeTap

The EyeTap (also known as Generation-2 Glass) captures rays of light that would otherwise pass through the center of a lens of an eye of the wearer, and substitutes synthetic computer-controlled light for each ray of real light. The Generation-4 Glass (Laser EyeTap) is similar to the VRD (i.e. it uses a computer controlled laser light source) except that it also has infinite depth of focus and causes the eye itself to, in effect, function as both a camera and a display, by way of exact alignment with the eye, and resynthesis (in laser light) of rays of light entering the eye.

Handheld

Handheld displays employ a small display that fits in a user's hand. All handheld AR solutions to date opt for video see-through. Initially handheld AR employed fiducial markers, and later GPS units and MEMS sensors such as digital compasses and six degrees of freedom accelerometer–gyroscope. Today SLAM markerless trackers such as PTAM are starting to come into use. Handheld display AR promises to be the first commercial success for AR technologies. The two main advantages of handheld AR is the portable nature of handheld devices and ubiquitous nature of camera phones. The disadvantages are the physical constraints of the user having to hold the handheld device out in front of them at all times as well as distorting effect of classically wide-angled mobile phone cameras when compared to the real world as viewed through the eye.

Spatial

Spatial Augmented Reality (SAR) augments real world objects and scenes without the use of special displays such as monitors, head mounted displays or hand-held devices. SAR makes use of digital projectors to display graphical information onto physical objects. The key difference in SAR is that the display is separated from the users of the system. Because the displays are not associated with each user, SAR scales naturally up to groups of users, thus allowing for collocated collaboration between users.

Examples include shader lamps, mobile projectors, virtual tables, and smart projectors. Shader lamps mimic and augment reality by projecting imagery onto neutral objects, providing the opportunity to enhance the object's appearance with materials of a simple unit- a projector, camera, and sensor.

Other applications include table and wall projections. One innovation, the Extended Virtual Table, separates the virtual from the real by including beam-splitter mirrors attached to the ceiling at an adjustable angle. Virtual showcases, which employ beam-splitter mirrors together with multiple graphics displays, provide an interactive means of simultaneously engaging with the virtual and the real. Many more implementations and configurations make spatial augmented reality display an increasingly attractive interactive alternative.

A SAR system can display on any number of surfaces of an indoor setting at once. SAR supports both a graphical visualisation and passive haptic sensation for the end users. Users are able to touch physical objects in a process that provides passive haptic sensation.

Tracking

Modern mobile augmented reality systems use one or more of the following tracking technologies: digital cameras and/or other optical sensors, accelerometers, GPS, gyroscopes, solid state compasses, RFID and wireless sensors. These technologies offer varying levels of accuracy and precision. Most important is the position and orientation of the user's head. Tracking the user's hand(s) or a handheld input device can provide a 6DOF interaction technique.

Input Devices

Techniques include speech recognition systems that translate a user's spoken words into computer instructions and gesture recognition systems that can interpret a user's body movements by visual detection or from sensors embedded in a peripheral device such as a wand, stylus, pointer, glove or other body wear. Some of the products which are trying to serve as a controller of AR Headsets include Wave by Seebright Inc. and Nimble by Intugine Technologies.

Computer

The computer analyzes the sensed visual and other data to synthesize and position augmentations.

Software and Algorithms

A key measure of AR systems is how realistically they integrate augmentations with the real world. The software must derive real world coordinates, independent from the camera, from camera images. That process is called image registration which uses different methods of computer vision, mostly related to video tracking. Many computer vision methods of augmented reality are inherited from visual odometry. Usually those methods consist of two parts.

First detect interest points, or fiducial markers, or optical flow in the camera images. First stage can use feature detection methods like corner detection, blob detection, edge detection or thresholding and/or other image processing methods. The second stage restores a real world coordinate system from the data obtained in the first stage. Some methods assume objects with known geometry (or fiducial markers) present in the scene. In some of those cases the scene 3D structure should be precalculated beforehand. If part of the scene is unknown simultaneous localization and mapping (SLAM) can map relative positions. If no information about scene geometry is available, structure from motion methods like bundle adjustment are used. Mathematical methods used in the second stage include projective (epipolar) geometry, geometric algebra, rotation representation with exponential map, kalman and particle filters, nonlinear optimization, robust statistics.

Augmented Reality Markup Language (ARML) is a data standard developed within the Open Geospatial Consortium (OGC), which consists of an XML grammar to describe the location and appearance of virtual objects in the scene, as well as ECMAScript bindings to allow dynamic access to properties of virtual objects.

To enable rapid development of Augmented Reality Application, some software development kits (SDK) have emerged. A few SDK such as CloudRidAR leverage cloud computing for performance improvement. Some of the well known AR SDKs are offered by Vuforia, ARToolKit, Catchoom CraftAR, Mobinett AR, Wikitude, Blippar Layar, and Meta.

Applications

Augmented reality has many applications. First used for military, industrial, and medical applications, it has also been applied to commercial and entertainment areas.

Literature

In 2011, there were works using AR poetry made by ni_ka from the Sekai Camera in Japan, Tokyo. The rose of these works come from Paul Celan, "Die Niemandsrose", and express the mourning of 3.11, 2011 Tōhoku earthquake and tsunami. In these works, there is a rose on the top of the Tokyo Tower, and touching Kitty float poetry words, and we can write the reply of this insteration. Pokémon Go make people know Augmented Reality, however ni_ka is a pioneer of AR literature.

AR Poetry

Archaeology

AR can be used to aid archaeological research, by augmenting archaeological features onto the modern landscape, enabling archaeologists to formulate conclusions about site placement and configuration.

Another application given to AR in this field is the possibility for users to rebuild ruins, buildings, landscapes or even ancient characters as they formerly existed.

Architecture

AR can aid in visualizing building projects. Computer-generated images of a structure can be superimposed into a real life local view of a property before the physical building is constructed there; this was demonstrated publicly by Trimble Navigation in 2004. AR can also be employed within an architect's work space, rendering into their view animated 3D visualizations of their 2D drawings. Architecture sight-seeing can be enhanced with AR applications allowing users viewing a building's exterior to virtually see through its walls, viewing its interior objects and layout.

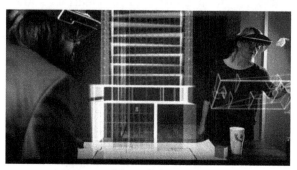

Meta 2 used for collaborative design.

Visual Art

AR technology has helped disabled individuals create visual art by using eye tracking to translate a user's eye movements into drawings on a screen. An item such as a commemorative coin can be designed so that when scanned by an AR-enabled device it displays additional objects and layers of information that were not visible in a real world view of it. In 2013, L'Oreal used CrowdOptic technology to create an augmented reality at the seventh annual Luminato Festival in Toronto, Canada.

iGreet's augmented reality greeting card suddenly becomes alive and hidden digital content appears when being viewed through the app.

AR in visual art opens the possibility of multidimensional experiences and interpretations of reality. Augmenting people, objects, and landscapes is becoming an art form in itself. In 2011, artist

Amir Bardaran's *Frenchising the Mona Lisa* infiltrates Da Vinci's painting using an AR mobile application called Junaio. Aim a Junaio loaded smartphone camera at any image of the Mona Lisa and watch as Leonardo's subject places a scarf made of a French flag around her head. The AR app allows the user to train his or her smartphone on Da Vinci's *Mona Lisa* and watch the mysterious Italian lady loosen her hair and wrap a French flag around her in the form a (currently banned) Islamic *hijab*.

Greeting Cards

AR technology has been used in conjunction with greeting cards. They can be implemented with digital content which users are able to discover by viewing the illustrations with certain mobile applications or devices using augmented reality technology. The digital content could be 2D & 3D animations, standard video and 3D objects with which the users can interact.

In 2015, the Bulgarian startup iGreet developed its own AR technology and used it to make the first premade "live" greeting card. It looks like traditional paper card, but contains hidden digital content which only appears when users scan the greeting card with the iGreet app.

Commerce

AR can enhance product previews such as allowing a customer to view what's inside a product's packaging without opening it. AR can also be used as an aid in selecting products from a catalog or through a kiosk. Scanned images of products can activate views of additional content such as customization options and additional images of the product in its use. AR is used to integrate print and video marketing. Printed marketing material can be designed with certain "trigger" images that, when scanned by an AR enabled device using image recognition, activate a video version of the promotional material. A major difference between Augmented Reality and straight forward image recognition is that you can overlay multiple media at the same time in the view screen, such as social media share buttons, in-page video even audio and 3D objects. Traditional print only publications are using Augmented Reality to connect many different types of media.

View Description image 1

Construction

With the continual improvements to GPS accuracy, businesses are able to use augmented reality to visualize georeferenced models of construction sites, underground structures, cables and pipes using mobile devices. Augmented reality is applied to present new projects, to solve on-site construction challenges, and to enhance promotional materials. Examples include the Daqri Smart Helmet, an Android-powered hard hat used to create augmented reality for the industrial worker, including visual instructions, real time alerts, and 3D mapping.

Following the Christchurch earthquake, the University of Canterbury released, CityViewAR, which enabled city planners and engineers to visualize buildings that were destroyed in the earthquake. Not only did this provide planners with tools to reference the previous cityscape, but it also served as a reminder to the magnitude of the devastation caused, as entire buildings were demolished.

Education

App iSkull, an augmented human skull for education (iOS OS).

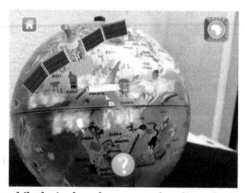
App iWow, a mobile device based augmented reality enhanced world globe.

Augmented reality applications can complement a standard curriculum. Text, graphics, video and audio can be superimposed into a student's real time environment. Textbooks, flashcards and other educational reading material can contain embedded "markers" that, when scanned by an AR device, produce supplementary information to the student rendered in a multimedia format. Students can participate interactively with computer generated simulations of historical events, exploring and learning details of each significant area of the event site. On higher education, there are some applications that can be used. For instance, Construct3D, a Studierstube system, allows students to learn mechanical engineering concepts, math or geometry. This is an active learning process in which students learn to learn with technology. AR can aid students in understanding chemistry by allowing them to visualize the spatial structure of a molecule and interact with a virtual model of it that appears, in a camera image, positioned at a marker held in their hand. It can also enable students of physiology to visualize different systems of the human body in three dimensions. Augmented reality technology also permits learning via remote collaboration, in which students and instructors not at the same physical location can share a common virtual learning environment populated by virtual objects and learning materials and interact with another within that setting.

This resource could also be of advantage in Primary School. Children can learn through experiences, and visuals can be used to help them learn. For instance, they can learn new knowledge about astronomy, which can be difficult to understand, and children might better understand the solar system when using AR devices and being able to see it in 3D. Further, learners could change the illustrations in their science books by using this resource. For teaching anatomy, teachers could visualize bones and organs using augmented reality to display them on the body of a person.

Mobile apps using augmented reality are emerging in the classroom. The mix of real life and virtual reality displayed by the apps using the mobile phone's camera allows information to be manipulated and seen like never before. Many such apps have been designed to create a highly engaging environment and transform the learning experience. Examples of the mobile apps, that leverage augmented reality to aid learning, include SkyView for studying astronomy and AR Circuits for building simple electric circuits.

Emergency management / Search and Rescue

Augmented reality systems are used in public safety situations - from super storms to suspects at large. Two interesting articles from *Emergency Management* magazine discuss the power of the technology for emergency management. The first is "Augmented Reality--Emerging Technology for Emergency Management" by Gerald Baron. Per Adam Crowe: "Technologies like augmented reality (ex: Google Glass) and the growing expectation of the public will continue to force professional emergency managers to radically shift when, where, and how technology is deployed before, during, and after disasters."

LandForm+ is a geographic augmented reality system used for search and rescue, and emergency management.

Another example, a search aircraft is looking for a lost hiker in rugged mountain terrain. Augmented reality systems provide aerial camera operators with a geographic awareness of forest road names and locations blended with the camera video. As a result, the camera operator is better able to search for the hiker knowing the geographic context of the camera image. Once found, the operator can more efficiently direct rescuers to the hiker's location.

Everyday

Since the 1970s and early 1980s, Steve Mann has been developing technologies meant for everyday use i.e. "horizontal" across all applications rather than a specific "vertical" market. Examples include Mann's "EyeTap Digital Eye Glass", a general-purpose seeing aid that does dynamic-range management (HDR vision) and overlays, underlays, simultaneous augmentation and diminishment (e.g. diminishing the electric arc while looking at a welding torch).

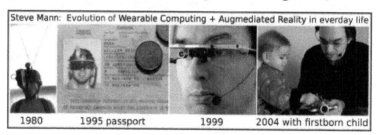

30 years of Augmediated Reality in everyday life.

Video Games

Augmented reality allows video game players to experience digital game play in a real world environment. Companies and platforms like Niantic and LyteShot emerged as augmented reality gaming creators.

Lyteshot in action.

Merchlar's mobile game Get On Target uses a trigger image as fiducial marker.

Industrial Design

AR can help industrial designers experience a product's design and operation before completion. Volkswagen uses AR for comparing calculated and actual crash test imagery. AR can be used to visualize and modify a car body structure and engine layout. AR can also be used to compare digital mock-ups with physical mock-ups for finding discrepancies between them.

Medical

Since 2005, a device that films subcutaneous veins, processes and projects the image of the veins onto the skin has been used to locate veins. This device is called VeinViewer.

Augmented Reality can provide the surgeon with information, which are otherwise hidden, such as showing the heartbeat rate, the blood pressure, the state of the patient's organ, etc. AR can be used to let a doctor look inside a patient by combining one source of images such as an X-ray with another such as video.

Examples include a virtual X-ray view based on prior tomography or on real time images from ultrasound and confocal microscopy probes, visualizing the position of a tumor in the video of an endoscope, or radiation exposure risks from X-ray imaging devices. AR can enhance viewing a fetus inside a mother's womb. It has been also used for cockroach phobia treatment. Also, patients wearing augmented reality glasses can be reminded to take medications.

Beauty

In 2014 the company L'Oreal Paris started developing a smartphone and tablet application called "Makeup Genius", which lets users try out make-up and beauty styles utilizing the front-facing camera of the endpoint and its display.

Spatial Immersion and Interaction

Augmented reality applications, running on handheld devices utilized as virtual reality headsets, can also digitalize human presence in space and provide a computer generated model of them, in a virtual space where they can interact and perform various actions. Such capabilities are demonstrated by "project Anywhere" developed by a post graduate student at ETH Zurich, which was dubbed as an "out-of-body experience".

Military

Rockwell WorldView Console showing space surveillance telescope video map overlay of satellite flight tracks from a 1993 paper.

In combat, AR can serve as a networked communication system that renders useful battlefield data onto a soldier's goggles in real time. From the soldier's viewpoint, people and various objects can be marked with special indicators to warn of potential dangers. Virtual maps and 360° view camera imaging can also be rendered to aid a soldier's navigation and battlefield perspective, and this can be transmitted to military leaders at a remote command center.

An interesting application of AR occurred when Rockwell International created video map overlays of satellite and orbital debris tracks to aid in space observations at Air Force Maui Optical System. In their 1993 paper "Debris Correlation Using the Rockwell WorldView System" the authors describe the use of map overlays applied to video from space surveillance telescopes. The map overlays indicated the trajectories of various objects in geographic coordinates. This allowed telescope operators to identify satellites, and also to identify - and catalog - potentially dangerous space debris.

Screen capture of SmartCam3D in picture in picture (PIP) mode. This helps sensor operators maintain a broader situation awareness than a telescopic camera "soda-straw". It was shown to essentially double the speed at which points can be located on the ground.

Starting in 2003 the US Army integrated the SmartCam3D augmented reality system into the Shadow Unmanned Aerial System to aid sensor operators using telescopic cameras to locate people or points of interest. The system combined both fixed geographic information including street names, points of interest, airports and railroads with live video from the camera system. The system offered "picture in picture" mode that allows the system to show a synthetic view of the area surrounding the camera's field of view. This helps solve a problem in which the field of view is so narrow that it excludes important context, as if "looking through a soda straw". The system displays real-time friend/foe/neutral location markers blended with live video, providing the operator with improved situation awareness.

Researchers at USAF Research Lab (Calhoun, Draper et al.) found an approximately two-fold increase in the speed at which UAV sensor operators found points of interest using this technology. This ability to maintain geographic awareness quantitatively enhances mission efficiency. The system is in use on the US Army RQ-7 Shadow and the MQ-1C Gray Eagle Unmanned Aerial Systems.

Navigation

LandForm video map overlay marking runways, road, and buildings during 1999 helicopter flight test.

Augmented reality map on iPhone.

AR can augment the effectiveness of navigation devices. Information can be displayed on an automobile's windshield indicating destination directions and meter, weather, terrain, road conditions and traffic information as well as alerts to potential hazards in their path. Aboard maritime vessels, AR can allow bridge watch-standers to continuously monitor important information such as a ship's heading and speed while moving throughout the bridge or performing other tasks.

The NASA X-38 was flown using a Hybrid Synthetic Vision system that overlaid map data on video to provide enhanced navigation for the spacecraft during flight tests from 1998 to 2002. It used the LandForm software and was useful for times of limited visibility, including an instance when the video camera window frosted over leaving astronauts to rely on the map overlays. The LandForm software was also test flown at the Army Yuma Proving Ground in 1999. In the photo at right one can see the map markers indicating runways, air traffic control tower, taxiways, and hangars overlaid on the video.

Office Workplace

AR can help facilitate collaboration among distributed team members in a work force via conferences with real and virtual participants. AR tasks can include brainstorming and discussion meetings utilizing common visualization via touch screen tables, interactive digital whiteboards, shared design spaces, and distributed control rooms.

Sports and Entertainment

AR has become common in sports telecasting. Sports and entertainment venues are provided with see-through and overlay augmentation through tracked camera feeds for enhanced viewing by the audience. Examples include the yellow "first down" line seen in television broadcasts of American football games showing the line the offensive team must cross to receive a first down. AR is also used in association with football and other sporting events to show commercial advertisements overlaid onto the view of the playing area. Sections of rugby fields and cricket pitches also display sponsored images. Swimming telecasts often add a line across the lanes to indicate the position of the current record holder as a race proceeds to allow viewers to compare the current race to the best performance. Other examples include hockey puck tracking and annotations of racing car performance and snooker ball trajectories.

AR can enhance concert and theater performances. For example, artists can allow listeners to augment their listening experience by adding their performance to that of other bands/groups of users.

The gaming industry has benefited a lot from the development of this technology. A number of games have been developed for prepared indoor environments. Early AR games also include AR air hockey, collaborative combat against virtual enemies, and an AR-enhanced pool games. A significant number of games incorporate AR in them and the introduction of the smartphone has made a bigger impact.

Task Support

Complex tasks such as assembly, maintenance, and surgery can be simplified by inserting additional information into the field of view. For example, labels can be displayed on parts of a system to clarify operating instructions for a mechanic who is performing maintenance on the system. Assembly lines gain many benefits from the usage of AR. In addition to Boeing, BMW and Volkswagen are known for incorporating this technology in their assembly line to improve their manufacturing and assembly processes. Big machines are difficult to maintain because of the multiple layers or structures they have. With the use of AR the workers can complete their job in a much easier way because AR permits them to look through the machine as if it was with x-ray, pointing them to the problem right away.

Television

Weather visualizations were the first application of augmented reality to television. It has now become common in weathercasting to display full motion video of images captured in real-time from multiple cameras and other imaging devices. Coupled with 3D graphics symbols and mapped to a common virtual geo-space model, these animated visualizations constitute the first true application of AR to TV.

Augmented reality has also become common in sports telecasting. Sports and entertainment venues are provided with see-through and overlay augmentation through tracked camera feeds for enhanced viewing by the audience. Examples include the yellow "first down" line seen in television broadcasts of American football games showing the line the offensive team must cross to receive a first down. AR is also used in association with football and other sporting events to show commercial advertisements overlaid onto the view of the playing area. Sections of rugby fields and cricket pitches also display sponsored images. Swimming telecasts often add a line across the lanes to indicate the position of the current record holder as a race proceeds to allow viewers to compare the current race to the best performance. Other examples include hockey puck tracking and annotations of racing car performance and snooker ball trajectories.

Augmented reality is starting to allow Next Generation TV viewers to interact with the programs they are watching. They can place objects into an existing program and interact with these objects, such as moving them around. Avatars of real persons in real time who are also watching the same program.

Tourism and Sightseeing

Augmented reality applications can enhance a user's experience when traveling by providing real time informational displays regarding a location and its features, including comments made by previous visitors of the site. AR applications allow tourists to experience simulations of historical events, places and objects by rendering them into their current view of a landscape. AR applications can also present location information by audio, announcing features of interest at a particular site as they become visible to the user.

Translation

AR systems can interpret foreign text on signs and menus and, in a user's augmented view, re-display the text in the user's language. Spoken words of a foreign language can be translated and displayed in a user's view as printed subtitles.

Privacy Concerns

The concept of modern augmented reality depends on the ability of the device to record and analyze the environment in real time. Because of this, there are potential legal concerns over privacy. While the First Amendment to the United States Constitution allows for such recording in the name of public interest, the constant recording of an AR device makes it difficult to do so without also recording outside of the public domain. Legal complications would be found in areas where a right to certain amount of privacy is expected or where copyrighted media are displayed. In terms of individual privacy, there exists the ease of access to information that one should not readily possess about a given person. This is accomplished through facial recognition technology. Assuming that AR automatically passes information about persons that the user sees, there could be anything seen from social media, criminal record, and marital status.

Notable Researchers

- Ivan Sutherland invented the first AR head-mounted display at Harvard University.

- Steven Feiner, Professor at Columbia University, is a leading pioneer of augmented reality, and author of the first paper on an AR system prototype, KARMA (the Knowledge-based Augmented Reality Maintenance Assistant), along with Blair MacIntyre and Doree Seligmann. He is also an advisor to Meta.

- Meron Gribetz, conceptualized the Meta mounted display headset. He is also founder and CEO of Meta, a Silicon Valley company that is known for producing innovative Augmented Reality products.

- S. Ravela, B. Draper, J. Lim and A. Hanson develop marker/fixture-less augmented reality system with computer vision in 1994. They augmented an engine block observed from a single video camera with annotations for repair. They use model-based pose estimation, aspect graphs and visual feature tracking to dynamically register model with the observed video.

- Steve Mann formulated an earlier concept of Mediated reality in the 1970s and 1980s, using cameras, processors, and display systems to modify visual reality to help people see better (dynamic range management), building computerized welding helmets, as well as "Augmediated Reality" vision systems for use in everyday life. He is also an adviser to Meta.

- Louis Rosenberg developed one of the first known AR systems, called Virtual Fixtures, while working at the U.S. Air Force Armstrong Labs in 1991, and published the first study of how an AR system can enhance human performance. Rosenberg's subsequent work at Stanford University in the early 90's, was the first proof that virtual overlays, when registered and presented over a user's direct view of the real physical world, could significantly enhance human performance.

- Mike Abernathy pioneered one of the first successful augmented reality applications of video overlay using map data for space debris in 1993, while at Rockwell International. He co-founded Rapid Imaging Software, Inc. and was the primary author of the LandForm system in 1995, and the SmartCam3D system. LandForm augmented reality was successfully flight tested in 1999 aboard a helicopter and SmartCam3D was used to fly the NASA X-38 from 1999-2002. He and NASA colleague Francisco Delgado received the National Defense Industries Association Top5 awards in 2004.

- Francisco "Frank" Delgado is a NASA engineer and project manager specializing in human interface research and development. Starting 1998 he conducted research into displays that combined video with synthetic vision systems (called hybrid synthetic vision at the time) that we recognize today as augmented reality systems for the control of aircraft and spacecraft. In 1999 he and colleague Mike Abernathy flight-tested the LandForm system aboard a US Army helicopter. Delgado oversaw integration of the LandForm and SmartCam3D systems into the X-38 Crew Return Vehicle. In 2001, Aviation Week reported NASA astronaut's successful use of hybrid synthetic vision (augmented reality) to fly the X-38 during a flight test at Dryden Flight Research Center. The technology was used in all subsequent flights of the X-38. Delgado was co-recipient of the National Defense Industries Association 2004 Top 5 software of the year award for SmartCam3D.

- Dieter Schmalstieg and Daniel Wagner jump started the field of AR on mobile phones. They developed the first marker tracking systems for mobile phones and PDAs.

- Bruce H. Thomas and Wayne Piekarski develop the Tinmith system in 1998. They along with Steve Feiner with his MARS system pioneer outdoor augmented reality.

- Dr. Mark Billinghurst is one of the world's leading augmented reality researchers, focusing on innovative computer interfaces that explore how virtual and real worlds can be merged. Director of the HIT Lab New Zealand (HIT Lab NZ) at the University of Canterbury in New Zealand, he has produced over 250 technical publications and presented demonstrations and courses at a wide variety of conferences.

- Reinhold Behringer performed important early work in image registration for augmented reality, and prototype wearable testbeds for augmented reality. He also co-organized the First IEEE International Symposium on Augmented Reality in 1998 (IWAR'98), and co-edited one of the first books on augmented reality.

History

- 1901: L. Frank Baum, an author, first mentions the idea of an electronic display/spectacles that overlays data onto real life (in this case 'people'), it is named a 'character marker'.

- 1957–62: Morton Heilig, a cinematographer, creates and patents a simulator called Sensorama with visuals, sound, vibration, and smell.

- 1968: Ivan Sutherland invents the head-mounted display and positions it as a window into a virtual world.

- 1975: Myron Krueger creates Videoplace to allow users to interact with virtual objects for the first time.

- 1980: Steve Mann creates the first wearable computer, a computer vision system with text and graphical overlays on a photographically mediated reality, or Augmediated Reality.

- 1981: Dan Reitan geospatially maps multiple weather radar images and space-based and studio cameras to virtual reality Earth maps and abstract symbols for television weather broadcasts, bringing Augmented Reality to TV.

- 1989: Jaron Lanier coins the phrase Virtual Reality and creates the first commercial business around virtual worlds.

- 1990: The term 'Augmented Reality' is attributed to Thomas P. Caudell, a former Boeing researcher.

- 1992: Louis Rosenberg develops one of the first functioning AR systems, called Virtual Fixtures, at the U.S. Air Force Research Laboratory—Armstrong, and demonstrates benefits to human performance.

- 1992: Steven Feiner, Blair MacIntyre and Doree Seligmann present the first major paper on an AR system prototype, KARMA, at the Graphics Interface conference.

- 1993: Mike Abernathy, et al., report the first use of augmented reality in identifying space debris using Rockwell WorldView by overlaying satellite geographic trajectories on live telescope video.

- 1993 A widely cited version of the paper above is published in Communications of the ACM – Special issue on computer augmented environments, edited by Pierre Wellner, Wendy Mackay, and Rich Gold.

- 1993: Loral WDL, with sponsorship from STRICOM, performed the first demonstration combining live AR-equipped vehicles and manned simulators. Unpublished paper, J. Barrilleaux, "Experiences and Observations in Applying Augmented Reality to Live Training", 1999.

- 1994: Julie Martin creates first 'Augmented Reality Theater production', Dancing In Cyberspace, funded by the Australia Council for the Arts, features dancers and acrobats manipulating body–sized virtual object in real time, projected into the same physical space and performance plane. The acrobats appeared immersed within the virtual object and environments. The installation used Silicon Graphics computers and Polhemus sensing system.

- 1995: S. Ravela et al. at University of Massachusetts introduce a vision-based system using monocular cameras to track objects (engine blocks) across views for augmented reality.

- 1998: Spatial Augmented Reality introduced at University of North Carolina at Chapel Hill by Ramesh Raskar, Welch, Henry Fuchs.

- 1999: Frank Delgado, Mike Abernathy et al. report successful flight test of LandForm software video map overlay from a helicopter at Army Yuma Proving Ground overlaying video with runways, taxiways, roads and road names.

- 1999: The US Naval Research Laboratory engage on a decade long research program called the Battlefield Augmented Reality System (BARS) to prototype some of the early wearable systems for dismounted soldier operating in urban environment for situation awareness and training NRL BARS Web page.

- 1999: Hirokazu Kato (加藤 博一) created ARToolKit at HITLab, where AR later was further developed by other HITLab scientists, demonstrating it at SIGGRAPH.

- 2000: Bruce H. Thomas develops ARQuake, the first outdoor mobile AR game, demonstrating it in the International Symposium on Wearable Computers.

- 2001: NASA X-38 flown using LandForm software video map overlays at Dryden Flight Research Center.

- 2004: Outdoor helmet-mounted AR system demonstrated by Trimble Navigation and the Human Interface Technology Laboratory.

- 2008: Wikitude AR Travel Guide launches on 20 Oct 2008 with the G1 Android phone.

- 2009: ARToolkit was ported to Adobe Flash (FLARToolkit) by Saqoosha, bringing augmented reality to the web browser.

- 2012: Launch of Lyteshot, an interactive AR gaming platform that utilizes smartglasses for game data.

- 2013: Meta announces the Meta 1 developer kit, the first to market AR see-through display

- 2013: Google announces an open beta test of its Google Glass augmented reality glasses. The glasses reach the Internet through Bluetooth, which connects to the wireless service on a user's cellphone. The glasses respond when a user speaks, touches the frame or moves the head.

- 2014: Mahei creates the first generation of augmented reality enhanced educational toys.

- 2015: Microsoft announces Windows Holographic and the HoloLens augmented reality headset. The headset utilizes various sensors and a processing unit to blend high definition "holograms" with the real world.

- 2016: Niantic released Pokémon Go for iOS and Android in July 2016. The game quickly became one of the most used applications and has brought augmented reality to the mainstream.

References

- R. Behringer, G. Klinker,. D. Mizell. Augmented Reality – Placing Artificial Objects in Real Scenes. Proceedings of IWAR '98. A.K.Peters, Natick, 1999. ISBN 1-56881-098-9

- Verlinden, Jouke; Horvath, Imre. "Augmented Prototyping as Design Means in Industrial Design Engineering". Delft University of Technology. Retrieved 2012-10-07

- Pang, Y; Nee, A; Youcef-Toumie, Kamal; Ong, S.K; Yuan, M.L (November 18, 2004). "Assembly Design and Evaluation in an Augmented Reality Environment". National University of Singapore, M.I.T. Retrieved 2012-10-07

- O'Neil, Lauren. "LCD contact lenses could display text messages in your eye". CBC. Archived from the original on 11 December 2012. Retrieved 2012-12-12

- Bond, Sarah (July 17, 2016). "After the Success Of Pokémon Go, How Will Augmented Reality Impact Archaeological Sites?". Retrieved July 17, 2016

- Chapman, Lizette (2015-01-28). "Augmented-Reality Headset Maker Meta Secures $23 Million". Wall Street Journal. Retrieved 2016-02-29

- Matney, Lucas (2016-03-02). "Hands-on with the $949 mind-bending Meta 2 augmented reality headset". TechCrunch. Retrieved 2016-03-02

- Berinato, Scott (January 29, 2015). "What HoloLens Has That Google Glass Didn't". Harward Business Preview. Retrieved 15 February 2015

- Lee, Kangdon (March 2012). "Augmented Reality in Education and Training" (PDF). Techtrends: Linking Research & Practice To Improve Learning. 56 (2). Retrieved 2014-05-15

- Wadhwa, Tarun. "CrowdOptic and L'Oreal To Make History By Demonstrating How Augmented Reality Can Be A Shared Experience". Forbes. Retrieved 6 June 2013

- Noelle, S. (2002). "Stereo augmentation of simulation results on a projection wall". Mixed and Augmented Reality, 2002. ISMAR 2002. Proceedings.: 271–322. Retrieved 2012-10-07

Permissions

All chapters in this book are published with permission under the Creative Commons Attribution Share Alike License or equivalent. Every chapter published in this book has been scrutinized by our experts. Their significance has been extensively debated. The topics covered herein carry significant information for a comprehensive understanding. They may even be implemented as practical applications or may be referred to as a beginning point for further studies.

We would like to thank the editorial team for lending their expertise to make the book truly unique. They have played a crucial role in the development of this book. Without their invaluable contributions this book wouldn't have been possible. They have made vital efforts to compile up to date information on the varied aspects of this subject to make this book a valuable addition to the collection of many professionals and students.

This book was conceptualized with the vision of imparting up-to-date and integrated information in this field. To ensure the same, a matchless editorial board was set up. Every individual on the board went through rigorous rounds of assessment to prove their worth. After which they invested a large part of their time researching and compiling the most relevant data for our readers.

The editorial board has been involved in producing this book since its inception. They have spent rigorous hours researching and exploring the diverse topics which have resulted in the successful publishing of this book. They have passed on their knowledge of decades through this book. To expedite this challenging task, the publisher supported the team at every step. A small team of assistant editors was also appointed to further simplify the editing procedure and attain best results for the readers.

Apart from the editorial board, the designing team has also invested a significant amount of their time in understanding the subject and creating the most relevant covers. They scrutinized every image to scout for the most suitable representation of the subject and create an appropriate cover for the book.

The publishing team has been an ardent support to the editorial, designing and production team. Their endless efforts to recruit the best for this project, has resulted in the accomplishment of this book. They are a veteran in the field of academics and their pool of knowledge is as vast as their experience in printing. Their expertise and guidance has proved useful at every step. Their uncompromising quality standards have made this book an exceptional effort. Their encouragement from time to time has been an inspiration for everyone.

The publisher and the editorial board hope that this book will prove to be a valuable piece of knowledge for students, practitioners and scholars across the globe.

Index